The Material Life of Human Beings

In this ground-breaking work, the distinguished anthropological theorist, Michael Brian Schiffer, presents a profound challenge to the social sciences. Through a broad range of examples, he demonstrates how theories of behavior and communication have too often ignored the fundamental importance of objects in human life.

In *The Material Life of Human Beings*, the author builds upon the premise that the most important feature of human life is not symbolic language but the incessant and diverse transactions that take place between people and myriad artifacts. The author shows that artifacts are involved in all modes of human communication – be they visual, auditory, or tactile. By creatively folding elements of postmodernist thought into a scientific framework, he creates new concepts and models for understanding and analyzing communication and behavior. Challenging established theories within the social sciences, Michael Brian Schiffer offers a reassessment of the centrality of *materiality* to everyday life.

The Material Life of Human Beings is essential reading for students and scholars within anthropology, sociology, and communications and archaeology. It is also a stimulating and provocative read for all those with an interest in the growing interdisciplinary field of material culture studies.

Michael Brian Schiffer is Professor of Anthropology at the University of Arizona. He is well known for his work in the fields of modern material culture, archaeological theory, and experimental archaeology and has published a number of books on these subjects, including *The Portable Radio in American Life* (1991), *Technological Perspectives on Behavioral Change* (1992) and *Taking Charge: The Electric Automobile in America* (1994).

The Material Life of Human Beings

Artifacts, behavior, and communication

Michael Brian Schiffer

With the assistance of Andrea R. Miller

London and New York

First published 1999
by Routledge
11 New Fetter Lane, London EC4P 4EE

Simultaneously published in the USA and Canada
by Routledge
29 West 35th Street, New York, NY 10001

Typeset in Bembo by Routledge
Printed and bound in Great Britain by Clays Ltd, St Ives plc

British Library Cataloguing in Publication Data
A catalogue record for this book is available from the British Library

Library of Congress Cataloging in Publication Data
Schiffer, Michael B.
The material life of human beings: artifacts, behavior, and communication /
Michael Brian Schiffer.
p. cm.
Includes bibliographical references and index.
1. Material culture. 2. Human behavior. 3. Communication and culture. I
Title.
GN406.S34 1999
306—dc21   98–51397
                                            CIP

ISBN 0–415–20032–6 (hbk)
ISBN 0–415–20033–4 (pbk)

We should resist neglecting or trivializing the commonplace. There are rewards for approaching nature with a naive curiosity and attempting to see the familiar in new ways.

(Provine 1996: 45)

Contents

Preface

In the mid-1980s, an undergraduate student, Kenneth Fordyce, spent some time hanging out in my archaeological laboratory. He was very bright and, being an older student who had taken countless classes across the university, uncommonly learned. One day we got into an animated discussion about why there were boundaries between the various social sciences. I argued that there were good reasons for a division of labor in investigating human affairs, and recited a litany of bromides that I had probably acquired as an undergraduate. Unimpressed, he stridently asserted that all social sciences study the same phenomena, but use different, sometimes mutually unintelligible, jargons. To this apparently outrageous claim, I responded with more platitudes, but Ken remained unconvinced.

In the years that have passed since this encounter, I have often wondered whether there is any ontological, epistemological, or theoretical justification for the tribalization of the human sciences. This question was never far from my mind as I pursued, in the late 1980s and 1990s, projects on the history of electrical products.

While researching the social, cultural, behavioral, and technological contexts of portable radios and electric cars through the decades, I came to appreciate that the explanation of these product trajectories required the integration of concepts and principles originating in diverse disciplines, including engineering, history, and several social sciences. Gradually I realized that Kenneth Fordyce had been on to something. At the very least, it appeared to me that the fragmentation of knowledge represented by traditional disciplines worked against the development of an integrated, scientific approach to explaining human behavior. I wondered if perhaps there were more systematic ways to build conceptual bridges across the social sciences.

Although I have lost respect for the sanctity and scientific utility of traditional disciplinary boundaries, the present work does have a center of gravity, a core orientation derived from one discipline: archaeology − behavioral archaeology in particular. In many ways, this is the ideal place to begin integrating the study of human behavior, for archaeology is the quintessential interdisciplinary discipline, having boundaries permeable to ideas and modes of discourse from virtually all other sciences and humanities: like *Star Trek*'s Borg, archaeologists assimilate information and principles from any discipline they encounter. What is more, archaeology's focus on artifacts equips its practitioners to undertake syntheses emphasizing the materiality of behavior and communication.

The present project began during 1994 after I had finished the book on electric automobiles (Schiffer, Butts, and Grimm 1994). That study, and the earlier one on portable radios (Schiffer 1991), had forced me to confront, in many ways both theoretical and empirical, the pervasiveness of artifacts in human communication. Fascinated, I began to read widely on communication, venturing into unfamiliar literatures in ethology, psychology, sociology, and communication. Although investigators in these disciplines were describing communication phenomena with different terms, I suspected that many concepts could be made mutually commensurable by development of an appropriate meta-language. On the other hand, I was dismayed that in no discipline had scholars fully grasped the importance of artifacts in all human communication. Investigators were merely dabbling with artifacts, forcing them to conform to conventional ontology and theory that had originated in research on speech. Thus, creating a meta-language for discussing communication in diverse disciplines would not be enough; I would have to construct new ontology and an artifact-based theory of communication.

Having plunged into alien literatures and disciplines before, I did not lack the hubris required for constructing a new and integrative theory of communication that ignores disciplinary boundaries and does not marginalize artifacts. While working through a preliminary version (Schiffer and Miller 1999), I realized that the theory could also handle human behavior. And so arose the present project: constructing a general theory that interrelates artifacts, behavior, and communication. The results of my deliberations and theory-building efforts are reported in this slim book, which treats subjects so fundamental that no social scientist could lack views on them.

My major message is that, by emphasizing artifacts, investigators can build scientific theories that provide more general and more satisfactory explanations of both communication and behavior. At the very least, the new formulations – archaeologically informed concepts and principles that cross-cut traditional disciplines – challenge social scientists to rethink conventional ontology and theory. Whether the present work actually leads to a more unified human science remains to be seen, but such attempts are necessary, however imperfect and incomplete. Indeed, I suggest that efforts at integration and synthesis now must be accorded a high priority if the worthy enterprise of explaining human behavior, scientifically, is to reach its full potential. It is time for us to demonstrate that the social sciences are much more than insular arenas in which smart people compete for good grants, ink, and prestige.

Scholars and scientists throughout the academy, in traditional disciplines such as communication, sociology, anthropology, archaeology, psychology, and philosophy, might find the ideas in this book to be provocative. Investigators in interdisciplinary areas such as complexity and evolution, ethology, artificial intelligence, and cognitive science will perhaps also encounter useful formulations. And, although containing a complete scholarly apparatus (i.e., sources cited in the text and a lengthy bibliography), the text itself should be accessible to anyone with an interest in learning new ways of conceptualizing communication and behavior. I also believe that this work has implications for developing new behavioral therapies, and so might interest health practitioners.

Acknowledgments

I am indebted to Andrea R. Miller, who has been my research assistant on this project since her freshman year at the University of Arizona. Andrea's activities, supported by the Laboratory of Traditional Technology, have run the gamut: tedious xeroxing in the library, arranging for inter-library loans, interviewing other social and behavioral scientists, writing sections of chapters, doing original library research, and commenting on countless chapter drafts. In short, this work would have proceeded much more slowly or even foundered without Andrea's help.

William H. Walker also deserves special thanks: not only did he furnish important new ideas and prod me to rethink basic concepts, but he also convinced me to bring fundamental principles of behavioral archaeology to a wide audience.

The Laboratory of Traditional Technology, in the Department of Anthropology at the University of Arizona, holds a Friday afternoon bull session. On various occasions during the past few years, drafts of several chapters were submitted to the unremitting criticisms of the assembled students and colleagues. I thank them one and all for helping me to clarify the book's main ideas and to improve their expression in prose.

A number of people worked their way through the entire manuscript or large chunks of it, furnishing me with invaluable criticism and suggestions: Ellen B. Basso, Kenneth Boden, Iain Davidson, Carol Gifford, W. David Kingery, Brian R. McKee, John Murphy, Frances-Fera Schiffer, Jeremy A. Schiffer, Louie Schiffer, James M. Skibo, John D. Speth, William H. Walker, and María Nieves Zedeño. I deeply appreciate their toil. In addition, I thank Vincent LaMotta, Patrick Lyons, and Monica Smith for commenting upon individual chapters.

Annette, my loving wife, also contributed much to this project. Doubtless it was her long-standing interest in animal behavior that provoked me in the first place to take a long look at communication in diverse species. I did so by casually observing animal behavior with Annette in the forested mountains of east-central Arizona, where we spend summers, and by undisciplined reading in ethology. These exposures to the lives of other creatures supplied me with inspiration of inestimable value. Annette also was a sounding board for many of the new ideas and encouraged me through tough times. Thank you, Annette; as always, my compass and companion in life.

Chapter 1

Introduction

The nature of human existence

For centuries, people have pondered the question, "What is it about human life that sets us apart from all other species in the animal kingdom?" In response to this question, social scientists, among countless other scholars, have supplied sundry answers (for recent discussions, see Betzig 1996; Cartmill 1990). Some investigators suggest that humans alone communicate symbolically and thus language is the definitive trait (e.g., Deacon 1997; Lieberman 1991; Noble and Davidson 1996: 8, 15); others argue that the ability to make tools is unique to our species; still others see only in people a capacity for self-awareness or consciousness (e.g., McGuire 1995; Noble and Davidson 1996: 215); and some say that culture is confined to humans.[1] One could fill a large book with a list of the anatomical, behavioral, and cognitive traits that have been advanced as humanity's distinctive features.

Attempts to distinguish the members of our species from others tend to founder when confronted with information on animal behavior. Communication is widespread if not universal among animals, especially mammals (e.g., Albone 1984; Hauser 1996; Moynihan 1985; Peters 1980; Sebeok 1968, 1977; Smith 1977; Snowdon 1990; Vauclair 1996), and a few primates in the laboratory can create and manipulate symbols (Deacon 1997: 340; Savage-Rumbaugh and Brakke 1996). Tool making in the animal kingdom is far from uncommon (e.g., Beck 1980: 105–116; McGrew 1992, 1993; Peters 1980), and tool *use* is ubiquitous (e.g., Beck 1980: 13–104; Beck 1986; Vauclair 1996: ch. 4). That other animals are self-aware or have consciousness remains controversial (see the papers in Ristau and Marler 1990), but this claim has its champions (e.g., Crisp 1996; Deacon 1997: 450; Griffin 1991, 1992; Parker *et al.* 1994; Radner and Radner 1989). And, on the basis of theory and considerable evidence, it has also been argued that some nonhuman species are culture-bearers (e.g., Boesch et al. 1994; Bonner 1980; Harris 1964; McGrew 1992), at least in the sense that a group perpetuates, through learning, behavior patterns not shared by other groups of that species (see

Galef 1990). One after another, supposedly unique human traits have been revealed by advancing knowledge of other species to be exaggerated or erroneous (Byrne 1995: 34–35).

Although some purportedly unique or near-unique human traits have withstood the recent onslaught of ethological findings (e.g., among primates only people have a fully opposable thumb and walk habitually upright on two legs [Fleagle 1998]), previous investigators have ignored what might be most distinctive and significant about our species: *human life consists of ceaseless and varied interactions among people and myriad kinds of things.* These things are called "material culture" or, better, artifacts (Rathje and Schiffer 1982: ch. 1). An *artifact* is provisionally defined here as any material, in contradistinction to spiritual or mental, phenomenon that exhibits one or more properties produced by a given species (for another expansive definition of artifact, see Deetz 1977: 10–ll). This definition allows one to refer not only to human artifacts but also to artifacts of bees or beavers. However, unless otherwise specified, "artifact" in the present work denotes *human* artifact.

What makes humans unique, then, is that we take part in diverse interactions with innumerable kinds of artifacts in the course of daily activities. Indeed, from a sacred ceremony to the most common craft, human activities – virtually without exception – have specific artifact requirements (Rathje and Schiffer 1982; Schiffer 1992b). As a result, every society, which consists of countless activities, develops hundreds or thousands or even millions of artifact types. Although other animals make and interact with a limited number of artifact types on a sustained basis (e.g., bee hives and honeycombs, beaver dams and lodges), in no other species do the variety of artifacts and the diversity and complexity of interactions begin to approach those found in even the most materially impoverished human society. Incessant interaction with endlessly varied artifacts is, I maintain, the empirical reality of human life and what makes it so singular.

To gain greater insights into this feature, let us employ some "thought experiments." First, imagine that members of a different – but also sapient – species are undertaking a philosophical examination of *Homo sapiens.* Our closest kin, the chimpanzee – "a most accomplished tool user" (Vauclair 1996: 82; see also McGrew 1993) – can serve this purpose. Chimps make tools of twigs, which they use to extract termites from their nests, and some even crack nuts with stones (McGrew 1992); so, the mere fact that people make and use tools would hardly be remarkable. Nor would there be surprise that humans reckon their kin and display a "Machiavellian intelligence" in social relationships, for chimps do the same (Byrne 1995: 222–225).

As the chimp philosophers ponder their hair-impaired cousins, they are more likely to notice that people employ artifacts for all undertakings, interposing them between every basic need – e.g., food, shelter, defense, reproduction, and establishing and manipulating social relationships – and its satisfaction (Schiffer 1992b). For example, in Western societies, even the acquisition and consumption of vegetable foodstuffs directly involves myriad things: farming implements and machines, pesticides and herbicides, trucks and warehouses, packaging materials, grocery display cases, grocery carts, bags, automobiles, refrigerators and cupboards, cooking and serving utensils, plates and bowls, silverware, garbage disposals, and so on. Similarly, religious ceremonies cannot be practiced without a host of appropriate paraphernalia, including special buildings, lights or candles, icons, sacred scrolls, hymn and prayer books, and priestly vestments. Even so basic an activity as sex often requires certain scents and clothing, beds and bedding, perhaps lubricants, and – for a few – whips and chains. Most surprising of all is grooming, an important chimp pastime (Byrne 1995: 200), which has taken a strange turn in human hands, for the latter are occupied in manipulating combs and brushes as well as lotions and potions. Chimps would doubtless observe that, in proliferating artifact types and using them in so many ways, humans in every known society have needlessly complicated their lives, taking time away from high-quality person-to-person interactions. What is more, the chimps might marvel that never during a person's lifetime are they not being intimate with artifacts.

The simian philosophers are also prone to draw a pessimistic conclusion about the ability of humans to study themselves. They might remark, for example, that the terms "interpersonal" interaction and "social" interaction, which permeate publications in the social sciences, are misnomers, for nearly always artifacts – at the very least body paint, clothing, and ornaments – accompany individuals in virtually every interactional setting. Humans, it appears to the chimps, interact not with other humans *per se* but with artifacts and humans compounded with artifacts. What is more, the artifacts attached to – and part of – people have demonstrable and sometimes far-reaching effects on interaction sequences and on the forward motion of activities. Thus, our chimps conclude, it is a mistake of cosmic proportions to arbitrarily abstract "interpersonal" and "social" interactions from human life and study them apart from the artifacts in which they are embedded.

If the nature of human existence involves varied and incessant transactions with numerous artifact types, why has this ontological truth eluded so many social scientists? Perhaps viewing ourselves from the vantage point of still another animal, in a second thought experiment, can help us to apprehend the problem. Let us suppose that tropical fish are learned and can philosophize. What would these fish conclude upon peering out of an aquarium at the surrounding room, a "family" room in an American home? They would observe humans, sometimes with painted faces, wearing clothing, watches, and jewelry. The people would be lounging on chairs and sofas, opening beer cans and pretzel packages and consuming their contents, sniffing food being cooked in the kitchen, puffing on cigarettes, handling and reading magazines and books, manipulating remote controls, gazing at a TV set, fiddling with tapes and VCR, walking on the rug, taking off and putting on sweatshirts and jackets, looking at pictures on the wall, dusting furniture, picking up and rearranging knickknacks, wrestling with a vacuum cleaner, and, all the while, intermittently uttering sounds.

Might not the fish wonder how social scientists, who like all other people spend the entirety of their time engaged with artifacts (especially books and chairs and computers), could be so oblivious to the medium that envelops them? People's lives are spent shaping and responding to this *material medium*, yet social scientists cannot see it for what it is, much less understand its pervasive influence (cf. Latour 1993: 54). Instead, human investigators lavish attention on the sounds that people produce, on the specialized artifacts that encode or record the sounds, and on the social, cultural, and biological bases of sound production, reception, and interpretation. Preoccupation with these phenomena, concludes our piscine philosophers, has seriously skewed the study of human behavior. Apparently, total immersion in the material medium has blinded social scientists to the distinguishing characteristic of their species – of their lives.

Fortunately, we need no further assistance from philosophical fish and chimps. As social scientists, we can work through the implications of an ontology founded upon the premise that what is singular about *Homo sapiens* is the constant intimacy of people with countless kinds of things – our immersion in the material medium. This new ontology can be used as a springboard for rethinking and relating the fundamental phenomena of human behavior and communication. As we shall see, an appreciation for the thorough embeddedness of behavior and communication in people–artifact interactions furnishes insights into both phenomena.

One obvious approach is to acknowledge that communication is behavior. Indeed, people move their tongues and lips, contort their faces, and wave their arms and hands, all of which fall comfortably within traditional definitions of human behavior as muscular movements. Intuitively satisfying and conforming to positions widely held in the social sciences and in ethology (e.g., Smith 1977), this move nonetheless hinders our ability to explore other relationships between behavior and communication. After all, a case can also be made for the reverse proposition (see Chapters 5 and 7), that *all human behavior is communication*, as in Hanneman's (1975: 21–22) claim that "when we interact with others, anything we do communicates...Behavior is communication and communication is behavior."

In the final analysis, however, statements to the effect that all communication is behavior or all behavior is communication are far too glib and vacuous to be useful in a scientific project. Thus, in the course of the present work, both communication and behavior are rethought and redefined; on the basis of this foundation, I specify exactly how both are related. But not until later chapters will we have in hand the terms needed for expressing that relationship precisely. If behavior and communication are in important respects related, then it might be possible to construct one theory that explains both phenomena. The overall strategy of this study, then, is to build a general theory of communication that also handles behavior. Conventional definitions of these phenomena leave out artifacts or treat them as epiphenomena, and thus are unacceptable in light of the new ontology. In contrast, I advance the sweeping – and counterintuitive – proposition that *virtually all communication and human behavior involve artifacts*. Building on this perspective, I integrate artifacts explicitly and thoroughly into the theory developed below. In short, this book makes the case that, in everyday life, both communication and behavior are related and both consist mainly of people–artifact interactions.

Material-culture studies

Because the social sciences beyond anthropology have in recent decades discovered artifacts, often called "material culture" (for a review, see Schiffer and Majewski n.d.), the participation of artifacts in communication and behavior no longer goes entirely unnoticed. Even so, material-culture studies as a genre have, from the perspective of the present work, several serious shortcomings.

In the first place, material-culture studies are largely marginalized in the major social science disciplines. This can be easily shown by a perusal of prominent literature in psychology, sociology, and anthropology.

The following serial publications were consulted for the period 1986 through 1995: *Annual Review of Anthropology*, *Annual Review of Sociology*, *Annual Review of Psychology*, *American Anthropologist*, *American Sociological Review*, and *American Psychologist*. These publications, which are believed to represent high-profile, mainstream research in the three disciplines, were searched exhaustively for papers treating material culture, artifacts, or technology (in anthropology publications, only papers in sociocultural anthropology and ethnoarchaeology – the archaeological study of living societies – were examined). The results demonstrate that material-culture studies are far from mainstream. In sociology and psychology, fewer than 1 per cent of the articles concern artifacts or technology. In anthropology, where material-culture studies have more than a century-long history and are augmented by ethnoarchaeology, the showing is better, with 7.7 per cent of the papers in the *Annual Review of Anthropology* and 6 per cent of those in *American Anthropologist* dealing with artifacts or technology (e.g., Hakken 1993; Lawrence and Low 1990; Miller 1995; Pfaffenberger 1992; Starrett 1995). If, as I maintain, every realm of human behavior and communication involves people–artifact interactions, then *all* studies in the social and behavioral sciences ought to attend diligently to artifacts. Evidently, this is not happening – even in sociocultural anthropology. What is more, one searches major journals in communication, such as *Communication Theory*, *Communication*

Monographs, and *Journal of Nonverbal Behavior*, in vain for papers that discuss artifacts seriously.

Second, beyond being marginalized, material-culture studies often suffer from a more severe problem: they simply project conventional ontology and theories into new empirical domains, treating people–artifact interactions as secondary to processes of culture. The manufacture and use of artifacts is regarded, for example, as just one more arena in which people negotiate culturally constituted meanings, such as individual and group identities (e.g., Appadurai 1986; Cordwell and Schwarz 1979; Csikszentmihalyi and Rochberg-Halton 1981; Dittmar 1992; Douglas and Isherwood 1979; Kaiser 1985; Lemonnier 1992; McCracken 1988; Miller 1994; Weiner and Schneider 1989). In these studies one does not dispute culture as *the* organizing principle of everyday life or contest its hegemony for formulating research questions. Even the term "material culture" subordinates artifacts to a cultural frame of reference, acknowledging objects but denying the materiality of human life. Apparently, material-culture studies have been domesticated and pose little threat to theoretical hegemonies, much less traditional ontology.

Third, as has been noted elsewhere (e.g., Rathje 1979; Schiffer 1992a, 1992b; Schiffer and Majewski n.d.), material-culture studies beyond ethnoarchaeology tend to be methodologically unsophisticated. For example, investigators seldom ground their generalizations in naturalistic, systematically obtained, and quantitative observations of people–artifact interactions. Instead, there is a reliance on statements gleaned from interviews, which are subject to innumerable but seldom elucidated biases (D'Andrade 1995: 184–193; T. Jones 1995; Neupert and Longacre 1994; Rathje and Murphy 1992; Schiffer 1978, n.d.). Moreover, descriptions of artifacts themselves, when provided at all, are superficial and incomplete. These methodological shortcomings are not surprising, given that the rigorous study of artifacts is not included in the training of social scientists (other than archaeologists).

Though marginalized, deeply invested in conventional ontology and theories, and methodologically unsophisticated, material-culture studies in the major social sciences have furnished empirical regularities, concepts, and insights that contribute to the present project. In addition, artifact studies undertaken in cultural geography (e.g., Rapoport 1990), folklore (e.g., Bronner 1986, 1989, 1992; Glassie 1975; Musello 1992), history (e.g., Quimby 1978; Schlereth and Ames 1985), and art history (Prown 1980, 1993) can be mined for the occasional nugget.

An archaeological perspective

I almost entitled this book *An Archaeology of Communication and Behavior*, and it would have been apt. Indeed, I contend that concepts and principles appropriate for building a theory of communication and behavior can come from archaeology. More than a few books claim to be "An archaeology" of this or "The archaeology" of that (e.g., Oudshoorn 1994; Perriault 1981) or purport to treat a subject "archaeologically" (e.g., Fahie 1884: viii). What these books mostly have in common is, first, a focus on origins or arcana, which the public – and even other scholars – associate with archaeology; and, second, they are not written by archaeologists. The present effort is an exception to both generalizations in that it treats neither origins nor arcana and its author *is* an archaeologist, specifically an anthropological archaeologist specializing in behavioral studies (see, e.g., Cameron and Tomka 1993; Gould 1990; Longacre and Skibo 1994; Schiffer 1976, 1992b, 1995a, 1995b; Skibo 1992; Skibo *et al.* 1995; Walker 1998; Zedeño 1997). Anthropological archaeologists ask both historical and scientific questions about past societies, seeking to reconstruct and explain their trajectories.

Whether their interests are in prehistoric, historical, industrial, classical, or modern societies, archaeologists are preoccupied with discerning how people and artifacts interact. Among social scientists, then, archaeologists are least alienated from appreciating the character of human involvement in the material medium. After all, only artifacts remain from ancient societies; to learn about life in the past, we must understand people–artifact relationships of all kinds (Reid *et al.* 1975; Schiffer 1976). Seemingly, an archaeological perspective might be of some value for probing the potential of the new ontology.

As an archaeologist, I can readily draw upon the formulations of people–artifact relationships that my discipline – especially behavioral archaeology – has produced, as well as exploit our methodological tools for studying phenomena of the material medium. In particular, I generalize the process of archaeological inference to all communication and, eventually, to all human behavior. A provisional definition of an inference, useful in Chapters 2 and 3, can be provided: an inference is a conclusion about something arrived at through reasoning from evidence.

Examples that illustrate the new concepts and formulations are drawn mainly from activities of daily life. By privileging the ordinary (cf. de Certeau 1984; Harris 1964; T. Jones 1995), I keep this work focused on what most people are doing most of the time – interacting with varied artifacts.

Like many archaeologists, I am a scientist. What is more, I offer no apologies for being a positivist, in the sense originated by Auguste Comte – someone striving to create positive knowledge for illuminating the empirical realm of human behavior. It is fashionable today for humanistic, especially postmodernist, scholars to bash the scientific enterprise, including the social sciences. Admittedly, many products of social science – i.e., purported laws and theories – are ethnocentric, temporocentric, or both (cf. Stephen and Harrison 1993), sometimes little more than empirical generalizations or Western indigenous knowledge writ large. Conceivably, the problem could be intrinsic to our subject matter: perhaps human behavior exhibits more intractable variability than other natural phenomena, such as the motion of heavenly bodies or the replication of DNA. Yet, one must acknowledge that, even if variability in human behavior is especially intractable, only relentless scientific research could reveal it as such. Thus, the present work fits comfortably within the natural science tradition. With seeming irony, however, I also admit to adopting a few postmodernist insights. Stripped of its gratuitous anti-science posturing and "heaps of badly written blather" (Stich 1996: 9), postmodernism can contribute useful ideas to social science (see Knapp 1996).

Let me acknowledge two additional biases. First, the approach I take here owes an undeniable debt to behaviorism. In agreement with behaviorists, I emphasize the need to distinguish rigorously between empirical observations of human behavior (e.g., stimulus and response) and interpretations of behavior's causes, such as "goal" and "intention" (Skinner 1953, 1974; Watson 1930; cf. Bostrom and Donohew 1992: 119–121; Harris 1964). However, in contrast to early behaviorists, but like their intellectual descendants such as cognitive psychologists and ethologists (e.g., Hulse *et al.* 1978), I believe that scientists can and should construct models for elucidating the knowledge and cognitive processes that connect stimulus and response (Littlejohn 1991: 73) – as long as the models can be evaluated, at least in principle, against behavioral observations (see Byrne 1995: 39). I also part company with behaviorists by emphasizing the importance of studying, with ethnographic methods, the entire suite of potential stimuli – especially artifacts – present in *natural* settings (Hutchins 1995; Sperber 1996: 98–99; Walker, Skibo, and Nielsen 1995: 6).

Second, in conformity with some strains of complexity theory (e.g., Lewin 1992), I argue that all human behavior arises from, and is embodied in, basic matter–energy transactions among interactors, not unlike the behavior of other animals (e.g., Gordon 1995; Theraulaz and Bonabeau 1995; see also Sperber 1996: 54). In pursuing this approach, investigators must address three fundamental questions: (1) which real-world phenomena are the interactors, capable of furnishing stimuli and responding? (2) What kinds of interactions take place between interactors? And (3) by what rules are the interactions governed?[2]

If one is willing to adopt conventional theory and ontology about human behavior, then these questions have straightforward answers. To wit, (1) the interactors are human beings; thus, "interpersonal" interactions are privileged and all others, such as those between people and artifacts, are treated as epiphenomena; (2) people interact by means of symbol-based cultural systems, like language; and (3) interactions are governed by the shared rules of language and other symbolic systems. These answers, if made explicit at all, are phrased in many ways throughout the social sciences, but the underlying ontological assumptions remain the same. Such answers are unacceptable here, however, because they render investigators oblivious to the materiality of everyday life. Clearly, the new theory must recognize the entire range of relevant interactors, allow for interactions of all kinds, and look beyond language for an understanding of interaction rules.

Readers may be nonplussed at the absence in the new theory of much vocabulary seemingly essential for discussing communication and behavior, such as meaning, sign, symbol, intention, motivation, purpose, goal, attitude, value, belief, norm, function, mind, and culture. Despite herculean efforts in the social sciences to define these often ethnocentric or metaphysical notions, they remain behaviorally problematic and so are superfluous in the present project.

This work also introduces many new technical terms, some of which label concepts that resemble, to varying degrees, others employed elsewhere in the social sciences (see Glossary). The introduction of new jargon, having a behavioral basis, allows us to shed the ontological and theoretical baggage that use of the old terms would inevitably carry.

Yet other new concepts and terms cross-cut the phenomenological world in ways that many readers might find unfamiliar, even puzzling. These formulations should be viewed as constituting a discipline-neutral meta-language, potentially useful to any researcher who aspires to explain variability in human behavior scientifically (see Glossary). Thus, this book furnishes – through new concepts – new ways of thinking that can help researchers to unify or integrate studies of artifacts, behavior, and communication under-taken across the social sciences.

A preview

In the presentation that follows, early chapters set forth in detail the most basic concepts, premises, and principles. These in turn are employed in later chapters for fashioning a new theory of communication and, eventually, of behavior. Because the work builds cumulatively, readers should resist the urge to skip ahead without having obtained the necessary conceptual foundation. Moreover, the reader is cautioned that definitions of important concepts, including artifact, behavior, and communication, undergo progressive refinement.

Chapter 2 elaborates the concept of the material medium, identifying the variety of interactors that participate and the kinds of interactions that take place, thereby answering questions (1) and (2) above. In addition, Chapter 2 sets forth relational definitions of human behavior that emphasize people–artifact interactions.

I examine in Chapter 3 "interpersonal" communication, showing that artifacts participate consequentially in every communication "mode" traditionally recognized by researchers. To wit, diverse artifacts contribute to the information that one person (the "receiver") obtains from another in everyday interactions. This demonstration makes clear the need to broaden the concept of communication to include the information that people acquire, through inference, from all kinds of interactors participating in the material medium.

In accord with the expanded view of communication, Chapter 4 argues that the process of archaeological inference is a more appropriate paradigm for studying communication phenomena than two people conversing – the language-based, "two-body" model that underlies all conventional theories. Basic premises and postulates are developed for the new theory.

A general theory of communication, built upon the new ontology and the premises of archaeological inference, is presented in Chapter 5. The receiver-oriented theory posits that all communication phenomena involve three interactor roles: sender, emitter, and receiver.

In order to give the reader a more grounded understanding of the new theory, Chapter 6 presents a series of nineteen "basic communication processes" (BCPs) in which people play the receiver role. The BCPs are illustrated with familiar examples from everyday life, which show how the theory enables investigators to analyze the varied communication phenomena that permeate the material medium.

Finally, in Chapter 7 I revisit the relationship between behavior and communication, demonstrating how an elaborated model of receiver response also explains behavior. Implications of the receiver-response model and the general theory are explored in relation to several significant issues: criteria of scientific explanation, the explanation of group responses, and the handling of "goals" and "purposes."

Together, Chapters 4–7 answer question (3) by identifying the rules – relational knowledge called "correlons" – that help to explain interactions.

What is human behavior?

Introduction

This chapter presents concepts and definitions crucial for developing a general theory of communication that can also handle human behavior. In keeping with the theme of this book, new definitions of behavior are grounded in people–artifact interactions. The discussions that follow put into empirical terms the intimacies between people and artifacts that make up so much of the material medium.

Definitions of behavior in biology and psychology focus on the individual organism, highlighting muscular motion and the functioning of internal organs. In the memorable phrase of Dawkins and Dawkins (1973: 83), behavior is "a temporal sequence of muscular contractions." By this definition, a blinking eye and a beating heart are human behavior no less than climbing a ladder or fishing for flounder. Although conceptions of behavior confined to the kinesics and physiology of individual organisms might be appropriate for biological and psychological research, they are manifestly unhelpful if one is striving to understand people–artifact interactions (Walker et al. 1995: 5–8).

In sociocultural anthropology and sociology, little effort goes into defining behavior, and most investigators do not even recognize this as a problem. Instead, energy is lavished on crafting definitions of culture and society; human behavior, when the term is used at all, is treated as a given. As one telling example, consider the book *New Rules of Sociological Method* by renowned theorist Anthony Giddens. "Behavior" or "human behavior," though occurring in *New Rules* a number of times (e.g., Giddens 1993: 33, 37, 65, 83, 101), is defined not once. Even when sociologists and anthropologists do furnish definitions, they almost always confine behavior to "interpersonal events" (e.g., Arensberg 1972: 9; see also McDermott and Roth 1978), which is far too narrow for our needs.

In the present work, behavior cannot be taken as a given, much less restricted to an individual's muscular contractions or "interpersonal events."

Rather, behavior is defined as *relational* phenomena at several scales. As Walker *et al.* (1995: 5) put it, "The boundary of a behavior does not lie at the edge of a moving organism but extends beyond it to include materials involved in activities" (see also Hutchins 1995: 287–293). These conceptual tools are indispensable for formulating fruitful questions about people's participation in the material medium. Let us now begin to tame the material medium, laying a foundation for crafting new definitions of behavior.

Interactors in the material medium

Chapter 1 established the ontological premise that people spend their lives immersed in the material medium, mostly engaging with innumerable kinds of artifacts and with other people who have been combined with, or modified by, artifacts (cf. Schiffer 1992b: ch. 1). Although it has been implied thus far that "material" means artifacts, this formulation seems somewhat confining in light of the entire range of interactions that occupy people daily. In expanding the material medium beyond artifacts, I define *material* in its broadest philosophical-scientific sense as any form of matter or energy. Thus, all phenomena exhibiting materiality – they are not patently mental or spiritual – can take part in interactions, and so are the stuff of the material medium. Any such phenomenon is termed an *interactor* (on concepts of interactor in evolutionary theory, see Hull 1988 and Sober 1984).

Three major families of interactors are recognized: people, artifacts, and externs. *People* are defined as individuals belonging to the species *Homo sapiens* and to its hominid predecessors.

Artifacts are phenomena produced, replicated, or otherwise brought wholly or partly to their present form through human means (adapted from Rathje and Schiffer 1982: ch. 1). Thus, all household items, from carpets to crucifixes, lightbulbs to beds, and cooking pots to paintings, are artifacts – as are neckties and nose-rings. Houses, churches, factories, and civic buildings, themselves stationary artifacts called structures or architecture, overflow with portable artifacts ranging from desks, widget-winders, and laptop computers to holy water and toilet paper. Most pets as well as domesticated plants and animals are also artifacts, for their breeding is at least partly under human control. Less obviously, when a person's body is altered by applying lipstick, piercing ears, receiving a tattoo, or styling hair, the resultant modifications become artifacts. Moreover, for some purposes we can also regard as artifacts any substances created by, but separated from, a person's body, such as hair, nail clippings, tears, fingerprints and noseprints, ear wax, scabs, sloughed-off epidermis, airborne scents and odors (from the skin, hair, breath, and axillary glands), saliva, sputum, urine, and feces. Finally, artifacts may also include human remains: corpses, mummies, skeletons, body parts, organs and tissues, ashes, and relics (Walker 1998).

The final type of interactor, *extern*, takes in phenomena that arise independently of people, like sunlight and clouds, wild plants and animals, rocks and minerals, and landforms. In actuality, many externs quickly become artifacts as they are modified through interactions with people or artifacts (see Chapter 6, BCP 3). The term "extern" allows the investigator to designate forms of matter-energy that participate in interactions but which are not obviously artifacts or people; thus, extern is a residual category whose precise definition need not occasion strenuous efforts.[1]

People, artifacts, and externs are combined in various ways to form *compound interactors*, which tend to interact as a single entity. For example, clothing, jewelry, hair style, and tattoos combine with the individual wearing them, and thus person-plus-artifacts becomes a compound interactor. Other examples of compound interactors are artifacts consisting of many parts brought together during manufacture, such as a stone-tipped spear, CD player, and automobile. Other compound interactors – one can call them *macroartifacts* – include horse and rider, car and driver, a cultivated field, and the air over industrial cities.

Interactions in the material medium involve diverse kinds of interactors, simple and compound, in every conceivable combination. From almost any vantage point, a person can look around and see occurring a plethora of person–person, person–artifact, person–extern, artifact–artifact, artifact–extern, and extern–extern interactions. Regrettably, social scientists have privileged people–people ("interpersonal") interactions, ignoring or marginalizing other kinds – even when they are relevant to explaining the forward motion of activities. In the present project, *all interactions involving people or artifacts are of transcendent importance*; only extern–extern interactions, which lack direct or indirect human involvement, are relegated to the background (even so, some examples are discussed in Chapter 6).

Interaction modes

Discrete interactions (Schiffer and Skibo 1987) are the observational units of the material medium – what the philosophical fish and chimps of the previous chapter observed. An *interaction* is any matter–energy transaction taking place between two or more interactors. There are five major *interaction modes*: mechanical, chemical, thermal, electrical, and electromagnetic.

Mechanical

Involving physical contact, mechanical interactions are ubiquitous in the material medium, making it possible, for example, to transform externs into artifacts and to assemble compound artifacts from component parts. Touching between people is also a mechanical interaction, one that figures importantly in human development and communication (e.g., Montagu 1978). Some mechanical interactions are subtler than the contact and modification of materials. Sound, after all, is mechanical – the vibration of air molecules (Coren *et al*. 1994); needless to say, this sort of interaction has dominated communication studies. In short, mechanical interactions, which vary greatly in their "intimacy," include the motion of a loudspeaker cone or vocal cords in the air, someone wearing eyeglasses, a drawer being opened, carving a turkey, and cars crashing.

Chemical

The material medium is also pervaded by chemical interactions, such as photosynthesis by crop plants, a pot of boiling rice, food being digested, a rusting anchor, and the reactions occurring in innumerable industrial processes ranging from tanning hides to making aspirin. Less obviously, smelling the aroma of a fragrant rose and the odor of someone ripe after a workout are equally based on chemical interactions, as are tasting a delicate chocolate mousse and a pungent pickle. Mechanical interactions sometimes involve chemical ones as well. For example, the simple act of chewing a piece of bread – so obviously mechanical – also entails chemical reactions between the masticated bread and salivary enzymes, as well as among the bread molecules and taste buds and olfactory receptors.

Thermal

In general, thermal interactions occur when one interactor warms or cools another. Examples include roasting a rabbit on a fire, someone snuggled in a sleeping bag or sucking on a popsicle, a refrigerator cooling its contents, a swimmer plunging into the ocean, a sidewalk swelling during the day and shrinking at night, and countless craft and industrial processes that use heat or cold to modify materials.

Electrical

An ever-increasing number of compound artifacts, from flashlight to Boeing 757, depend on electrical interactions – a flow of electrons or ions – among the discrete parts that make them up, such as wires, lightbulbs, batteries, relays, and computer chips. Although attention to the intricacies of electrical interactions would be out of place here, one should keep in mind that they are at the heart of all devices that use electricity.

   People can also participate directly in electrical interactions. During the late eighteenth century, electrical entertainment enjoyed a period of popularity in Europe and North America (Cohen 1990: 143–145; Heilbron 1982: 180). In one notorious example, the electrical demonstrator charged a comely woman with static electricity and then invited an unsuspecting young man to kiss her on the lips. Literally and figuratively, he was shocked as a spark passed between them in an "electric kiss." We are familiar with these kinds of static-electrical phenomena when touching objects in heated rooms after shuffling our feet on the carpet. Less amusing are electrical interactions that take place between people and externs (or artifacts) during thunderstorms or when handling faulty appliances. Among the modern artifacts that normally interact electrically with people are heart monitors and defibrillators, pain-reduction devices, lie detectors, and quack medical machines.

Electromagnetic

At last we arrive at the electromagnetic mode of interaction, seemingly as esoteric as the electrical one. However, electromagnetic radiation, as light, participates importantly in a great many complex interactions with people. For example, nearly all mechanical interactions involving sighted individuals depend also on the sense of vision. "Seeing" is thus an interaction between a person and the light reflected from or emitted by artifacts, externs, and other people (Coren *et al.* 1994). Because radio waves are also a form of electromagnetic radiation, many of our favorite toys take part in electromagnetic interactions, including radios, TVs, and cellular and cordless phones.

According to the investigator's interests, the major interaction modes (i.e., mechanical, chemical, thermal, electrical, and electromagnetic) can be subdivided and combined in countless ways. Later in this work, for example, I employ the categories of "visual" (one kind of electromagnetic interaction) as well as "tactile" and "acoustic" interactions (the latter two being mechanical).

In building a theory of communication, one should not privilege a priori one particular interaction mode (however defined), for all are relevant to understanding how people engage the material medium.

Complex interactions

As already intimated, interactions vary in complexity, depending on a number of factors. It should be recalled, for example, that many interactors – humans almost always – are compound, and this augments the interaction's complexity. Complexity also increases when more than two interactors take part, such as a person hammering a nail into a board, conversing with a friend by phone, or stirring a pot of soup. Additional complexity comes from interactions that involve more than one mode (regardless of the number of interactors); in licking a lollipop, for example, one can tally chemical (taste and smell) as well as mechanical interactions. As the number of interaction points increases, so too does complexity. Thus, while person and lollipop are engaged, the actual interactions are taking place between specific *interaction zones*, such as fingers, tongue, palate, lips, and nose. By delineating interaction zones, the investigator can handle complex visual interactions between, for example, a person and highly differentiated artifacts, like a newspaper, sculpture, or graffiti-laden wall (cf. Moriarty 1996). The literatures of ergonomics (e.g., Croney 1980; Pheasant 1986) and kinesics (e.g., Birdwhistell 1970) furnish potentially useful systems for describing some complex interactions involving people.

An intriguing feature of complex interactions is that one person is able to engage, simultaneously, in so many relationships with other interactors. This feature testifies to the massive parallel processing that takes place in the human nervous system (D'Andrade 1995: 140; Jeannerod 1997; see also Chapter 7).

Performance and performance characteristics

For an interaction to take place, each participating interactor must carry out one or more *performances* (Schiffer and Skibo 1997). For example, when two people, standing several feet apart, interact acoustically, the first generates sound waves, the second detects (and decodes) them, and the medium (i.e., air) conveys the sound waves from person to person. Clearly, this acoustic interaction requires the occurrence of all three performances (i.e., sound generator, acoustic medium, and listener).

A second example is furnished by a "visual interaction" (cf. Duncan 1969: 129) between two people; specifically, seeing a smile, which also necessitates a third interactor – a source of light, like a lamp. In "seeing a smile," one person's facial muscles move into the smile configuration; the lamp emits light, in the human-visible portion of the spectrum, of sufficient intensity to reflect off the smiling face and reach the second person; and the receiving person registers the reflected light and recognizes it as a smile.

The heating of vegetable soup supplies a third example. To keep it simple, I ignore the cook and light source; thus, the relevant interactors are the soup, a ceramic cooking pot, and an electric burner. The burner provides, without deforming, a steady source of thermal energy to the pot; the pot retains its integrity while containing the soup, becomes hot from the burner, and conveys heat to its contents; and the soup (vegetables and water) gradually absorbs heat from the pot, thus warming up.

Although the term already has many usages in the social and behavioral sciences (e.g., Giddens 1993: 20; Goffman 1959, 1974: ch. 5; Hall 1963; McDermott and Roth 1978), in ethology (e.g., Byrne 1995: 35), and in the arts, "performance" is retained here because of its centrality to behavioral theory in archaeology (e.g., Braun 1983; Schiffer 1995b, 1996a; Schiffer and Skibo 1987, 1997; Nielsen 1995; Walker 1998). For the present, *a* performance is defined as one interactor's minimal engagement with another in a specific interaction.[2]

In order to perform appropriately or skillfully, an interactor must possess certain capabilities known as *performance characteristics* (Braun 1983; O'Brien *et al.* 1994; Schiffer 1995b; Schiffer and Skibo 1987, 1997; compare to "behavioral predisposition" [Deacon 1997: 50] and "behavioral aptitude"

[Byrne 1995: 30]). A performance characteristic is a capability, competence, or skill that could be exercised – i.e., "come into play" – in a specific performance, and thus is behaviorally relevant in a given interaction (Schiffer and Skibo 1987, 1997). The previous examples allow us to illustrate performance characteristics. In the "seeing a smile" interaction, one person must be able to move his or her facial muscles into a smile configuration (unhappily, some people are born lacking the ability to smile – a performance characteristic that adversely affects many interactions [Babad *et al.* 1983]). And, in order to perform as a cooking pot, a vessel must have adequate resistance to thermal shock and ample heating effectiveness (Skibo and Schiffer 1995).

Some performance characteristics are rather general, in that they can come into play in many kinds of interactions (Schiffer and Skibo 1997). A scuff-resistant shoe, for example, can resist scuffing in diverse contacts. Likewise, someone who is capable of speaking Spanish can exercise this skill across a range of activities. Although some generalized performance characteristics can be identified, the investigator should focus first on the capabilities that make possible a specific interaction in a given activity.

Admittedly, the specification of performance characteristics, especially those of people, remains in its infancy (for some exceptions in industrial design, see Aghazadeh 1994; Peacock and Karwowski 1993). What is more, as compound interactors, individuals have emergent performance characteristics (holding the interaction constant). For example, in many interactions, a clothed person's performance characteristics differ greatly both from the same individual undressed and from the same clothing unworn.

When dealing with people and other animals, the investigator can make use of a family of *sensory* performance characteristics based on the senses of sight, touch (and pain), hearing, smell, and taste (Hayden 1998; Schiffer and Skibo 1997). Visual performance characteristics might include an interactor's abilities to stand out from its surroundings and thus "catch the eye" of an observer (Cott 1940: 436; Hayden 1998; Schiffer 1992b: 135; see also Carr 1995: 185–187), to direct the observer's attention elsewhere (Miller 1987: 101), or to be recognizable at a distance (Wobst 1977) – performance characteristics that come into play in many people–artifact interactions in retail stores (e.g., Hawkins *et al.* 1992). Tactile performance characteristics describe touch- (and pain-) related capabilities. For example, a shirt woven of silk should be able to perform as "silken" when touching someone's skin. Similarly, musical instruments have acoustic performance characteristics – e.g., to be easy (or difficult) to play; to be capable of making sounds like a clarinet; to be able to play as well as a Stradivarius violin – that are behaviorally relevant in purchase, practice, tuning, and recital activities. Many foods have olfactory performance characteristics that come into play during cooking and eating. In particular, when a halibut just bought at the market is unwrapped at home, it must be capable of smelling to the cook like a "fresh fish." All senses, and thus all sensory performance characteristics, have a physico-chemical basis in one or more of the major interaction modes (Coren *et al.* 1994).

Because, in the course of quotidian activities, we take for granted the performances of which interactions are composed, performance characteristics do not usually come to our attention unless an interactor performs inappropriately or unskillfully. Artifacts furnish abundant examples, as in a lightbulb that has burned out (inadequate visual performance), a tube of toothpaste that can no longer ooze its contents when squeezed (inept mechanical performance), and a moldy vegetable in the refrigerator that lacks sufficient freshness (poor visual, mechanical, and chemical performances). In responding to these below-par performances, people adjust their own performances accordingly, often implicitly.

Individuals also exhibit performance deficiences that call attention to underlying performance characteristics. Common examples include a vertically challenged shopper in a supermarket straining to reach a cereal box on a high shelf, a 16-year-old trying in vain to buy a pack of cigarettes at a liquor store, and someone who is chronically forgetful. Finally, in teaching children to read in elementary schools, it has been found that some students make little progress when taking part in ordinary interactions with books, teacher, and classmates. That is why school officials today pay close attention to a youngster's reading-relevant performance characteristics, usually testing lagging students to determine whether they are afflicted with a learning disability such as dyslexia. Performance deficiences can become conspicuous and explicit in situations of behavioral change (Schiffer and Skibo 1987). For example, in the transition from silent to talking motion pictures in the late 1920s, established actors were suddenly subjected to a "voice test." Studios were assessing whether an actor could perform skillfully in acoustic interactions with sound-recording technology (Eyman 1997). Many fine actors failed. Performance characteristics also come to our attention when a person exhibits an unusual capability, as in running 100 meters in under 9.90 seconds or easily memorizing a telephone book.

Numerous interaction-specific performance characteristics of artifacts have been defined, and their values can be measured along quantitative scales (e.g., Schiffer *et al.* 1994). And in some realms of life, *explicit* assessment of artifact performance characteristics looms large. Engineers designing a steel bridge discuss performance characteristics relevant to their proposed product's interactions with traffic, winds, and agents of deterioration (e.g., Petroski 1985, 1995). In designing upscale women's wear, such as evening gowns, people pay attention to how their creations might interact with potential consumers (cf. Chambers 1951); thus, they are concerned with visual performance characteristics such as novelty relative to last year's gowns, distinctiveness in comparison to the offerings of other designers, and the gown's ability to stand out from its display surroundings. Similarly, toothbrush designers may attend to graspability, ease of movement in the mouth, and the ability of the bristles to reach the sides of molars (for a general theory of artifact design, see Schiffer and Skibo 1997).

It is our task to tease out the performance characteristics that underlie all performances – and thus all interactions – in the material medium. Performance characteristics, after all, enable interactors to take part in the sequential performances that give rise to an activity's forward motion.

Performance characteristics should not be confused with an interactor's *properties*. A property – chemical, physical, biological – is something that, in principle, is intrinsic to an interactor, such as its shape, size, surface texture, chemical composition, molecular structure, cellular structure and organization, color, weight, and density. Thus, a property is defined in terms of the interactor itself (with respect to a measuring instrument and standard scale in the laboratory). In contrast, performance characteristics are defined relationally, for they refer to the capabilities of one interactor in its engagement with another in a specific real-world, not laboratory, interaction.

Properties are still of interest because they influence performance characteristics and thus performances. For example, the shape of a molded clay object affects its ability to perform visually, thermally, and mechanically like a teapot. Likewise, leg length strongly affects a person's ability to walk fast. In addition, I regard knowledge (including skill or tacit knowledge [e.g., Hutchins 1995; Keller and Keller 1996; Lave and Wenger 1991; Reber 1993]) as biochemical properties of a person's nervous system (see also Sperber 1996: 26); these properties determine whether someone can converse in Swahili, play ice hockey, or sculpt a madonna from marble.

Typically, a given performance characteristic is affected by more than one property (Schiffer and Skibo 1987, 1997). For example, whether an object can be seen and recognized at a distance depends on its size, color, and shape; and a person's ability to paint intricate landscapes on a canvas is influenced by a host of properties pertaining to the brain, optic nerve, eyes, arms, and hands. By the same token, a single property can affect several performance characteristics (Schiffer and Skibo 1987, 1997). Thus, the texture on the outside of a traditional ceramic cooking pot affects its heating effectiveness, thermal shock resistance, and resistance to thermal spalling (Schiffer *et al.* 1994). And a plethora of sports-related performance characteristics are influenced by a person's weight. It goes almost without saying that as an interactor's properties change, so too will its performance characteristics.

Insofar as people are concerned, I anticipate future research to show that many, perhaps most, properties – and thus performance characteristics – have both genetic and experiential causes (see Chapter 5; cf. Wilson 1978). For example, properties such as bone density and extent of musculature are affected by someone's genes as well as by activities of work, play, and eating. Such properties, of course, influence performance characteristics like weightlifting or jumping abilities. In other cases, the mix of genetic and experiential components might be skewed heavily toward one factor or the other (e.g., skin color vs. hair style). These formulations permit the investigator to reconceptualize issues surrounding nature–nurture influences on behavior. Specifically, I recommend that all questions be framed in terms of how both genes and experience affect the properties that influence a specific performance characteristic.

Analytic units

Behavioral system

Let us now turn to definitions of potentially useful analytic units. The question is: which *aggregates* of interactions in the material medium might be appropriate as foci for orienting scientific studies of communication and behavior? Although the problem of unit definition has neither a single nor a simple solution (e.g., Ramenofsky and Steffen 1998), the concept of *behavioral system* is a useful starting point.

The entire set of interactions taking place *with reference to a group of people*, during an interval of time, is defined as a behavioral system (Schiffer 1972). Thus, a behavioral system is composed of all people–artifact, people–people, people–extern, artifact–artifact, and artifact–extern interactions relating to the members of a specific household or community or society (for behavioral definitions of these organizational units, see Rathje and Schiffer 1982: ch. 3; Schiffer 1992b: ch. 1; Schiffer 1995a: ch. 15). It must be acknowledged that delineating the spatial boundaries of any behavioral system can be empirically challenging, since all human groups – at every spatial and organizational scale – interact with people and objects of other groups (e.g., Brumfiel and Earle 1987; Earle and Ericson 1977; Fry 1980). Needless to say, the investigator should specify the boundaries of a behavioral system in ways useful for answering research questions.[3]

A behavioral system's operation over time – i.e., the repetition of its constituent interactions – enables the group to reproduce and persist. It is, in the enduring phrase of Leslie White (1959), humankind's "extrasomatic adaptation," or, in modern evolutionary jargon, a human population's "extended phenotype" (Dawkins 1982; O'Brien *et al.* 1994; Schiffer 1996a). In responding to internal and external selective pressures, however, behavioral systems do change. From an evolutionary standpoint, all such changes can be regarded as alterations in the nature and frequency of particular interactions.

Activities

Between the discrete interaction – the minimal observational unit in the material medium – and the behavioral system, which designates large-scale analytical units, we require units of intermediate scale. The latter allow the investigator to create aggregates of interactions essential for framing fruitful questions about communication and behavior. Two such units are *activity* and *life history*.

An activity is a set of sequentially related interactions, occurring in a particular location, among a set of interactors that includes at least one person or artifact. In previous behavioral definitions, I stipulated that an activity must have an "energy source," such as a person or stove (e.g., Schiffer 1972: 57, 1976: 45, 1979, 1992b: ch. 4; Schiffer and Skibo 1997). This requirement is too restrictive for the present project because it implicitly assumes that an activity has to involve some kind of work, as in a mechanical interaction. To keep the concept as broad and flexible as possible, I now allow activity to consist of any kind of interaction. Admittedly, however, most activities of interest will be dynamic, involving energy sources such as a person, animal, fire, flowing water, wind, sunlight, and various machines. Commonplace activities include eating breakfast, sleeping, carving a wooden duck, writing a letter, rowing a boat, washing the dinner dishes, a toaster-oven at work, worshipping in church, playing a basketball game, and a robot installing components on a circuit board. A simple activity, "cooking stew," illustrates the many discrete interactions that can constitute an activity (Table 2.1).

Table 2.1 Major interactions of the activity "cooking stew" (adapted from Schiffer and Skibo 1997: 30). A source of light, redundant interactions, and the cook's clothing and ornaments are excluded.

Reference interactors	Other interactors	Interactions
Stove	Fuel	M
	Pot	M, T
	Stirring spoon	M, T
	Tasting spoon	M
Burning fuel (gas)	Pot	T, C
Pot	Stew	M, T, C
	Cook	M, T
	Stirring spoon	M, T
Stew	Stirring spoon	M, T
	Tasting spoon	M, T
	Cook	M, T, C
Cook	Stirring spoon	M, T, V
	Tasting spoon	M, T, V
	Stove	M, T, V
	Pot	V
	Stew	V, A
	Burning fuel	V, T

Note: Kinds of interaction are M = mechanical, C = chemical, T = thermal, V = visual, A = acoustic.

Activities also tend to be recurrent, in at least two senses: (1) within a behavioral system, such as a particular household, an activity (e.g., eating breakfast) is often carried out repeatedly, usually at regular times; and (2) the same activity can be conducted by different behavioral systems, e.g., many households in a community regularly eat breakfast.

An activity can be described on the basis of the number and types of interactors, the kinds of interactions taking place among them, the rate and duration of the activity, and its location (adapted from Schiffer 1975, 1979; Schiffer and Skibo 1997). For each interaction, the investigator can also specify, in principle, the performance characteristics that come into play and enable the activity's forward motion.

Like behavioral systems, activity is an eminently flexible concept that can be applied, depending on one's research question, to a small or large number of related interactions of varying durations: writing a letter, for example, is a simpler set of interactions of much shorter duration than a football game, but both are activities. Complex activities like a football game can be disaggregated into simpler activities, such as one fan eating popcorn, a play from scrimmage, the coach shuffling players in and out of the game, or the team's owner drinking with friends in a skybox. Activity is the basic unit employed throughout later chapters for analyzing communication phenomena (for additional definitions and applications of "activity," see, e.g., Bourdieu 1977; Hutchins 1995; McPhee and Corman 1995; Radzikhovskii 1987).

Life history

A *life history* is the specific sequence of interactions and activities that occurs during a given interactor's existence (Schiffer and Skibo 1997; cf. Schiffer 1972, 1975, 1987). It is commonplace in archaeology, for example, to infer important activities in the life histories of artifacts ranging from a house to a ceramic jar (e.g., LaMotta and Schiffer, n.d.; Schiffer and Majewski, n.d.; Walker 1995, 1998). Artifact life histories are usually divided into sets of closely linked activities called *processes*; in the case of a ceramic jar, processes include the collection of clay and other raw materials, clay preparation, forming the clay into a vessel, smoothing and painting its surface, drying and firing, transport, exchange, use, storage, maintenance, reuse, and discard (Schiffer 1972). Each process, then, is a set of activities that, in turn, comprises a set of interactions.

Human life histories are long and complicated, consisting of millions of activities and interactions; social scientists often divide them into life-cycle stages, such as infancy, childhood, and adolescence, and a host of stages defined for adulthood (e.g., Walsh 1983). Significantly, life-cycle stages mark major changes in the sets of activities in which a person participates (Rathje and Schiffer 1982: ch. 4).

Like interactions, life histories are amenable to aggregation. Thus, an investigator may refer to the life history of a single ceramic cooking pot in a community or to a generalized life history of an entire community's cooking pots; human life histories can be similarly aggregated (Walker 1995, 1998; Walker, Skibo, and Nielsen 1995). As aggregates, life histories are employed widely across the sciences (e.g., Bruton 1989; Peacock and Holland 1993; Shipman 1981) and in archaeology (for recent examples, see Gumerman 1997; LaMotta and Schiffer, n.d.; Schiffer and Skibo 1997; Walker 1995, 1998; Walker *et al.*, n.d.; Zedeño 1997).

Many interactions eventually modify an interactor's properties – and thus its performance characteristics. As a result, activities often affect an interactor's performances in subsequent activities (Schiffer and Skibo 1997; Walker 1995). This formulation, it should be clear, applies equally to artifacts and to people. For example, a butchering knife used repeatedly becomes dull, adversely affecting its ability to cut cleanly. Likewise, someone who repeatedly listens to very loud music suffers predictable damage to the inner ear. These altered biological properties, in turn, affect performance characteristics such as the ability to understand speech in a crowded party. More generally, in the course of taking part in activities, people acquire knowledge that influences subsequent performances. Human properties, and thus performance characteristics, are also affected by processes of development (Piaget 1952) and aging (e.g., Charness 1985). I stress that a given performance characteristic, as assessed at one time in an interactor's life history, is partly the product of modifications to its properties resulting from interactions in earlier activities.

Given that an interactor's properties and performance characteristics reflect, at least in part, its history of interactions, we can now formulate a definition of activities in relation to life histories. Because a life history is a sequence of activities, every activity must lie at the intersection of the life histories of its interactors. An activity can be defined, then, as the set of interactions taking place when life histories converge. This definition of activity is especially useful for the present project because it calls attention to the residual effects, on a given interaction, of an interactor's participation in previous activities (see Chapters 4 and 5).

Interactors and activities revisited

Kinds of interactors

An activity's interactors are drawn from three sets: platial, personal, and situational. Use of these terms enables the investigator to relate interactors, especially artifacts, to activities and activity locations.

Platial artifacts reside in a "place" (cf. Basso 1996; Binford 1982; Gallagher 1993; Meyrowitz 1990: 71–73; Thomas 1996: 85–91) – a specific location or set of locations, indoors or outdoors – and include portable artifacts stored there, semi-portable artifacts (e.g., furniture), and more-or-less permanent architectural features (Rapoport 1990). Common examples of platial artifacts include cooking pots and silverware, books and PCs, beds, tables and chairs, carpets, paintings, walls and floors, ceiling fans, fireplaces, tools in a workshop, museum exhibits, bridges and roads, houses on a street, footpaths, plants in a garden, and artificial lakes. More than a reservoir for potential activity artifacts, platial artifacts also figure significantly in human communication. In anticipation of discussions in later chapters, I note, for example, that from platial artifact performances people obtain information on a place's appropriateness for carrying out specific activities (Hutchins 1995; Krueger and Harper 1988: 63; Miller 1987: 101–102; Schiffer 1992b: 133).

Because people are compound interactors, the artifacts with which they are compounded – *personal artifacts* – also perform in activities. Personal artifacts include: (1) artifacts that are an actual and essentially permanent part of the human body, such as tattoos, scars, and modified teeth; (2) artifacts that are an actual but temporary part of the human body, including hair style, makeup and body paint, drugs, deodorant and perfume, earrings and noserings; and (3) artifacts that perform as if part of the human body but are very easily attached and detached, such as clothing, headgear, shoes, hair ornaments, necklaces, masks, and badges.

Personal artifacts have dramatic effects on an individual's properties and performance characteristics, and thereby greatly influence communication (for summaries and references, see Joseph 1986; Kaiser 1985; see also Barnes and Eicher 1992; Brain 1979; Craik 1994; David 1992; Polhemus 1978a, 1978b). In the following chapter, copious examples illustrate how personal artifacts affect someone's performances as well as an observer's inferences and responses.

Situational artifacts arrive with people or turn up at a place for the conduct of an activity. Common examples include canes and wheelchairs that come along with a person, ritual paraphernalia brought from a clan house to a dance in the village plaza, golf clubs toted to the course, car parts moving from one station to another along an assembly line, and a Thanksgiving turkey carried from kitchen to dining room. In anticipation of later discussions, I observe that situational artifacts take part in communication; for example, from their arrival people infer that a specific activity, such as eating a Thanksgiving dinner, can begin.

The artifacts taking part in a given activity – its *activity artifacts* – are drawn from personal, situational, and platial artifacts. By the same token, it must be stressed that an enumeration of the three artifact sets is activity-specific; thus, as the activity occurring in a place changes, so might the platial, personal, and situational artifacts. For example, the same hair ornament could be a personal artifact while being worn in one activity and a platial artifact while being stored during another.

Different kinds of activities draw, in varying proportions, on platial, situational, and personal artifacts. Not surprisingly, activities conducted frequently and repeatedly for long periods in the same location tend overwhelmingly to employ platial artifacts (in accord with some of Zipf's [1949] principles). In contrast, activities carried out intermittently in different locations, such as hunting deer, commercial fishing for tuna, and playing golf, often rely heavily on situational artifacts. Other activities depend mainly on personal artifacts, as in a young couple conversing. In most cases, activity artifacts consist of some mix of personal, platial, and situational artifacts.

It is also useful to identify platial, personal, and situational externs. Platial externs include a stream in which someone casts a fishing line, the streambank on which the fishing person stands, the mountains as viewed from the streambank, and the atmosphere (such as rain, wind, temperature). An example of a situational extern is an antelope that arrives at the watering hole where a hunter lies in wait. Finally, personal externs include pests, such as headlice and fungal infections, as well as dirt adhering to one's foot.

Not surprisingly, these interactor categories also apply to people. The idea of a personal person appears outlandish until one considers the prolonged dependency of human children, and the near-inseparability of infants from their mothers in most societies. However counterintuitive, then, a personal person is a possibility. So is a platial person, in that some people seem to be part of a place. An individual selling newspapers and magazines in a street-corner kiosk, for example, can be regarded as a platial person, as might a bank teller or ticket seller behind the counter in a train station. Although none of these people is really a part of these places, it is legitimate to consider them as such from the standpoint of people in other activities occurring nearby. If the activity of interest is a couple conversing on a bench in the train station, for example, the investigator could treat the ticket seller as a platial person. Finally, situational persons are those who arrive at a place to take part in an activity.

Delineating activities and their interactors

Because "activity" is the most important analytic unit for the present project, we must be able to delineate an activity's interactors, distinguishing them from uninvolved platial interactors. To help the investigator accomplish this task, I work through a simple example of one person writing a letter; the focus is entirely on identifying the activity artifacts.

Let us visualize a bespectacled professor seated at a desk in her home office, word-processing the answer to a letter. This activity is defined as all related interactions occurring in that place between the time the professor, carrying the incoming letter, sits down at the desk, and the time that she stands up, holding the new letter (sealed, stamped, and ready to be mailed). An obvious list of activity artifacts is the letter being answered, keyboard, monitor, computer tower, printer, paper, envelope, stamp, chair, and desk.

But, a little reflection reveals that, during the activity, these artifacts and the professor interact with other artifacts. For example, the professor obtains the stamp from a sheet reposing in a desk drawer, the chair and desk are in contact with the oak floor, her feet periodically touch the floor, she occasionally glances at a clock on a nearby bookcase and is listening to a stereo system behind the chair, and a floor lamp illuminates (directly and indirectly) the activity location. Computer components, lamp, clock, and stereo are plugged into a power strip. The room, it should also be noted, is insulated from the outdoors and from other rooms by walls, and contains a heating/cooling vent that periodically performs thermally. Paint on the walls and ceiling reflects some of the lamp's light onto the desk's work area; and bookcases and filing cabinets abound, loaded to the gills. Countless other artifacts, including mementos of trips and family pictures, rest on the desk and are occasionally looked at by the professor. In this longer list, some artifacts perform directly and consequentially in the activity, such as the lamp, power strip, envelope, desk drawer, clock, stereo, and oak floor, and it is reasonable to add these to the roster of activity artifacts. But still other artifacts, on and in the desk and elsewhere in the room, remain problematic.

In seeking further guidance, let us exploit the life-history concept, which can help us to distinguish between activity interactors and uninvolved platial interactors. In many cases, the investigator can pinpoint one or more interactors whose life history appears to impose a pattern on the activity's sequence of interactions. In the letter-writing example, the letter being written is the *focal interactor* because it seems to be choreographing the performances of other interactors, giving impetus to the activity's forward motion, and thereby advancing its own life history.[4]

By identifying a focal interactor, when possible, the investigator can more readily specify the degree to which interactions, and thus interactors, are consequential to its life history. Returning to the example, I define as *primary interactors* those whose performances are essential for advancing the life history of the focal interactor – the letter. These can be ascertained if the investigator goes backwards from the last interactions in the letter's life history. Thus, primary interactors include the professor, stamp, envelope, printer, computer tower, monitor, keyboard, lamp, and the letter being answered. Without the performances of these interactors, the letter could not have been completed.

The investigator can also recognize a set of *secondary interactors*; these play less direct, yet necessary, roles. Usually linked to primary interactors, secondary interactors can be listed without details: desk, chair, the professor's clothing and glasses, oak flooring, and power strip.

Finally, a set of *tertiary interactors* can be defined as ones whose performances are not entirely necessary for advancing the focal interactor's life history. Examples from the present case include clock, stereo, walls, and heating/cooling vent. From the standpoint of the letter-writing activity, the remaining artifacts in the professor's office — family pictures, books, filing cabinets, etc. — are considered to be uninvolved platial artifacts.

In practice, we will encounter difficulties in distinguishing among an activity's primary, secondary, and tertiary interactors, since all fall along a continuum of "necessary" involvement. What is most important is that the investigator enumerate, for any activity, the many interactors that perform more and less consequentially. Needless to say, in applying these categories to a specific case, the investigator exercises judgment informed by problem orientation.

When attempting to define any activity's boundaries, the investigator should come to appreciate that activities consist of a great many more artifacts, and far more interactions, than social scientists are accustomed to considering. Even an activity so seemingly simple and self-contained as "one person writing a letter" entails myriad artifact performances. Apparently, much of what social scientists have written about behavior is impoverished and misleading because it fails to take account of the articulation, deep and wide, between people and artifacts in activities of the material medium. Ironically, the occasional novelist displays more insight into activities by describing them as artifact-laden occurrences that also happen to include people.

Defining human behavior

An understanding of the material medium and its observational and analytical units (interactors, interactions, and interaction modes; behavioral systems at various scales; activities and life histories) furnishes us with countless possibilities for defining behavior relationally, but only two definitions are furnished here.

In the first, human behavior is taken to be *any performance of a person*. Further, to qualify as an instance of behavior, a specific performance must engage one or more other interactors *consequentially*. This latter proviso stresses that the concept of performance, as used here, has a relational basis.[5]

Clearly, the investigator must exercise good judgment in defining what is and is not consequential. For example, a hand waving in complete darkness, although moving air molecules, is not behavior because it cannot engage other interactors consequentially. However, if a hand-wave is observed and acted upon by someone else, then a consequential interaction has occurred — it has become a visual performance in an activity, and thereby qualifies as behavior.

Because I insist that a performance be consequential, this definition leaves out phenomena that other investigators would regard as behavior. Indeed, problem-solving, deciding, dreaming, contemplating, rehearsing tactile interactions, fantasizing, hoping, praying, and other cognitive processes fall within the scope of many definitions of behavior, though taking place almost entirely in the brain (see Fabrega's [1977: 420] concept of "cognitive behavior"). Although cognitive processes help to produce performance (see Chapter 7), they do not immediately or consequentially articulate with the material medium – unless someone is undergoing a brain scan. Thus, while the *explanation* of behavior patently requires the investigator to offer inferences about a person's interaction-relevant knowledge (Chapters 4 and 5) and to construct cognitive models (Chapter 7), one must take pains not to confuse or conflate cognitive phenomena with behavior itself.

Drawing upon previous discussions, we can create a second – and much more expansive – definition: human behavior consists of *all interactions in a given behavioral system*. Whereas the first definition leaves out phenomena that some investigators consider to be obvious instances of behavior, the second encompasses phenomena that many would prefer to exclude. By the second definition, for example, the behavior occurring in a household includes a refrigerator at work as well as a pile of books on a desk. Although counterintuitive, this definition does identify *all* phenomena in the material medium attributable, directly or indirectly, to human agency. Moreover, this definition makes it possible, I suggest, to operationalize fully the concept of the "extended phenotype," which plays a pivotal role in applying evolutionary theory to human behavior (Dawkins 1982; O'Brien and Holland 1995; Schiffer 1996a).

Although both definitions of behavior inform the present project, the first (i.e., behavior as a person's performance) is crucial for theory- and model-building in later chapters.

Summary

This chapter has shown that the material medium consists of three kinds of interactors: people, artifacts, and externs. Interactors can engage each other in one or more interaction modes, the major ones being mechanical, chemical, thermal, electrical, and electromagnetic. An interactor's participation in a specific interaction is known as a performance. Interaction-specific performances are enabled by performance characteristics, including sensory-based performance characteristics such as those relating to sight (visual), hearing (acoustic), and touch (tactile).

Although the discrete interaction is the minimal observational unit of the material medium, many studies require analyses to be undertaken at larger scales. For such analyses one can employ the larger-scale analytic units, including behavioral system, activity, and life history, which are aggregates of discrete interactions.

It is useful to have a vocabulary for describing the relationship of interactors, especially artifacts, to activities and activity locations. Toward that end, I have supplied the terms platial, personal, and situational, which apply to any kind of interactor. Heuristics based on the life history of a focal interactor help in delineating activity interactors.

Finally, to advance the present project, I furnished two specific definitions of human behavior: (1) any performance by any person, and (2) the interactions of all interactors in a given behavioral system.

With the new concepts and definitions in hand, we can now consider in some detail the participation of artifacts in "interpersonal" communication.

Chapter 3

Artifacts and "interpersonal" communication

Introduction

In this chapter, I lay a foundation for fashioning a theory of human communication that departs sharply from traditional views. The reason for taking this drastic step is simple: conventional communication theories are profoundly flawed because they rest on, or are adapted from, language-based models. To be sure, language is a marvel of natural selection; not only do people learn language as effortlessly as they learn to walk, but activities everywhere are punctuated by these peculiar acoustic performances. Scholars are drawn strongly to language, perhaps because they believe it directly reflects, through symbolism, uniquely human cognitive processes (e.g., Deacon 1997). Thus, it is no surprise that language use (as verbal performance) has been taken as the paradigm of communication and all other performances subordinated, both theoretically and methodologically, to verbal ones (Burling 1993).

As Nolan (1975: 100) warns, however, "we should not fall into the trap of thinking that language is the end-all and be-all of human communication." Regrettably, communication researchers have fallen squarely into that trap, and that is why mere tinkering with extant theories will not suffice. We require a new theory founded on the new ontology. In this chapter and the next, I identify generic problems in communication theories, many of which can be traced to their linguistic origins. The attempt to overcome these problems guides the formulation of a new and more general theory based on archaeological inference.

I begin by supplying a provisional definition of communication (for a range of definitions, see Hauser 1996: 6–10). To wit, communication enables an interactor – specifically, a person – to obtain information, through inference, from the material medium by registering the performances of people, artifacts, and externs. Students of communication might object to this definition because it takes in all sorts of phenomena that they prefer to call "information transfer" (e.g., Burgoon *et al.* 1996: 10; Eisenberg and Smith

1971: 12). I contend, however, that the conventional move, which confines communication to information transfer in person–person interactions (Burgoon *et al.* 1996: 9), is arbitrary and lacks a convincing theoretical justification. Worse still, once investigators isolate "interpersonal" interactions for study (in which I include "organizational" and "mass" communication), the remaining performances in the material medium tend to be ignored. This is regrettable because the forward motion of activities, and thus all behavior, depends upon people acquiring – and responding on the basis of – information gleaned from diverse interactors (Thomas 1996).

The most important feature of my definition is that a person potentially secures information from any performance of any interactor that she or he can register. The study of communication might reap benefits from this overdue simplification, which unifies the myriad phenomena from which people obtain the consequential information that influences their own performances.

In the present chapter, I appear to play the communication game by conventional rules, focusing narrowly on "interpersonal" communication. In fact, my game is a subversive one, demonstrating that there can be no such thing as pure "interpersonal" communication because of the involvement of artifacts in all person–person interactions. Specifically, I show how one person's artifact-laden performances yield information to a second person – the receiver (also referred to as an "other" or "observer"). I establish as well that the information a receiver acquires from someone during "interpersonal" communication comes not only from that person's performances as a compound interactor, but also from activity, situational, and platial artifacts (and externs).

The specific inferences that a human receiver constructs depend importantly on his or her relational knowledge. It is assumed for present purposes that receivers somehow come to possess the requisite knowledge; in Chapters 4 and 5 I discuss its general nature and acquisition processes.

Communication modes and performance modes

During the second half of the twentieth century, students of communication learned that people secure information from each other's facial expressions, gestures, gait, and so on. The communication "modes" beyond language are often termed, as a group, "nonverbal" communication (Burgoon *et al.* 1996; Burling 1993; Duncan 1969; Eisenberg and Smith 1971; Ekman and Friesen 1969; Harrison 1989; Harrison and Crouch 1975; Knapp and Hall 1992). Use of the label "nonverbal" regrettably reinforces the privileged standing of language in traditional treatments of communication.

Many investigators go so far as to regard "nonverbal" phenomena simply as factors that affect the interpretation of a verbal performance (e.g., Hanneman 1975). A few familiar examples easily show why this position is an untenable generalization. (1) When two people are conversing in sign language alone, information is embodied exclusively in the visual performances of personal artifacts, facial expressions, and gestures (Kendon 1993). (2) In the checkout line of a convenience store, the checker's only utterance might be to recite the total bill, which information is entirely redundant with the cash register's visual display. In this case, language merely adds emphasis to an artifact's performance. (3) During a basketball game, players obtain the most conse-quential information from the ball as well as the facial expressions, gestures, postures, gaits, and uniforms of other players. Although these examples could be multiplied indefinitely, there is no need to belabor the point. Clearly, investigators must disabuse themselves of the belief that nonverbal perform-ances always modify or augment verbal ones. Anyone who remains uncon-vinced should immediately read *A Natural History of the Senses* (Ackerman 1990). The time has come to shed our linguistic blinders and build a general theory that encompasses *all* performances having communicative effects.

Let us begin with a list of standard communication modes, which come close to exhausting the ways that a receiver can obtain consequential information from other people's performances (adapted from Duncan 1969): (1) verbal (language), (2) vocal, which includes yells, sighs, laughs, snorts, and so on, (3) paralinguistic (e.g., pitch, pauses, rhythm, loudness [Crystal 1975]), (4) facial expressions, (5) gestures, (6) touching (the tactile or haptic mode [Montagu 1978]), (7) postures and gait, (8) chemical (scents and smells and tastes), (9) proxemics – i.e., the use of space (Hall 1966), and (10) artifact (e.g., Burgoon 1978: 144; Burgoon *et al.* 1996: ch. 4; Harrison 1989: 121; Harrison and Crouch 1975: 93–94; Hymes 1967: 19).

From the standpoint of the present project we need to ask: how do the standard communication modes relate to the interaction modes defined in Chapter 2 – i.e., mechanical (including acoustic and tactile), thermal, chemical, electrical, and electromagnetic (including visual)? Fortunately, it is possible to establish some relationships, to effect a translation between the two systems. The verbal, vocal, and paralinguistic modes all are instances of acoustic performance; facial expressions, gestures, and postures are visual performances; tactile communication is performance of a mechanical kind; chemical communication is based on chemical performances; and visual performance is the basis of proxemics, especially interpersonal spacing. To this point, then, each standard communication mode corresponds to a single performance mode; thus, a straightforward translation is apparently possible.

The translation algorithm breaks down with the "artifact" mode, however, because even in "interpersonal" communication *artifacts can perform in all major performance modes*, as in the color of dyed hair or clothing, the "frou-frou" sounds made by Victorian silk undergarments (Joseph 1986: 57), the texture of a sweater, the warmth radiated by someone wearing a heavy coat in a heated room, and the scent of cologne. In addition, because people are compound interactors, their own performances are affected – in every mode –

by personal artifacts. Finally, even in electronic communication, such as telephony and teleconferencing, there is variation in the involvement of particular performance modes, i.e., acoustic, tactile, and visual (Hiltz *et al.* 1986). Evidently, the "artifact" mode is not comparable to the other communication modes.[1]

It appears that investigators have added artifacts to the list of modes in an *ad hoc* manner. Indeed, by assigning artifacts to a separate mode, communication researchers can, in theory and practice, easily marginalize them. I suggest that segregating artifacts in this way is an unwise move for anyone building a communication theory that aspires to complete generality. Not surprisingly, I maintain that artifacts must be drawn integrally into the consideration of every performance mode.

Because any performance that can be registered sensorily is capable of yielding information (Ackerman 1990; Sperber 1975: 86), the performance modes that follow, adapted from the interaction modes of Chapter 2, are based on the human senses. In anticipation of later discussions (e.g., Chapter 5), I suggest how performances in these modes affect not only the receiver's inferences but also his or her subsequent performances (i.e., the response).

Visual performance

As primates, the quintessential visual creatures, humans can be expected to obtain vast amounts of information through their eyes. A person's visual performance, as registered by a receiver, is affected by the body's physical properties, whether produced biologically or through participation in activities. For the sake of simplicity, one can refer to a person's visual performance as "appearance" (Kaiser 1985: 7). Needless to say, appearance is strongly influenced by personal artifacts, and these are emphasized in the following discussions. In addition, because all visual performances depend, for example, on light reflected from a person, they are also affected by activity and platial artifacts. Thus, people and their personal artifacts give different visual performances under different conditions of natural and artificial lighting, both indoors and outdoors. A case in point comes from Tucson, Arizona, where sodium–vapor street lamps reduce the light pollution affecting nearby astronomical observatories but, in this orange–yellow light, a person's face takes on a ghastly hue which can hinder interaction.

I now turn to some of the properties of the human body that affect appearance and the construction of varied inferences.

Properties of the human body

Facial features

Eyes, nose, mouth, cheeks, and so forth are readily altered by makeup. These modifications demonstrably affect a receiver's inferences about a person's attractiveness (e.g., Cash *et al.* 1989; cf. D. Jones 1995), age grade, ethnicity, and so forth. In some cases, inferences about a person's dispositions are inferred from makeup. For example, from the eyeliner worn by a Hispanic female gang member in northern California, knowledgeable receivers infer her intention and willingness to fight (Mendoza-Denton 1996: 55).

In Western societies, women's makeup tends to be more elaborate than that of men, but all genders fiddle with their faces, turning them into artifacts that supply information to receivers. Eyes get special attention: shadow, eye liner, and false lashes make them appear larger and more prominent; eyebrows are trimmed or plucked with special tweezers, and modified by eyebrow pencil; even eye color can be changed with tinted contact lenses. Eyeglasses of many sorts give people different "looks" that often vary by age, gender, occupation, and social class. Lipstick and lip color alter the color, glossiness, and apparent size of lips, an important zone of sexual interest; indeed, a woman's red lipstick readily draws a man's gaze. Powders, acne ointments, and zinc oxide creams affect the appearance of facial skin. Wrinkles are rendered less visible by special creams used by men and women, such as "age-defying liquid makeup." And a flaccid mustache can be stiffened with mustache wax. The number of different products that can be bought today for changing faces in Western societies is astounding, but faces are fixed throughout the world.

Among the Hagen of Highland New Guinea (Strathern and Strathern 1971), face painting figures importantly in elaborate ceremonial competitions between men of local groups. Hagen receivers registering an individual's overall visual performance – which includes the presentation of gifts as well as the wearing of wigs, aprons, and leaves – pass judgment on a man's impressiveness, inferring his suitability for assuming a leadership position.

Sometimes people take more drastic action by modifying their face's appearance through plastic surgery. It is not uncommon for a young Jewish woman to undergo rhinoplasty, an operation that makes her nose less prominent, giving it a more "gentile" appearance. And facelifts make old faces appear younger – at least for a while.

Ornaments affixed to the face with more or less permanence are common in societies around the globe. Among the Tapirapé, of central Brazil, lip ornaments are worn by men:

> The lower lip of the Tapirapé males was perforated at birth with a sharp monkey bone; then the hole was tied through with a string so it would not close. For the rest of his life a man wore a lip plug of one kind or

another, depending on his age. As a small boy he wore a slender lip ornament made of a wild pig or emu bone; then, as an adolescent, a smaller
one made of mother of pearl, and, finally, as an adult, a plain, small, round
plug, which simply closed the hole in his lip. Once in his life a boy would
wear the invaluable lip plug made of milky quartz at his coming of age
festival.

(Wagley 1983: 132)

Tapirapé observers could readily infer a male's age grade on the basis of the
kind of lip plug he was wearing.

In the West, earrings traditionally have been worn by women, but in the
1980s teenagers and young adults of both sexes increasingly adopted
earrings, sometimes in profusion. Also proliferating were rings and studs for
the nose, tongue, lip, eyebrow, navel, and more intimate zones. A few years
ago, a young man visited my office wearing a gold stud in his tongue, the
first I had ever seen. Its visual performance was like a magnet, drawing my
gaze ineluctably to his tongue. I have to confess that my every response was
affected by the need not to show mirth. In many traditional societies, lip
rings (labrets) as well as ear spools and disks perform prominently by
distending, respectively, lips and ear lobes – sometimes to an amazing extent
(Rubin 1988). Among the Inka, all men wore earplugs, but men of the
nobility could be identified because their earplugs were huge, sometimes
reaching 5 centimeters in diameter, and made of gold or silver (Mason 1968:
149–150). Clearly, from facial ornaments in societies worldwide, others
obtain information about gender, sexuality, age grade, social group affiliation,
social roles and rank, and so on.

A face that appears as "attractive" to observers is apt to positively affect
interactions in many situations, just as an "unattractive" face may have adverse
effects. A large and growing literature, mostly based on experiments
conducted in the United States, has brought to light these distressing patterns
(e.g., Chung and Leung 1988; Hunsberger and Cavanagh 1988; Kalick 1988;
Roszell et al. 1989; Zahr 1985). In a typical experiment, investigators presented
a group of fifth-grade teachers with a report card of average grades along with
the student's purported photograph. "Attractive" children were inferred to
have a higher IQ, better relations with peers, and higher potential for
education than "unattractive" ones (Clifford and Walster 1973). Outside the
laboratory, these effects can be dire, as demonstrated in a recent case from the
People's Republic of China. A young man with "sky-high marks, solid
references, and a strong character" (Mickleburg 1996: 2) was denied admission
to Chinese universities. The aspiring undergraduate unfortunately suffered
from a severe birth defect that "left him cross-eyed, with a misshapen, almost
mangled face" (Mickleburg 1996: 2). In the West, this young man doubtless
would have been advised to undergo plastic surgery. It goes almost without

saying that virtually all facial modifications and ornaments contribute to inferences about attractiveness.

Facial hair

Management of facial hair is an important part of daily activities in many societies. As recently as the early 1960s, almost every American man shaved his entire face, removing all traces of hair. Beginning in the late 1960s, men exercised more freedom in facial hair management, and a few began to sport beards. Today, one can find examples of virtually every conceivable variant of facial hair; however, mutton chops, though popular during the nineteenth century, have not made a comeback. Women in middle and later years may have facial hair removed or bleached, thereby reducing its visibility. Middle-aged men sometimes dye graying beards and mustaches and, as a result, may appear more youthful.

Teeth

The number, sizes, shapes, and placement of teeth along with dental hygiene and health have marked effects on the visual performance of dentition. In Western societies, toothpastes and innumerable other products help people to create whiter, cleaner teeth. The ancient Maya took a different approach, filing teeth into geometric shapes and sometimes inlaying them with jade and other semi-precious stones (Romero 1970). In wealthier strata of industrial societies, the placement of teeth is modified by orthodontia, involving the wearing for many years of conspicuous braces and retainers. Orthodontia is usually practiced on youth, who learn all too quickly that braces affect interaction. Some still recall their debut with braces at school, when peers responded with jeers and jokes. Teeth are also repaired and replaced today by assorted ceramic, metal, and plastic prostheses. Needless to say, the appearance of teeth contributes to inferences about overall beauty and attractiveness and thus affects interaction.

Top of the head

In most societies, people devote much time, energy, and resources to modifying the hair upon their heads. In creating a coif, hair is curled or uncurled, styled, plied with sundry substances from rare oils to mud to animal dung, bleached or colored, allowed to grow long or cropped short, braided, and laced with ornaments such as clips and combs, barrettes and bone awls, and ribbons and "pony elastics." Within a society, hair treatments vary by gender and often by age, ethnicity, and social class. Among many groups, special occasions – ranging from weddings to funerals to senior proms – call forth intensive hair-preparation activities. Because particular hairdos are necessary for so many ceremonies, observers can infer that someone is or is not properly coifed for the occasion. During the late 1960s and 1970s in the United States, some receivers inferred a person's politics as well as attitudes toward illegal drug use on the basis of hair length. In short, the coiffed head is an important personal artifact from which others draw conclusions that affect their responses.

Above and beyond coifs, headgear such as hats, crowns, headdresses, and wigs gives people nearly infinite possibilities for decorating their domes. In the former Yugoslavia, ethnic groups donned traditional hats, from which ethnicity could be discerned at a safe distance (Wobst 1977); as we are painfully aware, these inferences allowed the receiver to distinguish friend from foe.

Throughout the first half of the twentieth century, hats in America were an indispensable part of the urban male's ordinary attire (Watson 1994). From a man's hat, one could sometimes learn his occupation, region of residence, and wealth. After a decades-long hiatus, hats are making a comeback in daily life, and can furnish others with information on age grade or generation, vocations and avocations, sports-team preferences, political beliefs, and so on. Among my favorites are baseball caps bearing timeless witticisms such as "I'm so horny even the crack of dawn ain't safe." Headgear of all kinds can easily influence interaction. I, for one, tend to steer clear of any muscular man wearing a hat, adorned with the stars and stripes, that taunts "Try burning this U.S. flag."

Head shape

The head itself is treated in some societies as a modifiable object. In the technology of head deformation, a baby's head is shaped by tight binding to cradle boards or by placement in special wooden molds or stones (Dembo and Imbelloni 1978: 155–157; Ubelaker 1978: 68–71). The result is an adult head that boasts various degrees of flattening or elongation. In Renaissance France, a receiver could identify the district from which a person hailed on the basis of head shape (Brain 1979: 90).

Skin

In everyday conversations, we tend to treat skin color as a biological given, an individual's invariant property. Yet, skin color can be modified, not only by sunlight, but also by tanning lamps, makeup, and chemical darkeners and lighteners. Many observers have pointed out the irony of black Americans using artifacts to lighten their skin color while "whites" employ different ones to darken theirs. That skin color affects inferences, and thus interaction, has been extensively documented (e.g., Fix and Struyk 1993; Gross and Mauro

1989; Sovern 1973; Von Furstenberg *et al.* 1974) and requires no further comment.

Tattooing is among the oldest and most widespread technologies for altering skin (Mascia-Lees and Sharpe 1992; Rubin 1988). Usually a permanent modification, tattoos are created by introducing pigment into the skin with a needle or other sharp tool. In many societies, tattoos are applied in stages corresponding to changes in an individual's role and status. For example, among the Motu of Port Moresby, New Guinea, tattooing of women

> begins when the child is small, the hands and arms being tattooed first since they are body parts which are less symbolically important and also less sensitive to pain. At a later stage the belly and chest and back are done. When the girl is considered marriageable, her buttocks and legs and face are tattooed. A feast is given to mark the final stage: the marriageable, permanently marked woman is decked out in finery and parades cere-monially up and down the village. Then for five days she sits on the ve-randa of the house, displaying herself and her ornaments.
>
> (Brain 1979: 50).

It is apparent that, from a woman's appearance, another Motu can readily infer her marital status.

In Polynesian societies, there was a strong correlation between a person's social rank and the kind and extent of tattooing (Buck 1959; Handy 1923). The body of a paramount chief, for example, could be entirely covered with tattoos of great intricacy. Needless to say, an extensively tattooed chief commanded great respect.

Tattooing is also practiced in industrial nations, including Japan (Fellman 1986), western Europe, and the United States. Until recent decades, in the United States tattoos were taboo except for men in the military, prisons, and gangs (Steward 1990). Differences in designs allowed an observer to infer the group to which a tattooed person belonged (e.g., a branch of the service), and often a tattoo included someone's name, perhaps a loved one. Today, tattooing occurs among both men and women of varied social classes, and the designs are greatly diversified (e.g., Lautman 1994); as a result, the range of inferences possible from tattoos has correspondingly expanded, including a teenager's "coolness," sexual availability, and a biker's preference for motorcycle brands.

Among many dark-skinned peoples, another technology – scarification – is sometimes employed to transform skin into artifact (Gillin 1948: 310; Rubin 1988). In scarification, the skin is cut so as to produce after healing a raised scar having the appearance of a pea or small button; these welts can be created in patterns anywhere on the body. Among the Tiv, an African society, the designs are made in geometrical patterns in the shapes of animals (Bohannon 1988). It is possible to infer from a Tiv's scarification design something about his or her social roles. For example, a woman's belly is not scarified until she reaches puberty.

Where customary clothing leaves large areas of skin exposed, bodies are often painted, usually with meticulously prepared clays, oils and pigments, and ground-up plants. In its innumerable colors, designs, and places of application, body painting, which began at least 30,000 years ago (Mithen 1996: 182), supplies much information to other members of a society. For example, among the Bangwa, a group in Cameroon, people apply paint to their bodies during rites of passage, such as "births and marriages, the crowning of their chiefs and the ritual fattening of adolescent girls" (Brain 1979: 19). When a Bangwa dies, dark clays are rubbed on the mourners' bodies. From the color and patterning of the paint, another Bangwa can infer the kin relationship of a mourner to the deceased (Brain 1979: 19). Among the Andaman Islanders, a hunting–gathering society, bodies are elaborately painted with pigments and clays. Women do the painting, apparently in a spirit of competition, and artistic innovations are welcomed (Radcliffe-Brown 1933). Doubtless, an Andaman Islander could easily infer who was responsible for painting a particular person's body.

Body hair

Body hair is selectively removed in some societies by shaving. In the United States, for example, many women shave or wax their legs and underarms, and some shave their pubic areas; and, increasingly, young men shave their chest hair. Not surprisingly, these practices affect inferences about attractiveness.

Stature and size

Animals throughout the vertebrate world often deploy fur, feathers, and limbs during dominance displays (Peters 1980: 294). As a result, they appear larger, and others often respond submissively. In human societies, a person's apparent height is an important visual performance characteristic that affects interaction (Burgoon and Ruffner 1978: 140). It is perhaps no accident that stature, in English, also denotes importance, for we generally equate power and influence with a person's – especially a man's – height. Indeed, it has been shown that taller male politicians more readily attract followers (Kaiser 1985: 73).

Predictably, personal artifacts enable someone to alter his or her height. For example, men can buy special shoes that add a few inches to apparent height without being obvious. A woman, of course, can wear platform shoes or "high heels;" the latter also alter other aspects of her appearance, especially when she is seen from the rear while walking. The use of headdresses, hats, and huge coifs can also extend someone's visual performance vertically.

Activity, situational, and platial artifacts contribute to a person's apparent stature. In some very formal activities, individuals who occupy specific high-status roles commonly sit or stand on special furniture, platforms, or mounds that are elevated relative to other participants and spectators. Familiar examples include the judge in a courtroom, the clergy in many churches, the speakers in a political debate, and the sovereign in a throne room.

Build

People everywhere engage in activities that affect particular muscle groups, alter bone structure, or change fat content, all of which influence appearance. In early industrial societies, a blacksmith might be visually distinctive because of his enormous arm and upper-body muscles, gained from relentlessly pounding iron. Not a few modern Americans buy expensive machines for exercising muscle groups or visit gyms and health clubs, and many of us are obsessed with managing body fat through exercise, food intake, drugs, or even surgery. Particular zones of the body may receive special attention. The female breast, for example, once merely augmented with a padded brassiere, can now be "enhanced" or diminished surgically. Even in basic proportions, then, the human body is modified by activities and becomes itself a personal artifact.

Torso and limbs

A person's torso and limbs undergo changes by participation in activities repeatedly carried out over decades; interactions can affect even the shape of bones and thus limbs (Boyd 1996; Larsen 1987). Although people can adopt the clothing and headgear of a cowboy ("I see by your outfit that you are a cowboy"), it takes decades of sitting astride a horse's back to create bow legs.

Individuals in some societies adopt, or are subjected to, technologies that alter torso and limbs, sometimes permanently. In traditional China, the feet of aristocratic girls were deformed by binding (Gillin 1948: 312), which eventually caused the smaller toes to wither to uselessness. In this form, the female foot furnished a characteristic visual performance that was necessary for courtship and marriage among the elite. Upper-class Victorian women, after being shoehorned into corsets, better approximated the hourglass shape that many Western men find attractive – perhaps, it has been claimed, for biological reasons (Singh 1993). Circumcision and clitoridectomy affect the appearance of sexual organs and so influence interactions in ritual and intimate activities.

The most drastic alteration of this kind is the sex-change operation. Even with the extensive hormone treatment that accompanies the surgical procedures, a biological male cannot be transformed into a biological female or vice versa. Rather, with gender-appropriate clothing, a "sex"-changed person's appearance comes to resemble that of the opposite sex, and so can affect a receiver's inferences and responses.

Since at least the early Upper Paleolithic, which began more than 30,000 years ago, people have been modifying their torso and limbs with clothing and ornaments (e.g., Mithen 1996: 173–174; White 1989). In some societies, clothing might be as simple as a loin cloth or penis sheath, the traditional attire of many tribal societies in New Guinea, such as the Kapauku (Pospisil 1963). Members of many groups today can choose from clothing available in countless colors, natural and artificial materials, and designs. On the basis of differences in dress, receivers make an enormous number of inferences, including a person's motives for interacting, wealth, sex and gender, social class or rank, social power, nationality, ethnicity, religion, attractiveness, sexuality, leisure activities, age or age grade, and occupation and social role (e.g., Burgoon and Walther 1990; Cahill 1989; Hill *et al.* 1987; Joseph 1986; Kaiser 1985; Kaiser *et al.* 1985; Wobst 1977).

Social psychologists have undertaken many experiments that demonstrate how inferences and interaction are affected by clothing (for useful syntheses, see Joseph 1986; Kaiser 1985). In an exemplary study carried out on the streets of Brooklyn, New York, Bickman (1974) examined how pedestrians complied with requests made by male experimenters wearing different outfits. There were three outfits: (1) civilian, wearing a sports jacket and tie, (2) milkman, dressed in white and carrying a basket of empty milk bottles, and (3) guard, resembling a policeman's uniform with badge and insignia. The experimenters – four of them alternated outfits – gave one of three commands to pedestrians (Bickman 1974: 50): (1) "Pick up this bag for me," pointing to a small paper bag on the ground; (2) indicating a nearby confederate, "This fellow is over-parked at the meter but doesn't have any change. Give him a dime;" and (3) at a bus stop, "Don't you know you have to stand on the other side of the pole? The sign says 'No standing.'"

Great variation was found in compliance. Not unexpectedly, the "guard's" percentage of compliance ranged from 56 to 89 percent; the "milkman's" from 21 to 64 percent; and the "civilian's" from 20–36 percent. These patterns are profound and provocative, underscoring that differences in outfits worn by the same person, emitting the same utterance in the same activity and place, can lead an observer to remarkably different inferences about occupation and social power, thereby affecting responses. I suspect that observations of more natural activities are likely to reveal even stronger patterning in the effects of clothing on inferences and interaction.

Examples of how clothing influences responses abound in history and popular culture. In *Jezebel*, a 1937 Warner Brothers film, Bette Davis's character and her escort were shunned at a dance because she was wearing a red dress when only a white one was appropriate. During the American War of Independence, Hessian soldiers, mercenaries for the British, wore blue and red coats that resembled those of Delaware troops. In the Battle of Long Island, the

British, not surprisingly confused by the uniforms, managed to capture some of their own soldiers (Joseph 1986: 135). Usually, however, uniforms enable receivers to distinguish sharply a wearer's social roles, both within and between bureaucratic organizations (Joseph 1986: 2). In many societies, costumes are worn on ceremonial occasions, and these are the subject of inferences. The Tapirapé of Brazil possess several male ceremonial societies, each of which owns specific spirits – of animals and enemies slain in combat. When a Tapirapé man dons a mask and costume, others can identify the spirit he represents. For example, "The wild pig spirit...could be distinguished by tufts of pig bristle stuck into the headdress and by rattles made of pig hooves which the dancer wore around his ankles" (Wagley 1983: 110).

In Western and westernized societies, items of clothing, such as T-shirts, seem to invite inferences about the wearer's political and religious beliefs, fashion tastes, places they or their friends and family have visited, and even musical preferences; these inferences especially influence interaction between strangers. A teenager confided to me that he could discern, immediately upon entering a party, the people with whom he was most likely to strike up a conversation. And what was his evidence? The rock-and-roll bands advertised on their T-shirts.

Jewelry and other ornaments such as necklaces, pendants, armbands, finger rings, and bracelets influence the appearance of the upper chest, arms, fingers, and legs. These kinds of artifacts enable others sometimes to infer the wearer's religious or ethnic affiliation, marital status, wealth, social role, previous travels, and so on. Among the Trobrianders of Papua New Guinea, observers infer a man's political connections and wealth from the quality of his shell necklace (Weiner 1988: 60). Closer to home, when I see a man with a Rolex watch, heavy gold chains around his neck, and many fingers adorned with rings of gold and precious gems, I am apt to conclude that his gains were ill-gotten.

Nail polish, on fingers and toes, also affects visual performance. Among young women in some ethnic groups in the United States, nail "care" today has become an artform. Not only are long artificial nails skillfully affixed to the ends of fingers, but they are often painted with intricate designs. From nails performing in this way, receivers fashion diverse inferences.

Prosthetic devices such as artificial limbs and hooks alter a person's appearance and can have dramatic effects on interaction.

People as macroartifacts

People compounded in activities with horses, bicycles, motorcycles, automobiles, and so on, furnish – as macroartifacts – distinctive performances, forming the basis of many inferences. When a middle-aged adult is seen commuting to work on a bicycle in the United States, some onlookers draw conclusions about the rider's views on energy and the environment. Car and driver of course yield myriad kinds of information to receivers. Commonly, the driver's wealth and lifestyle preferences are inferred from the car's make and model, presuming that she is also inferred to be its owner. Surprisingly, some people who lived through the Second World War still conclude, in the 1990s, that an American driving a Japanese car has committed an act of treason.

As compound interactors themselves, automobiles carry window stickers, decals, bumper stickers, rearview–mirror tags, licenses and license frames, and nameplates, all of which readily yield information. Numerous indeed are the conclusions an observer can draw about a car's owner and family members, such as place of employment, neighborhood of residence, schools attended, ethnic and religious affiliations, political party, membership in clubs, and philosophical tenets. In addition, receivers can also infer the car's state of registry, dealer and city where it was sold new or sold last, where the car is serviced, and when it was bought new. Any and all of these inferences, based on the visual performance of person plus car in a public place, can affect interactions.

Kinesics

Movements of various parts of the body, from facial features to gait, affect appearance and thus contribute to the information obtained by observers (e.g., see Birdwhistell 1970; Burgoon *et al.* 1996; Duncan 1969; Ekman and Friesen 1969; Fridlund 1994; Hall 1966; Knapp and Hall 1992; Polhemus 1978b). In popular culture, these kinds of visual performances are called "body language" (Fast 1971). The present discussion focuses on (1) facial expressions and (2) gestures, postures, and gait.

Facial expressions

People are capable of moving a surprising number of muscles, voluntarily and involuntarily, that alter the appearance of eyes, eyebrows, mouth, cheeks, chin, and forehead. These together create facial expressions, some of which may be universal (Ekman 1993; Ekman *et al.* 1969; Harrison and Crouch 1975: 91; LeDoux 1996), and a few seem to be shared with our closest primate relatives (van Hooff 1962). Although facial expressions apparently have some genetic basis, significant variability is introduced by learning (Ekman 1993; Fridlund 1994; Matsumoto 1991; Tucker and Riggio 1988). From facial expressions, including gaze, a receiver acquires information on a mix of permanent and transitory characteristics, such as friendliness, sincerity, and mood (Barrett 1993; Burgoon *et al.* 1996: 235–236). Ekman and Friesen (1969: 74) argue that people everywhere infer seven different affective states from someone's facial expressions: happiness, anger, surprise, fear, disgust, sadness, and interest (for other classifications of "basic emotions," see LeDoux 1996: 112–114).

In most human societies, however, facial expressions seldom exist in anything like a "natural" state, since they are often modified by makeup, tattoos, shaving practices, and ornaments. These personal artifacts are sometimes tailored to specific activities, such as face paint used in a marriage ceremony, or they can be a more or less permanent part of an individual's appearance, as in a scar, labret, tattoo, or ear spool. The use of tobacco products also affects facial expressions and thus inferences. Someone silently sucking on a pipe, for example, is often judged by others to be deep in thought. And who can forget Humphrey Bogart with a cigarette dangling from his mouth – a visual performance that some still take to be the epitome of masculinity. Masks, of course, prevent others from drawing any of the usual conclusions from facial expressions, and so strongly influence interactions.

Gestures, postures, and gait

Movements of head, fingers, hands, arms, torso, and legs contribute greatly to an individual's visual performances, which furnish receivers with information about, for example, a person's age, mood, and psychological state (Ekman and Friesen 1967; Kendon 1993; McNeill 1992; Montepare and Zebrowitz 1993; Polhemus 1978b). Ekman (1985), for example, has shown how inferences about the truthfulness of someone's utterance can be based on kinesics.

Although the roles of gestures, postures, and gait in human communication have been studied extensively by social scientists in recent decades, the effects of personal artifacts on these visual performances have tended to be overlooked. I suggest that clothing, shoes, face and body painting, tattoos and scarification, and ornaments can appreciably influence these performances. An obvious case is the restraining effects that clothing can have on the ability to execute certain gestures and postures. Plentiful examples come from dance and drama, where costumes affect a performer's motions. In another example, Victorian women, corsetted and often plied with eight or ten skirts, were unable to engage in the movements needed for carrying out many domestic chores. Veblen (1994: 148–149) suggested long ago, in 1899, that other Victorians observing the obvious disabilities of a woman so attired would infer that she was free from the need to engage in manual labor and was therefore a member of the leisure class. Less extreme examples are not hard to find. An arm movement made while wearing a short-sleeve shirt gives a different visual performance than the identical arm movement in a long-sleeve shirt; and both performances differ from those made in the nude or in a tuxedo. Similarly, a hand movement in which the fingers are festooned with large and colorful rings differs visually from one with false fingernails and red nail polish. Particular postures and gaits also vary visually according to a person's headgear, clothing, and shoes. Being compound interactors, people clearly cannot make facial expressions, perform gestures, or adopt postures and gaits unaffected by personal artifacts. Moroever, the reader can readily envision how personal artifacts might affect inferences, for example, about age and gender.

Activity artifacts also have important effects on kinesics. In his cross-cultural survey, Hewes (1957) indicated that posture responds to activity artifacts such as woodworking and gardening tools, hammocks and beds, chairs and stools (see also Leroi-Gourhan 1993; Roux *et al.* 1995). Not surprisingly, from these visual performances, receivers readily infer the activities people are carrying out. For example, an observer concludes that a Jewish woman in her home on Friday evening, bending over candlesticks and striking a match, is lighting the Sabbath candles. Similarly, a man walking up to a teller's window in a bank, holding a gun in his outstretched hand, is often inferred to be engaged in a robbery.

Gait (as well as posture) is also influenced by activity artifacts. Purses, luggage, backpacks, umbrellas, parasols, canes, walking sticks, wheelchairs, walkers, and baby carriages all contribute to varied visual performances that supply information to others. A person walking haltingly with a white, red-tipped cane is inferred to be blind, and other pedestrians respond by stepping aside. Platial artifacts, such as the surface of an activity area, can affect one's gait – and thus appearance. For example, a person's appearance differs greatly, depending on whether she is strolling on the boardwalk, walking in a department store, or climbing a trail.

Acoustic performance

The mainstay of research on communication has been acoustic performance, which was originally taken to be entirely verbal, the uttering of words and sentences. By and by linguists discovered that other acoustic performances – e.g., coughs and cries, grunts and pants, whistles and sneezes, yawns and yells, and belches – also participate in communication, and these, which came to be labeled "paralinguistic" (Trager 1958) or "vocal" (e.g., Burgoon *et al.* 1996: 59–67), came under scrutiny. Also contributing to acoustic performance are other paralinguistic phenomena such as pitch, rhythm, and loudness (Crystal 1975). Although today attuned to all sorts of sounds and their manner of execution, students of communication remain largely oblivious to the fact that acoustic performance is significantly affected by artifacts.

Oral sounds in particular are modified by personal artifacts such as face masks, scars from accidents, plastic surgery, tooth modification, dentures, braces, drugs, and tongue and lip ornaments. In addition, the sounds emanating from someone's mouth are altered by countless activity artifacts, including food being chewed, gum, megaphones, and telephones.

In discussing acoustic performance, it should not be forgotten that people, by interacting with activity artifacts, can make sounds without using their voices. And these acoustic performances, no less than speech and paralinguistic phenomena, influence inferences and responses. For example, my paternal great-grandfather, in presiding over meals of his large, boisterous family, would sometimes pound the table with a fist; by all accounts he usually got the immediate attention of other diners. Likewise, through musical instruments people have been modifying their acoustic performances for many thousands of years. Any instrument actuated by modulated human breath, such as the trumpet or clarinet or kazoo, obviously creates new possibilities for performing acoustically, but all other musical instruments contribute to the sounds a person makes (as a compound interactor). Similarly, people talking or singing together create an acoustic performance differing from that of one person performing alone.

Platial artifacts also affect acoustic performance. For example, in temples, churches, concert halls, amphitheaters, and lecture rooms, seemingly passive artifacts such as ceilings, walls, tapestries, and drapes all influence acoustic performances taking place there (see, e.g., Beranek 1962). Many university professors have had the misfortune of lecturing in vast rooms with poor acoustics; the latter are sometimes so bad that students fail to hear correctly many of the lecturer's utterances. These situations can sometimes be ameliorated by the use of megaphones, electronic amplification systems, and other artifacts. In addition, one needs to consider the effects of sound-producing platial interactors, such as a radio, TV, jukebox, live band, animals, breaking waves, wind, traffic, other people talking, and machinery. In short, people performing acoustically – e.g., talking, singing, making music – do so in places and during activities that can appreciably affect the information that others obtain from their performances. For that reason alone, human acoustic performance cannot exist in any "pure" form, completely bereft of artifact influences.

Tactile performance

In the course of various activities, people have occasion to touch each other; this mechanical interaction is known as tactile or haptic performance. Some obvious examples come from the contact occurring between mother and child during breastfeeding, husband and wife while love-making, and boxers in the heat of battle. Yet, our daily lives are constantly punctuated by touches from others, and these kinds of interactions demonstrably participate in communication (Burgoon and Walther 1990; Heslin and Alper 1983; Jones and Yarbrough 1985; Montagu 1978; Summerhayes and Suchner 1978; Thayer 1986).

Tactile performances commonly involve clothing and other personal artifacts, and so are seldom "pure." For example, the pat on a colleague's shoulder is mediated by clothing, and the first touches in love-making are often affected by the feel of fabrics.

Activity artifacts take part in countless other tactile interactions, as in the surgeon's scalpel, tools for cutting hair, and sexual appliances. At the most general level, of course, person–artifact interactions in many activities are tactile, from baking bread to reading a book; I contend that these interactions, too, take part in communication (see Chapters 5 and 6).

There is no doubt that platial artifacts also have effects in this performance mode. One need only consider two business people, one a man, the other a woman, who have the same tactile encounter in different places. In an elevator, the man's hand may gently come in contact with the woman's backside with no effect at all, whereas the exact same touch in the office might provoke a startled response, perhaps an accusation of sexual harassment.

Regardless of whether one yet accepts that any contact between a person and artifact is a communication phenomenon, it must be granted that artifacts take part in countless tactile interactions affecting inferences and responses.

Chemical performance

Chemical performance plays a large role in the communication of other animals, including mammals (e.g., Albone 1984; MacDonald 1980). That chemical performance, particularly smell, also participates in human communication and can affect interaction is also now beyond dispute (e.g., Ackerman 1990; Coren *et al.* 1994: 279–281; Doty 1985; Kirk-Smith and Booth 1980; Rogel 1978; Stoddart 1990; Van Toller and Dodd 1992). Chemical performances are sensed mainly by the smell (olfactory) and taste (gustatory) organs. The chemical senses are evolutionarily the most ancient, and supply much information, often nonconsciously (Ackerman 1990).

It is widely believed that humans have a poor sense of smell, but that summary judgment is misleading. Although people cannot detect airborne molecules in minute concentrations like bears and dogs (Coren *et al.* 1994: 269–270), we are nonetheless able to discriminate and recall an enormous number of different chemical performances – all based on the contact of specific molecules with our smell receptors. Thus, humans have a broad-band chemical sensor of relatively low sensitivity.

Like other animals, human bodies produce separable substances – gases, liquids, and solids – that perform chemically and can be regarded as artifacts (see Chapter 2). The most obvious artifact of this type is the odor produced by bacterial action upon secretions of the axillary (armpit) glands (Spielman *et al.* 1995). In addition, sebaceous glands in human skin secrete more than 200 different fatty acids; and it is likely that each person's mix of fatty acids is unique, thereby giving everyone a distinctive aroma (Albone 1984: 65). Volatile molecules from these complex substances contribute to "body odor," and people can readily distinguish between male and female varieties (Coren *et al.* 1994: 279–280). When we kiss or nuzzle another, we are also registering some of that person's chemical performances.

Needless to say, body odors influence inferences and interaction. It has been shown that infants are able "to recognize their mothers' body odors and to orient towards them" (Schleidt and Genzel 1990: 145). Experiments have also demonstrated that, on the basis of body odors, American adults draw sometimes far-reaching inferences (Ackerman 1990: 22–23). For example, McBurney *et al.* (1977) found that observers of both sexes were willing to infer, from the armpit odors of males, various personal characteristics such as sociability, cleanliness, intelligence, and attractiveness to the opposite sex. Another study showed that the body odor of male job applicants affected the responses of women interviewers (Albone 1984: 133). Medical diagnosticians sometimes discern diseases on the basis of body odors (Ackerman 1990: 54; Labows and Preti 1992).

A person's breath is another source of chemical performance that varies by sex and affects interaction (Doty *et al.* 1982). Human hair and the scalp also perform chemically (Labows and Preti 1992), but these performances have been little studied for their involvement in communication.

People in many societies tinker with their own odors, removing, altering, and replacing them with other chemically performing artifacts in a process that Labows and Preti (1992: 69) have termed "reodorization." In the United States, possibilities for reodorization are endless because drug and grocery stores offer hundreds of products having odor-changing effects. Among the more common are soaps, bath oils, shampoos and conditioners, hair sprays, skin moisturizers, massage oils, sunscreen, insect repellent, perfume, cologne, aftershave lotion, toothpaste, breath mints, mouthwash, chewing gum, pain-relieving creams and ointments, foot powder, scented menstrual products, douches, and fresh wipes. Needless to say, artificial scents are employed by peoples worldwide, often in activities where close-range interactions take place.

Some chemically performing products, like lip balm, lipstick, cigars and cigarettes, and sunscreen, influence a person's taste to others, and thus can affect intimate encounters. Chemical performances produced by body and breath odors are also sometimes affected by ingesting particular foods and medicines. Alcoholic beverages, raw onions, garlic, and sundry spices can affect someone's interactions unless his or her chemical performances are modified by still other artifacts such as mouthwash and mints.

From diapers to teddies, clothing can also effect changes in a person's chemical performances by concealing, accumulating, or revealing bodily scents and odors and by supplying scents of their own. When clothing of wool and fur was more common in the United States, people wearing such items sometimes carried around the unmistakable aroma of moth balls. In urban areas today, the clothes of the homeless sometimes reek of stale body odors, and this doubtless affects the responses of passersby to their panhandling efforts.

The chemical performances of activity, situational, and platial artifacts can at times mask or modify a person's scents and odors. Among the obvious artifacts that perform in this way are scented candles, cleaning products, incense, tobacco smoke, food being cooked, carpet and upholstery cleaners, an open fire, pets and barnyard animals, human and animal wastes, potpourri, flowers, unfinished wood, and fresh paint. But, a great many other everyday objects also give off scents. As Ackerman (1990: 39) has noted, "only 20 percent of the perfume industry's income comes from making perfumes to wear; the other 80 percent comes from perfuming the objects in our lives," from scented toilet paper to "new car" smells sprayed into old clunkers.

Conclusion

In constructing a general theory of communication, I suggest that we must accord equal weight, in principle, to all performance modes. Global assertions that speech is the "most important conduit" of communication (Deacon 1997: 353) or that "nonverbal" performances supply the majority of information (Mehrabian and Ferris 1967) should be discounted. Thus, the importance of one performance mode over any others is always an empirical question *anchored to an activity*: on the basis of which performances, in which modes, does a person obtain information, make inferences, and respond? I suggest that receivers in most activities acquire consequential information from interactors – including artifacts – performing in several modes.

Like the earliest ethnographers, who often grudgingly relegated "material" culture to a single chapter in their monographs, communication researchers have placed artifacts into a separate – but decidedly unequal – mode. Both strategies have made it easy to neglect artifacts, diverting attention away from their embeddedness in all behavior and communication.

Building on the new ontology, this chapter has demonstrated that artifacts affect the properties – and thus performance characteristics and performances – of people in all modes. Not only have I shown the importance of personal artifacts in every performance mode, but I have also argued that activity and platial artifacts also affect a person's performances as registered by a receiver. In addition, this chapter has established that, on the basis of someone's artifact-laden performances, a receiver derives diverse inferences that affect interaction. Quite clearly, "interpersonal" communication – in any communication or performance mode – cannot be rigorously studied unless the investigator attends closely to artifacts.

Even if we fully integrated artifact performances into discussions of "interpersonal" communication, the effort to build a general theory would founder. That is because the information a receiver obtains is not limited to the performances of people as directly affected by personal, activity, situational, and platial artifacts (and externs). Rather, performances of these latter interactors themselves independently supply information to receivers. This recognition furnishes us with a strong mandate for building an archaeologically informed communication theory. The presentation of just such a theory occupies the next two chapters.

Chapter 4

Some first principles

Introduction

The previous chapter has demonstrated that the concept of "interpersonal communication" is profoundly misleading. To wit, when someone performs in the material medium, personal, platial, and activity artifacts can materially affect that person's performances in all modes. What is more, in most places various artifacts and externs are performing, whether or not their performances are affecting those of people. From this plethora of performances, another person – a receiver – constructs inferences that affect his or her response, thereby contributing to an activity's forward motion.

A fully general communication theory must therefore explain how receivers obtain, through inference, consequential information from the multimodal performances of people and other interactors. That receivers build inferences is scarcely a novel claim. Indeed, the inferential component of communication has long been recognized, for example, in "attribution" theory (e.g., Ehrenhaus 1988; Littlejohn 1991: 154–160; Wyer and Carlston 1979; for an anthropological version, see Sperber and Wilson 1995). Rather, the novelty surrounding inference in the present project lies in my claim that the most appropriate paradigm for modeling communication is *archaeological* inference.

Generalizing the process of archaeological inference into a new communication theory might seem like an odd undertaking; after all, the people that prehistorians study have usually been dead for some time. Yet, because of the very materiality of excavated finds, archaeologists have had to create concepts, knowledge, and methods for extracting information about the past from a bewildering array of interactors performing today. Throughout the centuries, we have learned how to make inferences from virtually anything that has survived from the past, be it human bone, stone spear points, broken pottery, a house's foundation, dirt on a path, pollen grains, or pack-rat nests.

As we shall see in Chapters 5 and 6, people everywhere acquire information in daily activities from as wide a range of interactors. Thus, the process of archaeological inference seems to be more generally representative of communication than two people conversing – the implicit basis of attribution theory and essentially all other modern communication theories, especially those from outside anthropology (e.g., Berger 1991; Berger and Chaffee 1987; Casmir 1994; Cherry 1966; Harper 1979; Heath and Bryant 1992; Littlejohn 1991). Employing archaeological inference as a paradigm, this chapter sets forth basic principles for forging a general theory of communication.

The nature of archaeological inference

> "Someone's been sleeping in my bed" said Mama Bear in her middle-size voice.
>
> (Jerrard 1992: 13)

From an archaeological standpoint, the enchanting childhood tale of *Goldilocks and the Three Bears* tellingly demonstrates how, almost from infancy, people appreciate that an artifact can furnish information about previous interactions in its life history. Thus, archaeologists have refined, elaborated, and formalized a process of obtaining information that has its roots in everyday communication.

In recent decades, archaeologists have clarified the process of inference, emphasizing the importance of both evidential and cognitive components (e.g., Fritz 1972; Hard *et al.* 1996; Patrik 1985; Rathje and Schiffer 1982; Schiffer 1972, 1975, 1976: ch. 2, 1987: ch. 2, 1996b; Sullivan 1978; Thompson 1956, 1958; Wylie 1985, 1992). On the basis of these studies, one can construct a definition of inference that departs somewhat from the provisional definition presented in Chapter 1. I now define an inference as any information about a past interactor, interaction, or performance that is supported by evidence and relational knowledge. "Past" denotes any amount of elapsed time, from a millisecond to a million years or more.

The evidential basis

The hard evidence for fashioning inferences consists of the present-day performances of artifacts and other interactors, for these are the remnants of past behavioral systems. From the visual and mechanical performances of bits of bone and chips of stone in laboratory activities today, for example, archaeologists learn how our earliest hominid ancestors hunted and butchered animals (e.g., Brantingham 1998; Sept 1992). Similarly, by studying the chemical performances of food residues absorbed by the wall of a ceramic cooking pot, we can sometimes infer which plant and animal species had been cooked (e.g., Heron and Evershed 1993; Skibo 1992). As evidence of prehistoric interactions, archaeologists have available only today's performances of interactors in field and laboratory activities; even so, we manage, like Mama Bear, to make well-founded inferences.

All inferences are made possible by the simple fact that the interactors that archaeologists study have life histories that extend from past times into the present. During activities that preceded archaeological study, as in the manufacture and use of a cooking pot, interactions left their marks by modifying the pot's chemical and physical properties. Modified properties are said to be the *traces* (Schiffer 1987: 14–15; Sullivan 1978: 194–201) of previous interactions, and traces are formed throughout the life histories of people, artifacts, and externs. As properties, traces affect a wide range of performance characteristics and performances (e.g., visual, tactile, chemical) in the archaeologist's field and laboratory activities; traces are thus the evidential basis of inference. Just as Mama Bear concluded that there had been contact between an animate interactor and her bed from the bedspread's visual performance, so too archaeologists infer that a stone tool had been used to butcher an animal on the basis of the artifact's visual (through a microscope) performance, or that a pot had been employed for cooking rice through chemical performances of food residues. Thus, any past interaction that leaves a trace on – i.e., modifies any property of – an interactor is potentially inferable.

The simplest kind of trace is a chemical or physical alteration, such as a rumpled bedspread, a stone tool with a dull edge, a man's dueling scar or capped tooth, scratches on a porcelain plate, a corroded penny, axe marks on a tree trunk, barnacle encrustations on a boat, and paint on a canvas. These are known as *formal* traces because they modify an interactor's formal – i.e., chemical–physical–biological – properties. Archaeologists recognize three additional kinds of traces: locational, relational, and quantitative (Rathje and Schiffer 1982: ch. 4; Schiffer 1987: ch. 2).

A *locational* trace refers to an interactor's find-spot, its place of occurrence. Thus, an arrowhead found where it was last used, in a hunting–butchering area, retains, in that locational information, additional evidence for inferring use-related interactions in comparison to an identical arrowhead found in a trash pile.

Closely related to locational traces are *relational* (or associational) traces, which describe interactors that occur together. For example, if a prehistorian of the American Southwest finds in a single grave some lumps of clay, pieces of pigment, scrapers, and shiny pebbles, he is apt to infer that the interred person was a potter (e.g., Shafer 1985). In this case, the association of these artifacts with each other and with the human remains in the grave is a trace of their participation in past activities, both pottery-making and grave-side ritual.

Finally, there are *quantitative* traces – e.g., frequencies and relative frequencies of interactors. An archaeologist who uncovers one warped and bloated ceramic jar is apt to infer that it had been burned, perhaps in a trash heap, after use. On the other hand, if the archaeologist finds in one place 1,500 jars, similarly warped and bloated, she would likely conclude that they had been waste products of a pottery factory.

In short, traces of several kinds record interactions in the life histories of interactors, and the latters' performances *today*, in field and laboratory activities, are the evidence for inference. It is important for us to appreciate that, in everyday life, we also employ as evidence the same range of interactor performances when making inferences. For example, on the basis of visual performances that depend on formal *and* quantitative properties of currency, we infer whether a supermarket cashier has given us the correct change. Similarly, the items of furniture associated in a living room (formal, quantitative, locational, and relational traces) supply visitors with evidence, through visual performance, of the owner's furniture-purchasing and arranging activities.

The cognitive basis

The process of inference requires much more than evidence, as an example from prehistory makes clear. Three centuries ago, early archaeologists in Europe pondered odd-shaped, fist-sized stones picked up from ancient river gravels, and concluded that their peculiar formal properties had been caused by lightning or elves (Daniel and Renfrew 1988). Today, archaeologists examine these very same stones, registering the same visual and tactile performances, but infer that they had been modified by contact with other stones (hammerstones) wielded by hominid hands. The stones have not changed in three centuries; rather, there has been a complete replacement of the relational knowledge that archaeologists employ for making inferences from them.

Correlates are relational statements of archaeological knowledge with which an interactor's present-day performances can be linked to its past interactions (Schiffer 1976: ch. 2, 1995a: chs 3, 4, 15). Returning to the *Goldilocks* example, we can appreciate that Mama Bear employed correlate-like knowledge to link her rumpled bedspread to the performance(s) of the inferred trespasser. In making this inference, she had clearly assumed something to the effect that "interaction with an animal could have modified the bedspread in the observed manner." Presuming that the bed had been made when she last left it, Mama Bear was able to infer a trespasser's transgressions.

Correlates, the cognitive component of inference, vary along several dimensions. First, some are relatively simple statements, such as the regression equation linking the length of a person's pace to his or her height. Complex correlates also abound. For example, when examining use-related traces on a stone tool's working edge – e.g., striations, polish, and micro-chipping – the archaeologist employs a family of correlates, obtained through thousands of experiments, for identifying the kind of material that was worked, such as dry hide, wet hide, meat, plant, or bone (e.g., Keeley 1980; Vaughan 1985).

Second, correlates differ in degree of generality. Some correlates, like those relating use interactions to their traces, have a broad scope and can be applied whenever one finds artifacts made of similar materials, whereas others are far more particularistic, applicable to just a single society or region (e.g., early Puebloan people of the American Southwest manufactured pottery with black-on-white decoration).

Third, some correlates are rather concrete, with a high empirical content (e.g., the sawing motion of a stone knife produces, on its blade, striations parallel to the cutting edge [Tringham *et al.* 1974]). In contrast, other correlates are abstract and theory-like (e.g., industrial societies have millions of diverse waste streams that converge and become more homogeneous in artifact content as they approach disposal localities [cf. Schiffer 1987: 64–70]).

And fourth, correlates fall along a continuum from deterministic to statistical and probabilistic. It is helpful to regard all correlates as statistical–probabilistic, with determinism being the special case in which a correlation coefficient or a probability equals 1.0.

Despite variation in the complexity, generality, concreteness, and determinism of correlates, all archaeological inferences rest on such relational knowledge. Indeed, one or more correlates inhere, implicitly or explicitly, in every inference (Schiffer 1976: ch. 2).

In everyday life, people usually use correlate-like knowledge implicitly, without awareness; as a result, this relational knowledge has to be modeled by the investigator. One does this by positing a hypothetical correlate or correlates to account for the linkage assumed in an inference – just as I did above for the correlate that had to have been employed, however implicitly, by Mama Bear.

Though incomplete and somewhat sketchy, the preceding account of archaeological inference serves as a solid foundation on which to construct a new communication theory. In the remainder of this chapter, I draw upon additional principles and propositions of archaeological inference in order to establish the new theory's basic tenets, which are elaborated in the next chapter.

Toward a general communication theory

Inference and correlons

I begin by making explicit what, so far, has been but implied: in communication, a receiver constructs inferences – implicitly or explicitly, consciously or nonconsciously, with or without awareness – from interactor performances using correlate-like relational knowledge. Whereas correlates in archaeology tend to be established generalizations, based on independent research undertaken in experiments, ethnoarchaeology, and cross-cultural studies, the relational knowledge used in everyday communication need not be well founded (see Chapter 5). To avoid confusion, I apply the term "correlon" to the relational knowledge, or rules (see Chapter 1), underlying any communication phenomenon (compare to "procedural records" [Greene and Geddes 1993: 30–31], "decision rules" [Busemeyer and Myung 1992: 177], and "representation" [Byrne 1995: 39; Gallistel 1990: ch. 2; Jeannerod 1997: 8–9; Karmiloff-Smith 1992: 15–26; Pearce 1987; Roitblat and von Fersen 1992; Sperber 1996: 24–27]. Correlates, then, are merely the subset of correlons used in archaeology.

A correlon can be modeled by the investigator as a relational statement(s) that (like a correlate) may range from general to particular, simple to complex, concrete to abstract, and deterministic to statistical–probabilistic. The "relationship" between a correlon's terms may be of many sorts, including quantitative, part–whole, class and subclass, subset and superset, sequential or transitive, analog to digital, digital to analog, and sameness and difference (e.g., D'Andrade 1995; Deacon 1997: 265; Fox 1979: 153; Hutchins 1995: ch. 2; Vauclair 1996: 160). As relational knowledge, the concept of correlon subsumes "procedural" and "declarative" knowledge, but is obviously broader than both; indeed, correlons also include "schemas" (D'Andrade 1995: ch. 6), "indigenous knowledge" (Sillitoe 1998), and "frames" (Goffman 1974). Perhaps correlons can even encompass the nonconscious cognitive structures posited by structuralists (e.g., Glassie 1975; Lévi-Strauss 1963; Sperber 1975).

A few additional features of correlons can be mentioned. As already implied (Chapter 2), correlons can be learned, hardwired through genes, or arise as some combination of both. Surprisingly, there is no necessary link between a correlon's degree of determinism and extent of hardwiring. Thus, learned correlons can be deterministic (e.g., in the United States, unimpaired automobile drivers stop at red lights in heavy traffic) and hardwired correlons can be probabilistic (e.g., although people are hardwired to laugh when others are laughing [Provine 1996: 44], we do not do so invariably [Deacon 1997: 236–244, 429]).

Correlons can also include "nonverbal imagery" (Keller and Keller 1996: 133–137) pertaining to any performance mode (Deacon 1997: 265), such as "cognitive maps" (Byrne 1995: 179–180); as a result, verbal accounts of correlons may be highly imperfect (cf. Crick 1982: 300–301; Deacon 1997: 157; Jeannerod 1997: 96; Karmiloff-Smith 1992: 23; Moriarty 1996; Stich 1996: 14, 154). That we have no precise vocabulary for describing smells (Ackerman 1990: 6–8), for example, should alert us to the limitations of language for modeling correlons. Also difficult to put into verbal terms are the many correlons having an emotional "flavoring" (LeDoux 1996: 201), such as a correlon that causes someone to become weepy at the sight of a deceased parent's picture or one that yields an angry outburst when someone spies a swastika (on the emotive performances of artifacts, see Prown 1993; Shanks 1992). Despite the shortcomings of language, our efforts to model correlons (see Chapters 5 and 7) will rely somewhat on *ad hoc* verbal accounts until better descriptive devices are devised.

Many correlons, it should be noted, have generative capabilities, such as those facilitating verbal performance. Indeed, a grammar is simply the linguist's model of the shared correlons that people in a speech community use for generating novel – yet skillful – utterances. Other complex and highly abstract correlons having generative capabilities include indigenous theories, also called "folk" or "common-sense" theories (D'Andrade 1995: ch. 7; Stich 1996: ch. 3). For example, it has been hypothesized that Americans hold a variety of indigenous theories about the comings and goings of consumer products that enable them, in daily conversations, to contruct *de novo* explanations for phenomena not previously encountered or studied, such as the failure of early twentieth-century electric cars to find much of a market (Schiffer, n.d.). Correlons can also be employed generatively, perhaps through metaphor and analogy (cf. Mithen 1996: 214–215), to create new correlons. Likewise, new correlons can arise through cognitive processes such as contemplating, problem solving, and praying.

Because they consist of relational knowledge, correlons are also used to forecast future performances or interactions (cf. Jeannerod 1997: 3; Mithen 1996: 124). This predictive capability, which is by no means confined to correlons held by humans (Byrne 1995: ch. 10; Smith 1977; Stich 1996: 125; Vauclair 1996), comes into play when an interactor is responding (Chapter 7). For example, in a clothing store, a salesperson's response to the approach of a customer (i.e., visual and acoustic performances) is influenced by forecasts of the person's propensity to make a purchase. In addition to permitting the construction of inferences and forecasts, correlons have other functions in the explanation of responses (Chapter 7).

Finally, because correlons allow people to pile abstraction upon abstraction *ad infinitum*, there are no restrictions on the content of inferences (Baudrillard 1983; cf. Sperber and Wilson's [1995: 87] "representations of representations"). At the very least, correlons, which both subsume and presume categories, enable inferences of recognition or identification (Chapters 5 and 7). But receivers also attribute properties of animals to humans and vice versa or even impute supernatural capabilities to any interactor. Inferences about paranormal or supernatural capabilities appear insupportable when judged by the canons of modern science, yet they may be quite "real" to the people who construct them, and can demonstrably affect responses (Sperber and Wilson 1995; Walker 1998).

In complex societies, indigenous theories having predictive powers can sometimes be transformed into, or give rise to, explicit scientific theory (see Schiffer 1992b: ch. 7 on techno-, socio-, and ideo-science). Despite near-heroic efforts, however, philosophers of science have established no deep discontinuities in *structure* between indigenous and scientific theories: both kinds consist, in my terms, of abstract and usually complex correlons (cf. Stich 1996: ch. 2). Rather, what distinguishes accepted scientific theories is the robust linkage of their posited entities and processes, often through experimental laws (*sensu* Nagel 1961), to supporting empirical evidence. The latter is of course judged relevant and sufficient by a community of scientists (Kuhn 1970).

Because a correlon (or correlons) is the investigator's model of an interactor's relational knowledge relative to a given communication phenomenon, there is no need for us to assume anything about its actual physical form or distribution (cf. Newell 1990: 223). The strongest claim I am willing to make is that correlons, in any animal, are "activation patterns" (Stich 1996: 111) or "associative paths" (Deacon 1997: 265) connecting neurons in different areas of the nervous system.

The context: activity and place

The process of archaeological inference is situated in activities that occur mainly in the field and laboratory, where the investigator registers the varied performances of her finds. This feature is easily generalized: the context of communication is a specific activity transpiring in a given place.

Although students of communication have acknowledged for decades the need to consider the "context" (Haslett 1987: 85–111; Heath and Bryant 1992: 57; Krueger and Harper 1988: 62–63; Meyrowitz 1990; Stamp *et al.* 1994: 173), "social context" (Jakobs *et al.* 1996), "situation" (Kendon 1985: 231; Williams 1975: 59), "stage" (Goffman 1959), "scene" (Kellerman *et al.* 1989), or "setting" (Ekman and Friesen 1969: 53; Smith 1977: 15, 78) of communication, these factors tend to be defined too narrowly, and often exclude performances of platial interactors (for exceptions, see Harrison and Crouch 1975; Rapoport 1990). A general theory must give more than lip service, for example, to people who are present but not conversing and to other artifacts and externs whose performances can be registered in the activity area – for any such performance could be consequential. Equally unsatisfactory are definitions of context so broad that they include psychological traits of participating people (e.g., Haslett 1987: 110–111; Lievrouw and Finn 1990; Olson 1994: 173; Worchel 1986). For our purposes, the context of a communication phenomenon (defined in the next chapter as a "communication process") consists of an activity *and* a place.

Both archaeological inference and communication in general are anchored to an activity and place in the present, but the resultant inferences may describe activities carried out earlier and/or elsewhere. For example, when I hear a woman speak with a "southern" accent, I infer that she was raised below the Mason–Dixon line. Similarly, when observing a green-haired student in my class, I conclude that somewhere else he had a close encounter with hair dye. It is essential that one distinguish carefully between *inferred* activities and the activity context of communication; the latter activity, extant in the present and tied to a place, is the *reference* activity in analysis.

Number of interactor roles

In archaeological inference, interactors play *three* major roles: (1) an interactor in the past that imparted information by modifying the properties of a second interactor (e.g., a potter fashions clay into a jar), (2) the second interactor (e.g., the ceramic jar), whose performances today materially embody that information, and (3) a third interactor (the archaeologist), who registers the second interactor's performances and, employing correlates, constructs an inference or inferences and thereby obtains information.

In contrast, conventional communication theories, based on human language, recognize only two major interactor roles and both are played by people (e.g., see Stamp *et al.* 1994). According to these theories, the transfer of information from person to person can take place either directly, often face to face, or mediated by a technology such as a telephone, radio, or television (Gumpert and Cathcart 1990). Thus, communication involves people playing but two roles: one who originates the communication and another who receives it; I refer to this formulation as the "two-body" model. Students of human and animal communication have termed the two roles, variously, "sender" and "receiver" (Burgoon *et al.* 1996: 10; Halloran 1985: 31; Hymes 1967: 24; Olson 1994: 77; Vauclair 1996: 99), "transmitter" and "receiver" (Peters 1980: 289), "communicator" and "recipient" (Smith 1977: 11), "source" and "receiver" (Hanneman 1975: 24; Krippendorff 1975: 375), and "encoder" and "decoder" (Harrison and Crouch 1975: 82; Rosenthal and DePaulo 1980).

I suggest that the three-role archaeological model can handle far more actual instances of communication, with fewer contortions and anomalies, than can the two-body model (for examples, see Chapter 6). Among the three-role model's obvious advantages is its ready accommodation of the ubiquitous communication phenomena in which people get information from artifacts. The three-role model also displays greater generality and versatility by shedding light on other behavioral phenomena that can be treated as instances of communication, such as divination, medical diagnosis, brainwashing, literary and art criticism, musical performance, playing games, product manufacture, and inference in history and geology (see additional examples in Chapter 6). Finally, the three-role model, being more general, easily subsumes the two-body model (Chapters 5 and 7).

A simple example can underscore the strengths of the three-role model. Let us ponder the visual performance of infants and their clothing (cf. Joseph 1986: 39). Suppose a jogger in New York's Central Park were to observe two young adults taking their newborn child for a stroll in a carriage. In many cases, the jogger could discern the baby's sex from his or her clothing. Employing deterministic correlons widely shared by Americans, the jogger could readily conclude that a blue-attired baby is a boy, and one dressed in pink a girl. The emissions of a compound interactor (baby plus clothing), in a public place, has patently resulted in information transfer – the jogger has learned the infant's sex.

The challenge to the two-body model is that the baby was not the person who caused the information to be present in his or her visual performance. The sender was in fact the parents, either of whom might have dressed the infant. In this case, evidently, there are three major roles: sender (the parents), receiver (the jogger), and a third one (the infant plus clothing) – as yet unnamed. How might someone force this case to conform to the two-body model? A transparent move is to regard the clothed infant as a mediating artifact, but this solution is *ad hoc*. A more general solution, one capable of handling many seemingly problematic cases, is to employ a three-role model.

The immediate task is to label the three interactor roles. Following many investigators, I apply the label *sender* to the first role – the interactor that originally imparted the information. The information is "broadcast" by performances – we can also call them "emissions" – of the interactor playing the second role, which is termed the *emitter* (cf. Foucault 1972: 145; Gouran *et al.* 1994: 246; Wobst 1977: 322). Finally, and again in accord with much current usage, I retain the term *receiver* for the third role, the interactor that constructs inferences. The receiver role also includes a response – a subsequent performance based partly on the inferred information.

With the three-role model, the investigator can treat the two-body model as a special case useful for studying certain communication phenomena, such as speech and craft activities. To accommodate a conversing couple more easily, for example, the investigator may collapse sender and emitter into a combined sender–emitter role played by one individual. And in craft activities, such as applying makeup or carving a wooden duck, it is often convenient to regard the craftsperson as both sender and receiver (for additional examples of combined roles, see Chapter 6).

Which interactors may play the roles?

In conventional theories, only people are allowed to play the major roles. That people privilege people is an anthropocentrism, perhaps forgivable in many everyday contexts. In a scientific context, however, it prevents investigators from achieving an understanding of how consequential information is actually transferred among interactors in activities. Indeed, human receivers routinely secure information from the performances of artifacts and externs (Hymes 1967: 25), treating them as senders, emitters, or sender–emitters. There is simply no theoretical justification for restricting role playing to people.

Thus, consistent with the project of fashioning the most general theory possible, I stipulate that any role can be played by any interactor having appropriate performance characteristics. Insofar as senders and emitters are concerned, this proviso is unproblematic: virtually any interactor can modify, or be modified by, any other. To serve as a receiver, however, an interactor has to possess a sensory apparatus and be capable of responding; thus, only some artifacts and externs, such as computers and coyotes, can be receivers.

In everyday life, people obtain information from the emissions of externs, treating them as sender–emitters. On the basis of a wild bird's acoustic performance, for example, someone acquainted with bird calls can identify not only the species but also whether it is in distress. In a second example, let us consider a woman, about to finish dressing before going to work, who steps outside to check the weather; from the atmosphere's emissions, she readily learns about temperature and precipitation. I submit that these cases cannot be made intelligible by conventional theories. Indeed, the only move possible is to argue that such transfers of information, because they lacked two people, were not really *human* communication. This move is unacceptable because the people patently acquired information from externs that affected their responses and thus the forward motion of activities. In the theory being developed here, externs can be the sender or sender–emitter as easily as an artifact or a person.

Artifact receivers are another anomaly for conventional theories, yet examples abound. I especially recall the Cadillac car of 1956, which dimmed its headlights when an oncoming vehicle – the emitter – approached at night. Light from the oncoming car's headlights was registered by a photoelectric cell that, through electrical and mechanical interactions, automatically dimmed the Cadillac's own headlights. In this case, the Cadillac's response demonstrates that it had secured consequential information from the other car. Today, of course, countless devices are capable of much more marvelous feats based on "sensing" diverse emissions; of these I mention only the ubiquitous smoke detector, which continuously gets information from the atmosphere in its immediate environs, responding with an alarm when appropriate – and sometimes when not. Needless to say, quite a few artifacts in industrial societies can be receivers.

In conventional theories, an artifact plays only a supporting role, that of "mediating" the conversation between sender and receiver – e.g., a telephone or magazine article (Fortner 1994; Gumpert and Cathcart 1990; Harrison and Crouch 1975). However, as archaeologists have repeatedly pointed out, artifacts play both major and supporting roles in communication – even when conversation is absent (e.g., Binford 1962; Carr and Neitzel 1995; Conkey and Hastorf 1990; Fletcher 1996; Gould 1990; Hayden 1998; Hodder 1982, 1987, 1989; Ingersoll and Bronitsky 1987; Leone 1977; Leone and Potter 1989; Miller 1985, 1987; Nielsen 1995; Rathje and Schiffer 1982; Schiffer 1991, 1992b; Schiffer, Butts, and Grimm 1994; Schiffer and Miller 1999; Schiffer and

Skibo 1997; Shanks 1992; Thomas 1996; Wiessner 1984; Wobst 1977). A case in point is the omnipresent suburban "stop" sign. When an automobile driver approaches one and is selecting a response to its visual performance, she most likely treats the sign itself as a sender–emitter. Likewise, in nonindustrial societies, a hunter traversing a traditional trail acquires consequential information from ancient ruins, shrines, petroglyphs, and the trail itself without having to identify a specific human sender (cf. Zedeño 1997). Even when a person is recognized as the sender, one cannot simply regard the artifact–emitter as mediating the communication between two people. Thus, the more general perspective must be that artifacts can play major communication roles; mediation is merely the special case of an artifact playing the emitter role when the sender is a person.

In some conventional theories, artifacts are regarded as a separate mode or channel that links sender and receiver or as one of several nonverbal modes or codes (e.g., Burgoon 1978: 144; Burgoon *et al.* 1996: ch. 4; Harrison 1989: 121; Harrison and Crouch 1975: 93–94; Hymes 1967: 19), but these moves neglect artifact participation in all other communication modes (see Chapter 3) and ignore the counterintuitive possibility that some codes might cross-cut modes (cf. Zuckerman *et al.* 1991). That is, one code could allow a receiver to obtain information from performances in many modes. What is more, the term "code" itself may be little more than a misleading metaphor for describing the rules (i.e., correlons) that link emissions to receiver responses (Chapter 7; see also Sperber and Wilson 1995). And, as Nolan (1975: 106) also observes, language-type rules may be inadequate for describing how someone is able to obtain information from another person performing simultaneously in several modes – e.g., acoustic, tactile, and visual – or, I might add, from several interactors performing in many modes at once.

If people can acquire information from performances of artifacts and externs (treating them as emitters, senders, or sender–emitters), and if artifacts and externs can serve as receivers, then traditional theories must be judged deficient for leaving out common – and therefore important – communication phenomena. Apparently an archaeological viewpoint, which does not privilege human interactors as major role players, is a preferable basis for building a general communication theory.

Receiver orientation

Although the theory being fashioned here allows any kind of interactor to play the three major roles, the roles themselves are not of equal analytical significance. For reasons that will soon become clear, my theory is receiver oriented (Burgoon and Ruffner 1978: 14). In contrast, conventional communication theories tend to focus on the sender's actions and intent (e.g., Eisenberg and Smith 1971: 13–20), and on how the sender can get the message across to the receiver. That the sender's role is usually privileged is not surprising since students of communication have for centuries supplied people with insights and rules for improving their skills in writing and public speaking (Delia 1987; Harper 1979). Although all scholars today recognize that the receiver actively participates in communication (e.g., Olson 1994), an archaeologically informed theory fastens relentlessly on the receiver's point of view and subordinates all else to it.

In adopting a receiver orientation, however, I emphatically distance my formulations from much of "reception theory" (Olson 1994) in philosophy and literary criticism, which at times more than flirts with solipsism, and from symbolic interactionism, which in its subjectivity is sometimes mired in abject mentalism (e.g., Katovich and Reese 1993; Lal 1995). As I demonstrate below, one can build receiver-oriented theories and models that are testable.

An uncompromising receiver orientation, it must be acknowledged, is congruent with neither Western indigenous theories nor the conventional communication theories they have sired. Indeed, a receiver orientation is counterintuitive because it inverts everyday ways of construing communication phenomena. Thus, the effort required to comprehend and use a theory so strange must be richly repaid by the explanatory insights it affords. The remaining chapters develop the surprising and fruitful implications of a receiver orientation; for the present, a few arguments must suffice.

A focus on the receiver helps one to frame inquiries into any instance of communication. What is more, by focusing on the receiver, the investigator comes quickly to appreciate that information obtained through inference can lead directly and immediately to a response, thereby contributing to an activity's forward motion. As a result, a receiver-oriented theory allows one explicitly to tie communication to all other human behavior (see Chapters 5 and 7).

A telling defect in most sender-centered theories is the assumption that communication is not occurring unless the sender "intends" to send a message (Hall 1992: 57–58). The absurdity of this requirement in the use of historical or archaeological evidence is obvious: few people in the past performed in order to enlighten the historians and archaeologists of today. However, the intentionality requirement also leads to absurdities in modern settings, as an example from everyday life illustrates.

When my wife and I walk through our neighborhood in the evening, we often notice dinnertime odors wafting through open windows of nearby homes. Sometimes we play a little game, attempting to discern what is being cooked. Although our specific inferences might be wide of the mark – although I insist that the smells of potatoes being fried and toast being burned are unmistakable – there is no doubt that we have drawn correct conclusions about dinner being prepared in a particular house from the chemical performances of food. According to the sender-oriented view, however, no communication could have taken place in this activity unless the cook had intended to heat up food in order to enlighten passersby. A receiver orientation furnishes a better basis for handling such cases: regardless of the cook's intent, he or she is the sender, and the cooking food comprises the emitters. It should also be noted that, as is generally appreciated, human facial expressions and gestures are often performed in an entirely implicit manner (e.g., Ekman 1985, 1993; Fridlund 1994; Harrison and Crouch 1975; LeDoux 1996), making the question of sender's intent more than a little problematic. And, needless to say, the concept of intent has no relevance to communication when artifacts or externs are the senders (for examples, see Chapter 5 and 6), although receivers sometimes impute intent to such interactors (Edwards 1994).

That the sender has an intent to communicate is an unacceptable condition to place on a general theory of communication. People may or may not intend to send information to other interactors (Heath and Bryant 1992: 49), and they may or may not be aware that they are doing so (cf. Byrne 1995: 119–124). As Hutchins (1995: 233) remarks, "A good deal of our behavior has communicative function without communicative intent." Although indigenous knowledge may include correlons for inferring intent (see Chapter 5), *scientific* principles for discerning intent are utterly lacking now and may never be available. As a consequence, disputes about what someone intended in a given case are unresolvable (Schiffer and Miller 1999). In the final analysis, what matters most is that a receiver has acquired consequential information from emissions. That is why, I submit, any theory purporting to encompass the entire range of communication phenomena must, like archaeological inference, be receiver-oriented (cf. Herman and Morrel-Samuels 1996).

Archaeologists are well aware that different investigators, registering emissions from the same interactors in an identical laboratory activity, can arrive at disparate inferences and respond differently. The cause of these discrepancies is variation in the cognitive component (Thompson 1956, 1958) – i.e., in the investigators' correlates. Thus, a receiver-oriented theory can easily account for varied inferences and responses by appealing to differences in the receivers' correlons (Schiffer 1976: ch. 2; see also Greene and Geddes 1993).

Finally, because a receiver-oriented theory is more general, it is capable, under conditions to be specified in Chapter 5, of subsuming the sender orientation.

Multiple lines of evidence

An archaeologist is happy to use as evidence for inference any performance of any surviving interactor; indeed, the more lines of evidence, potentially the stronger the inference can be (Hard *et al.* 1996; Rathje and Schiffer 1982: ch. 8). In communication, I suggest, receivers also make use of multiple lines of evidence; these consist of many emitters performing in many modes, depending on their formal, locational, quantitative, and relational properties. In daily activities, people effortlessly integrate these varied lines of evidence, constructing inferences and forecasts.

It is no accident that human senses, like those of most other animals, can operate in a massively parallel fashion. Our responses to other interactors — indeed, our very survival in the material medium — depend on constant monitoring of many emissions and thereby maintain the forward motion of life-sustaining activities. That we can register more or less simultaneously the multimodal performances of multiple emitters, among which artifacts loom large, supplies us with an enormous stream of potentially relevant evidence for fashioning inferences and forecasts, and generating responses.

Life histories and role playing

In archaeological inference, the emitter's performances in field and laboratory activities are strongly affected by previous interactions in its life history. We may generalize this statement to all major roles. To wit, the performance of an interactor playing any role depends *partly* upon its life history, including its immediately preceding performances. The remaining determinants of a performance are found in the activity itself — i.e., in other emissions (see Chapter 7).

Summary and conclusion

This chapter has presented a précis of the process of archaeological inference, showing that it involves the extraction of information from multiple lines of evidence employing relational knowledge. I argued that this process is a better paradigm for constructing a general theory of communication than that of two people conversing (the "two-body" model). The principles, tenets, and assumptions of archaeological inference highlighted in this chapter are important desiderata for crafting the general theory. These are, in abbreviated form, as follows. (1) All inferences inhering in communication depend on relational knowledge, instances of which are called correlons. (2) Inferences also have an evidential basis that rests, ultimately, on the formal, spatial, quantitative, and relational properties of interactors. (3) Inference, and thus any communication phenomenon, has as its context a specific place and activity. (4) Three major interactor roles can be recognized in communication phenomena: sender, emitter, and receiver. (5) Interactors (person, artifact, or extern) can play any role provided that they possess the requisite performance characteristics. (6) The study of communication should be receiver oriented; that is, research questions need to be formulated in relation to the receiver's point of view. (7) The receiver makes inferences on the basis of multiple lines of evidence — i.e., emitters performing in various modes. (8) An interactor's specific performance while playing a communication role depends in part on previous interactions and activities in its life history. From these raw materials, I fashion in the next chapter a general theory of communication.

Chapter 5

A general theory of communication

I have suggested that the process of archaeological inference is a more suitable paradigm for studying communication than the two-body, language-based model derived from Western indigenous knowledge, whose variants permeate the social sciences (for examples, see Burgoon *et al.* 1996; Casmir 1994; Crowley 1994; Dance 1967; Littlejohn 1991; Ruben and Lievrouw 1990). Moreover, in the previous chapter I set forth the basic principles of archaeological inference, generalizing them to all communication phenomena. These discussions have furnished a foundation for building, in the present chapter, a receiver-oriented theory of communication that aspires to complete generality.

Roles and role playing

To recapitulate briefly, the theory's three interactor roles are sender, emitter, and receiver. The sender imparts information by performing in interactions that modify the emitter's properties. These interactions leave behind traces – be they formal properties, location, quantity, or associations – that affect the emitter's subsequent performances (emissions), potentially in many modes. Applying correlons to these emissions, the receiver constructs inference(s) about the sender and sender–emitter interactions, and can also formulate forecasts. On the basis of information obtained from inferences and forecasts, the receiver responds.

A principal task in fleshing out the theory is to specify how, in general, the roles may be played. I propose that role playing is governed by four rules:

1   With some qualifications (see below), any role can be played, in principle, by any kind of interactor – person, artifact, or extern. Even an animal or inanimate object sometimes can be a receiver (Chapter 4).
2   People can play the three roles explicitly or implicitly, consciously or nonconsciously, and voluntarily or involuntarily. As Stamp *et al.* (1994: 199) remark, "The thesis that individuals often operate mindlessly…, without conscious awareness of their own or others' behavior is widely

accepted among both psychologists and communication researchers" (see also Jeannerod 1997; Karmiloff-Smith 1992: 22; Nolan 1975: 113–115; Stich 1996). Clearly, the manner of role playing must be determined, ethnographically, on a case-by-case basis.

3   An interactor – especially a person – can simultaneously play more than one role in an activity (see Chapter 6, BCPs 11–19). For example, in the case of two people conversing, the receiver can regard the speaker as playing a combined sender–emitter role.

4   Any role can be played by more than one actual interactor. This rule allows us to handle group performances, as in a church service, tennis tournament, conference call, or symphony orchestra concert. Usually, emitter roles are played simultaneously by many interactors, especially platial, activity, and personal artifacts.

Communication processes

The three roles come together in a *communication process* (cf. Hanneman 1975: 24), which is the passage of consequential information from interactor to interactor, culminating in a receiver's response. A communication process is situated in the reference activity, which must be designated by the investigator.

Four sequential *events* make up a communication process:

1   *Inscription* (cf. Musello 1992: 37). The sender imparts information by modifying the emitters' properties (formal, locational, relational, or quantitative).

2   *Emission*. The emitters perform in one or more modes; these performances are termed "emissions."

3   *Reception*. The receiver, registering the emissions of activity and platial interactors, constructs inference(s) and forecast(s) employing correlons.

4   *Response*. On the basis of the information yielded by the inference(s) and forecast(s), the receiver responds. The response is itself a performance, often in many modes.

The events of a communication process can be illustrated with an everyday activity in a beauty salon: a beautician applying makeup to a customer's face in front of an onlooker. Several communication processes can be discerned in this activity, but I delineate only one. In addition, although many interactors are performing, the example focuses on just the three people: Sally the beautician, Elaine the customer, and Rachel, the latter's close friend. Let us designate Rachel, the onlooker, as the receiver. To Rachel, who observes Sally at work, the application of makeup to Elaine's face is an inscription event; that is, the interactions between a sender (Sally) and an emitter (Elaine) have caused information to be imparted to (or inscribed on) the emitter. Emission occurs throughout the makeup application process, as Elaine's modified face performs visually. Reception takes place when Rachel registers Elaine's visual performances and constructs an inference regarding, for example, Sally's skill as a beautician. When Rachel passes judgment about the quality of Sally's work, with words of praise performed emphatically along with gestures and facial expressions, she has furnished a response.

Any communication process can be broken down into a set of inscription, emission, reception, and response events, but the investigator's research interests dictate the required level of detail. In the example just furnished, explaining Rachel's response might not require that communication events be resolved more finely. However, in studies of a different communication process, the investigator might need to resolve the face-painting activity into Sally's individual brush strokes, each of which incrementally modifies Elaine's face and thus her visual performance. One could enter the microscale even further, by focusing on each interaction between Sally and her brush, between brush and makeup container, and between brush and Elaine's face. Investigations at finer scales would make perfect sense, for example, if one were studying information transfer in craft activities (e.g., Keller and Keller 1996). In that case, Sally — a craftsperson — could be treated as both receiver and sender: each brush stroke applies paint to Elaine's face (inscription) and thereby modifies its visual performance (emission); Sally observes the new visual performance and constructs an inference (reception), which provides the information needed to place the next brush stroke (a response). Clearly, the general theory gives the investigator the conceptual tools for delineating communication processes and events at any scale needed to answer research questions.

Although an inferred inscription event might be distant in time and place from the remaining events in a communication process, the latter is always embedded in a specific activity: *the one in which the receiver takes part*. Thus, only in the reference activity anchored by the receiver can one identify a communication process and specify the roles played by other interactors. I also underscore that an investigator may be able to isolate, in the reference activity, multiple communication processes (sequential and/or simultaneous), perhaps with a given interactor playing different roles in each. This kind of analysis enables the investigator to tame the complexity of communication processes embedded in real-world activities (see Chapter 6).

Specifying a communication process only from the receiver's point of view may seem restrictive, but it is not. Because all role playing involves performance, the investigator can delineate a communication process in such a way as to enable *any* human performance to be regarded as a receiver's response. Thus, the theory can also explain a sender or emitter performance as long as it is framed as a receiver response in a *different* communication process. This is the move, of course, that allows us at last to establish a precise relationship between behavior and communication (for more on this, see Chapter 7).

Indeed, by treating any performance of a person as a receiver's response, we forge an identity between communication and behavior.

Constructing inferences in communication processes

Depending on the case, receivers construct inferences that range from very simple to highly complex (Burgoon *et al.* 1996: ch. 9). On the simple end of the scale, the inference/forecast might merely indicate that the other interactor is ready to switch roles. To wit, in a two-person conversation, the receiver might conclude from the acoustic performance, facial expression, gestures, and personal artifacts of the sender/emitter that it is time to talk again (cf. Harrison and Crouch 1975: 78). In contrast, many communication processes require the receiver, such as a homicide detective, to construct laboriously a complex set of inferences about how, precisely, a victim was slain. Thus, inferences about the murderer's (sender) interactions in inscription events are based on emissions from multiple interactors, including the victim's body and personal artifacts, activity artifacts, and platial artifacts and externs. These examples emphasize that inferences can implicate senders and inscription events occurring in the reference activity or in other activities greatly removed from the receiver in time and place.

Even when registering mainly acoustic performances (as in a telephone conversation), the receiver still fashions inferences. At the most basic level, the receiver builds inferences about the sender/emitter's ostensible message. What is more, depending on the receiver's correlons, she can sometimes conclude from voice alone the sender's age, sex, social class, region of enculturation, and relative social power (Philips 1980; Trudgill 1983) – not to mention arrive at judgments about the message's "truth" or "authenticity" (e.g., Soppe 1988). Receivers also make inferences about another's personality on the basis of voice (e.g., Scherer 1972). Needless to say, these diverse inferences all can influence the receiver's response.

Experiments have shown that tactile interactions also require inference (cf. Ackerman 1990: 94). When a person reaches out and grasps something, this performance depends on inferences about the object's size, shape, and distance. Specifically, these nonconscious inferences/forecasts guide the shaping of fingers and extension of the arm (Jeannerod 1997: ch. 2).

I now discuss each role in greater detail and present additional premises.

The receiver

Analysis of a communication process can begin when the investigator designates a receiver in the reference activity.

As noted in Chapter 4, an interactor must possess a sensory apparatus and be capable of responding in order to play the receiver role. Thus, animals and some artifacts – e.g., computers and smoke detectors – can be receivers, often having hardwired correlons. In the case of a smoke alarm, deterministic correlons that link the smoke's chemical or visual emissions to the alarm's acoustic response are literally hardwired, embodied in specific electrical and mechanical interactions between its parts. The inference – that there is a fire – is entirely implicit in the reception event and in the smoke alarm's response. The reception capability of animals is also sometimes hardwired in the sense that, during the animal's early development, particular (often deterministic) correlons are genetically emplaced in its nervous system; such correlons allow the animal to construct inferences for given emissions, which can lead to a reflex response (Domjan 1993: 26–29). Other correlons employed by animal receivers are, of course, learned (Peters 1980; Sebeok 1968; Smith 1977). Thus, we return to one of the most general tenets of the theory: a reception event requires correlons and yields inferences, regardless of whether the receiver is a person, animal, or artifact.

Although a fully general theory must accommodate the artifacts and externs that serve as receivers in behavioral systems, much of the remaining discussion is tailored to human receivers. This focus allows the theory to be amplified in a direction essential for explaining behavior (see Chapter 7).

The reception event can lead to three outcomes:

1   The registered performances have no effect on the receiver that can be detected by an investigator. In this case, there is no communication event (Stevens 1950: 689) because the information transfer was inconsequential.

2   Reception contributes to learning, thereby causing a biochemical change in the person's nervous system and thus the creation of new correlons (or the remodeling of old ones). Because an investigator cannot discern the precise biochemical changes induced by an instance of learning (notwithstanding recent advances in brain imaging – e.g., Haberlandt 1994: 63–66), the direct detection of learned correlons is unlikely to be possible any time soon. Thus, the only accessible evidence of learned correlons resides in a receiver's subsequent response(s). Perhaps that is why so many investigators of human and animal communication have long included the response event in their studies (e.g., Frings and Frings 1977: 3; Hanneman 1975: 24; Smith 1977: ch. 10; Stevens 1950: 689). This point brings us to the final case, from which the second is, in important respects, operationally indistinguishable.

3   The receiver constructs inferences (and forecasts) and responds during an immediately subsequent interaction. It is useful to regard the emission(s) as having *cued* the response (cf. Albone 1984: 130, 166, 229, 238; Burgoon *et al.* 1996: 189; Easterbrook 1959: 188–189; Miller 1985: 181, 1987: 101; Rapoport 1990: 219; Rathje and Schiffer 1982: 63; Schiffer and Skibo 1997; Thomas 1996: 59; compare to "contextual cue" – e.g., Domjan 1993; Giddens 1993: 110). Needless to say, the same registered emission(s) can contribute to learning *and* cue a response (Keller and Keller 1996:

17–18). For example, a child (the receiver) touching a hot stove (the emitter) for the first time simultaneously acquires correlons about stove performance and retracts the injured member.

Factors influencing the responses of human receivers

Three major sets of factors affect what a human receiver registers, the inferences/forecasts created, and the response.

The first set of factors is learning through experience; needless to say, the person's immediately preceding performances are especially important. To illustrate the effects of correlons acquired experientially, let us imagine that someone eating dinner at a friend's house is passed a bowl of steamed okra (the emitter). In this activity and place, the guest, as the receiver, can respond appropriately in one of several ways to the bowl of okra's visual, chemical, mechanical, and thermal performances. For example, if the guest was unfamilar with okra, she might take a small serving to taste. However, if she already possessed correlons mapping to okra emissions, she might pass the plate along or take a large serving, depending on her okra-related correlons. Another alternative is available to the okra-averse, and that is to take a small portion but not eat it. In any event, the specific response depends on the correlons a person has acquired during previous life-history activities. Individual differences in experiential learning can be large and consequential, despite expectations of uniformity. For example, learned correlons that permit inferences of facial attractiveness exhibit much variation, even in ethnically homogeneous populations (e.g., Strzalko and Kaszycka 1992).

Learned correlons are obtained through direct experience – e.g., earlier encounters with okra, engagements with tools and materials in craft activities, taking part in religious rituals (Lave and Wenger 1991) – and by indirect experience involving interactions with teachers, friends, family members, books, magazines, television, and so on. Indirect experience supplies correlons that often come into play in contexts never before encountered. For example, when a tourist visits England for the first time and fills a prescription, he employs the correlon, learned from a travel guide, that a pharmacist is called a "chemist."

The acquisition of correlons through learning goes on consciously and nonconsciously as well as explicitly and implicitly (LeDoux 1996; Reber 1993), and much of it takes place nonverbally (Bloch 1990; Keller and Keller 1996; Lave and Wenger 1991). It is noteworthy that tactile and visual interactions with objects figure importantly in experiential learning by infants (e.g., Boyatzis and Watson 1993; Hall 1991; Karmiloff-Smith 1992: ch. 3; Piaget 1952; Saarnio and Bjorklund 1984; Streri and Spelke 1988; Tomasello *et al.* 1993; Williams and Kamii 1986). As properties of a person, learned correlons are the basis of many performance characteristics and thus responses (Schiffer and Skibo 1997).

There is enormous variation in the complexity and duration of learning processes. Indeed, the acquisition of correlons may involve one interaction or a large set of complex interactions and activities, as in the contrast between learning about a stove's thermal performance and obtaining the "know-how," by trial and error, for painting faces competently. Learning varies not only in complexity but also in duration (Lave and Wenger 1991). For example, learning to play a musical instrument well enough to perform as a soloist in a world-class symphony is usually a decades-long process, whereas the name of a new television program can be acquired in a few seconds. The ability to learn from life-history interactions is clearly a crucial premise of the present theory, but specific processes and mechanisms of learning are not an integral part of the theory itself.

The second set of factors affecting responses pertains to a person's genetically constituted, biological properties. As noted in Chapter 2, an individual's genes are partly or wholly responsible, through their effects on someone's formal properties, for many performance characteristics – i.e., can the person yell loudly, sing sweetly, or jump three feet in the air? A familiar example of a hardwired correlon is color blindness (Coren et al. 1994: 157–160). People afflicted with these genetic variants have impaired color reception, and this affects their responses in activities such as taking color-blindness tests, identifying birds, and connecting color-coded wires. All sensory modes exhibit inter-individual variation (Ackerman 1990; Coren et al. 1994), much of it doubtless hardwired. Genetic factors range in their degree of determinism, sometimes merely contributing to the ease with which new correlons can be learned experientially (compare to "learning bias" [Deacon 1997: 338], "prepared learning" [LeDoux 1996: 236–238], "predisposition" [Sperber 1996: 92], and learning "constraint" [Karmiloff-Smith 1992: 11–12, 40–41]; see also Fox 1979: 143; King 1994: 43; Tooby and Cosmides 1989; Wilson 1978: 47). For example, an individual born into a musical family can become a virtuoso on an instrument with much less practice than someone not so favorably endowed. Regardless of the degree of determinism, responses can be influenced by genetic variability in sundry properties and thus in performance characteristics.

The third set of factors is alterations to the properties of a person's body. Such changes result from developmental and aging processes (which may have a large genetic component), as well as interactions in activities throughout one's life history. During aging, for example, predictable changes take place in the senses (Coren et al. 1994: 571–575; Corso 1981), altering hardwired correlons. Hearing, for one, becomes less acute as one gets older, often with reduced reception of high frequencies. Because of such differences in sensory-related performance characteristics, people vary in responses. To take the most obvious example, a person unable to hear a soft voice in face-to-face conversation may respond by interjecting "what?" at frequent intervals. Similarly, age-related changes in brain structure, muscle mass, and hormones affect countless performance characteristics (e.g., Bergeman 1997; Charness 1985). Not surprisingly, the National Football League has had few George Blandas, a man able to perform well as a place kicker in his fifth decade. In addition, accidents, illness, eating patterns, drugs, exercise, surgery, mutilation, and so on can change a person's formal properties in ways that demonstrably alter performance characteristics, and thus the potential for generating particular responses.

To sum up, then, a person's response as a receiver in a specific communication process is significantly affected by his or her life-history activities and biological properties. Of course, personal artifacts also affect responses (through their effects on performance characteristics), but they are not discussed until Chapter 7.

Tuning

Because of the difficulty in distinguishing between the influences of genes and experience on specific correlons and performance characteristics, and because doing so is unnecessary for the present project, I bundle all causal factors into one overarching category called *tuning* (compare to "attuned" and "attunement" – Deacon 1997: 126; Kendon 1985; Thomas 1996: 41, 45–46, 55; cf. Lieberman 1991: 45; Newell 1990: 27). The tuning process refers to a person's acquisition of correlons, whether they are obtained genetically, experientially, or through both processes.

An *appropriately* tuned receiver is someone who possesses the correlons needed for constructing inferences/forecasts from, and responding skillfully to, emissions in a specific communication process (compare to low vs. high competence [Romney *et al.* 1986, 1987], "cognitive complexity" [Stamp *et al.* 1994: 195–196], "behavioral mastery" [Karmiloff-Smith 1992: 24–26], and novice vs. expert [Whittaker *et al.* 1998]). People who lack appropriate tuning – i.e., are less skilled – nonetheless still respond on the basis of whatever tuning they possess (on skilled performance, see Greene and Geddes 1993; Keller and Keller 1996: 55).

In everyday activities, people are constantly being "retuned" experientially as new correlons are acquired and old ones modified. In a typical example, the correlons one forms from a stranger's visual emissions (i.e., "first impressions") are often modified – sometimes quickly – on the basis of additional performances. As Diane Ackerman (1990: 275–276) recounts:

> I remember seeing Omar Sharif in *Doctor Zhivago* and *Lawrence of Arabia*, and thinking him astonishingly handsome. When I saw him being interviewed on television some months later, and heard him declare that his only interest in life was playing bridge, which is how he spent most of his

spare time, to my great amazement he was transformed before my eyes into an unappealing man. Suddenly his eyes seemed rheumy and his chin stuck out too much and none of the pieces of his anatomy fell together in the right proportions.

Presumably, this retuning affected Ackerman's subsequent responses to images and films of Omar Sharif.

Sometimes retuning takes longer than Ackerman's epiphany. A common example of lengthy retuning comes from people's responses to questions about the platial artifacts in their neighborhood, such as, "How do you feel about that huge water tower?" When the water tower is first erected, many neighbors are likely to respond by labeling it a nuisance or an eyesore. Through the decades, the water tower performing visually every day contributes to a gradual retuning, until the response of many neighbors is apt to become something like, "It's part of the neighborhood, and we just take it for granted." Finally, if the water tower is threatened with demolition, some neighbors might claim that "The tower is an historic property – our heritage." The acquisition of difficult skills also involves and exemplifies long-term retuning, such as identifying red wines, conversing in a new language, writing a book, playing chess, and pole vaulting (see Hutchins 1995: chs 6–7).

Despite the temptation to equate tuning with enculturation or socialization, one should resist doing so for several reasons. First, tuning includes biological, even genetic components. The need to take into account such factors when explaining behavior is seldom acknowledged by sociocultural anthropologists and sociologists, but can no longer be ignored. Indeed, lest they risk losing credibility among the wider sciences, social scientists must find ways to integrate the findings of, for example, behavioral genetics (e.g., Nelson 1994; Plomin *et al.* 1997) and aging research (e.g., Bergeman 1997) into their formulations. The concept of tuning, I suggest, opens the door to easy integration. For example, as people's biological properties undergo changes with aging, they are gradually retuned in ways that affect many performances, such as those often attributed to changes in "personality."

Second, the concept of tuning enables investigators to comprehend cases where the sharing of correlons transcends the social units (i.e., cultures and societies) in which enculturation and socialization are believed typically to take place. As a result, one can easily make sense of similarities in the responses of people in different nations who participate in the activities of universalist religions, commercial banking and finance, or philately without resorting to *ad hoc* devices such as "subculture."

And third, enculturation and socialization highlight the experiences that people as members of groups in a culture or society *share*, enabling us to explain why different *groups* – defined on the basis of age, sex, gender, ethnicity, class, urban or rural, occupation, etc. – have dissimilar sets of correlons and responses. The concept of tuning is much broader, not only because it includes the biological component, but also because it applies at the scale of the individual, explicitly recognizing a person's capacity for fashioning uncommon correlons and for generating idiosyncratic responses (see also D'Andrade 1995: 149; Fletcher 1996: 79; Keller and Keller 1996; Sperber 1975: 87). Thus, the extent that people in a behavioral system share any tuning – i.e., a specific set of correlons – is always an empirical matter (cf. Sperber 1996: 49, 57–58). The concept of tuning easily handles both extreme individual differences (e.g., the multiplicity of responses to the visual and tactile performances of a modern sculpture) and widespread patterns (e.g., Americans almost uniformly respond to a nearby spider's visual performance by killing it or backing away, not by popping it into their mouths) – and everything in between. That two people *share* a correlon implies only that, as receivers, they would respond alike in the same communication process; no assumption is made that the correlon(s) is identically constituted in their nervous systems.

In appreciating that tuning accommodates individual variation, we should not forget that many correlons are widely shared, and this contributes to patterning in a behavioral system's interactions. Precisely such uniformities in tuning allow investigators to fashion explanations of group-response patterns in relation to specific emissions, especially of artifacts (see below).

Hierarchical organization and keying-in of correlons

Another important factor contributing to patterned responses is the manner in which correlons are organized and deployed. In accord with the organization of human memory and probably cognition in general (Deacon 1997: 297; Hardcastle 1996: ch. 3; Newell 1990: 7, 117; cf. Greenfield 1991; Kellerman *et al.* 1989; Saarnio and Bjorklund 1984), I hypothesize that a person's correlons are organized hierarchically and thus are "keyed in" sequentially by the performances of different emitters. (The actual mode of information processing may be serial or parallel [cf. Bloch 1990; Byrne 1995: 149], but it is more conveniently modeled as a sequence.) At the most general level, emissions of platial interactors, including people, key in correlons that supply the receiver with information for inferring a place's identity (Miller 1987: 101–102), such as church, bedroom, skid row, or golf course (Kaiser 1985: 139; compare to "environmental scenes" [Tversky and Hemenway 1983] and to "physical contexts" [Krueger and Harper 1988: 63]). Once the place is identified, emissions from activity interactors result in a second sorting of correlons, and from the latter a specific activity is inferred. When a place is identified as a "bedroom," for example, correlons are keyed in that identify activities such as sleeping, making the bed, vacuuming the floor, or reading a magazine. After these context-defining correlons have been keyed in, the process continues until correlons are keyed in for identifying particular interactors and interactions.

Why is it essential for people to identify the hierarchically related categories of place, activity, interactor, and interaction? I submit that skillful performance requires a receiver to employ a different set of correlons, and thus generate different responses, for each place, activity, interactor, and interaction. Thus, every combination of categories calls forth a corresponding – perhaps unique – set of correlons and thereby yields more or less tailored responses (see Chapter 7). In this way, receivers are able to respond skillfully to emissions in any communication process in any context. Indeed, imagine what might happen if people responded identically in amusement parks, churches, and bedrooms, or to lovers, friends, and strangers. To say the least, the responses of people failing to make these identifications would be judged by others as highly unskilled or inappropriate.[1]

To illustrate in greater detail the process of keying in correlons (compare to "code-switching" in sociolinguistics [e.g., Blom and Gumperz 1972]), let us suppose that a man – an appropriately tuned receiver – is observing a second man. The latter, as an emitter in this communication process, is holding his right hand aloft, rapidly moving it back and forth (cf. Goffman 1974: 37). Without additional information, there is no way to know what inference(s) the receiver constructs from this gesture and what response is likely, for the same emitter (with identical personal artifacts) can carry out that exact performance along the side of a road, on the beach, at the railing of a ship, or in a classroom. When the receiver registers the performances of platial interactors, however, he is able to identify the place and key in place-specific correlons. Next, on the basis of activity interactor performances, the receiver identifies the activity. To wit, is the ship arriving or departing? Is the person in the classroom a student in the midst of taking an exam or responding to a teacher's question? After the activity is identified – let us assume that the emitter is arriving on a ship – activity-specific correlons are keyed in. Even then, the receiver needs to attend to other performances of the waving man, including those of his personal artifacts along with facial expressions and other gestures. Together, these emissions permit the receiver to situate the person in the activity, which in turn keys in the set of interactor-specific correlons. The latter make it possible for the gesturing man to be identified with respect to context-relevant categories (e.g., a baggage handler, an unknown passenger, his friend John) on the basis of visual and acoustic emissions (cf. Joseph 1986: 71–72). These identifications allow the hand-waving performance itself to key in interaction-specific correlon(s) that enable the receiver to obtain information from the gesture, such as a greeting from his friend John, returning from a Caribbean cruise.

As the previous example makes clear, the keying-in process operates on (or is driven by) countless emitters performing in many modes. What is more, emitter roles are often played by artifacts, whose performances contribute importantly to the identification of places, activities, interactors, and interactions.

I hypothesize that, during the course of everyday activities, correlons are usually keyed in implicitly or nonconsciously, with the receiver unaware of the process. This is so because the sorting of correlons, so necessary for producing a skillful response, must be done rapidly and unobtrusively; thus, it is essentially automatic. However, the process can become explicit, conscious, or provoke awareness when people are confronted by novel places, activities, interactors, or interactions – or novel combinations of them (Keller and Keller 1996: 112–116). An example comes from the experiences of a traveler, staying overnight in an unfamiliar motel room. During the dark of night, he responds to the discomfort of a full bladder by arising from bed, barely awake, and heading to the bathroom. But, after a few steps, he finds his way barred by an unfamiliar chest of drawers. In this case, the traveler's platial correlons had keyed in automatically as if he were at home. Once he recognizes the unfamiliar place, he can explicitly navigate his way to the bathroom.

Additional evidence that the processing of emissions is hierarchical, beginning with the application of place- and activity-specific correlons, is furnished by instances when someone ordinarily encountered on a daily basis is not recognized at first when seen in a different place and activity (Watkins *et al.* 1976). Because recognition does occur eventually in these contexts, I conclude that correlons can be sorted in varied sequences but at an appreciable increase in processing time and, more importantly, a delay in the response. Natural selection, I suggest, favored the more efficient hierarchical processing algorithm while at the same time preserving an individual's ability to sort correlons "manually" as required for coping with novel situations.

More cumbersome correlon-sorting mechanisms should also come into play in learning. Indeed, there is evidence that platial and activity correlons are learned after interactor and interaction correlons. For example, "children display the same abhorrence toward waitresses in white as toward nurses with whom they have had unpleasant experiences" (Joseph 1986: 164). Gradually, children acquire the platial and activity correlons needed for skillful performance in different contexts (e.g., see Gross and Ballif 1991).[2]

An appreciation for the keying-in process permits us easily to explain the co-presence in the same person of utterly incompatible correlons (see also Sperber 1996: 70–74, 149–150); such correlons would come into play only when keyed in by emissions in different contexts. For example, the correlons that someone has acquired experientially in walking, riding a bicycle, and driving a car in a city lead, usually, to skillful performances in these activities. However, if those correlons could be modeled – i.e., approximated verbally and made explicit – we would likely encounter incompatibilities in, for example, the response to stop signs. To wit, when *walking*, ignore stop signs and watch for cars; when *riding a bicycle*, never stop unless there is a cop around or a vehicle is about to enter the intersection; and when *driving a car*, always come to a stop or a near-stop. Similarly, many urban people have acquired conflicting correlons about forests. On the one hand, reading novels like *Heidi* and nature tracts may lead to correlons that associate forests with pleasurable experiences, such as singing birds and the glories of nature unspoiled. On the other hand, familiarity with *Grimm's Fairy Tales* along with sundry media accounts of campers being mauled by bears can give rise, in the same person, to correlons that endow forests with sinister qualities as places filled with occult forces and dangerous beasts. These contradictory correlons coexist without causing dissonance because they are seldom if ever explicit at the same time and because they come into play in different contexts. A person possessing both kinds of correlons might never enter a forest alone at night, but could enjoyably take nature walks with friends in the daytime. These examples allow us to appreciate that the present theory predicts and makes intelligible the common occurrence of incompatibilities in a person's relational knowledge – correlons – that would be anomalies for most other communication theories.[3]

The emitter

From the receiver's vantage point, the outside world consists of myriad emissions, in diverse performance modes, providing a barrage of potential evidence on which his or her tuning – and the keying in of correlons – can operate. When the receiver's interactor- and interaction-specific correlons are at last keyed in, usually the performances of one emitter – a *salient* emitter (cf. Joseph 1986: 21; Newell 1990: 274; Smith 1977: 190) – lead to specific inferences/forecasts and cue the response; other emitters often recede into the background, having played their roles in *that* communication process by keying in the receiver's context-defining correlons.

One can also distinguish between active and passive emitters. An *active* emitter has a sensory apparatus and is able to respond, and so can be a receiver. On the other hand, *passive* emitters, which lack a sensory apparatus, cannot be receivers, nor can their performances be cued. Nonetheless, active or passive emitters can be salient in a particular communication process. Active emitters, especially people, ordinarily furnish emissions in many modes simultaneously, but only some such emissions are true performances – the ones that engage other interactors consequentially, thereby contributing to an activity's forward motion.

How does an emitter come to carry out a specific performance in a given context? Not surprisingly, these emissions are influenced by the same factors that affect receiver tuning and responses: life-history interactions and physical–chemical–biological properties.

An emitter, such as an artifact, can be inscribed during any activity of its life history, from the procurement and shaping of its raw materials, to manufacture and use, to maintenance and disposal (Schiffer 1972, 1975). Thus, an artifact's emissions can embody information inscribed by many senders (Musello 1992).

As we shall soon see, this potential multiplicity of senders poses insuperable problems for the two–body model (cf. Kelly 1981:83).

The sender

The sender role is privileged in conventional communication theories, and much effort is lavished on discerning the sender's intent. In the present theory, however, the sender role cannot be privileged because it depends, ultimately, on the receiver's ability to infer the interactor responsible for a particular inscription event. Without a designated receiver, there can be no sender because the sender is a product of the receiver's inference.

This strong claim about the dependence of senders upon receivers perhaps seems bizarre when applied to two people conversing face to face, where at any given instant it appears possible for the participants and an investigator to specify the sender (assuming a combined sender–emitter role). However, I emphasize that a conversing couple is but a special case of communication, and even in this case the sender can be ambiguous (see Chapter 6, BCP 1). The more general claim of sender dependence is retained because it applies to a vastly greater array of communication phenomena, as the following examples illustrate.

Let us assume that an archaeologist visiting my laboratory is the receiver in analytic activities; in responding to artifact emissions, she writes down inferences. The object of study – the salient emitter – is a large earthenware pot of recent Cypriot manufacture bearing a spout and handle, which performs visually like a large pitcher. When the visiting archaeologist, who is trained in ceramic analysis (i.e., appropriately tuned with relevant correlates), examines this vessel through a hand lens, she registers various visually performing traces of previous interactions in that vessel's life history. For example, on the pot's base she observes a heavily abraded area that contains striations generally oriented toward the spout. The archaeologist's correlates (e.g., Schiffer and Skibo 1989), applied to these striations, enable her to infer that the pot had been abraded by a relatively rigid, sandy surface, such as a hard–packed dirt floor. By focusing on the location and orientation of the striations, she also concludes that the pot had been frequently tipped during use. Although the pot's visual performances lead to inferences about inscription events, the sender can be identified only as one or more anonymous people who participated in the vessel's use activities. Indeed, the pot had been used for several seasons on a Cypriot dig by many dozens of people.

But suppose that instead of examining the vessel's base, the archaeologist inspects an area, below the neck, lacking abrasive traces. Here she sees small, low–density patches of striations oriented in many directions. Armed with interaction-specific correlates (Rye 1981: 86), she infers that these striations were caused by contact between a scraping tool, probably of wood, and the vessel's still soft surface. She further concludes that this hypothesized scraping tool was wielded by the potter. In this instance the receiver is able to infer one person in the past responsible for the inscription event.

In the example of the Cypriot pot (the salient emitter), the archaeologist–receiver can construct inferences about multiple senders who inscribed the pot during various life-history activities. Thus, the sender – or, more properly, the senders – were inferred by the receiver after she had keyed in correlates mapping to the emitter's visual performances. This example demonstrates that senders emerge only after the receiver has built activity- and interaction-specific inferences.

Archaeological inference, as it turns out, is not an aberrant case of communication, but exemplifies a more general process. Indeed, another case drawn from modern life helps us to appreciate the advantages of always regarding senders as receiver dependent. Recall from the last chapter the jogger–receiver in Central Park, viewing an infant clad in sex-linked clothing (the salient emitter) who is accompanied by two young adults, a male and female. Applying the appropriate correlons to the infant's clothing, the jogger infers the child's sex. But who is the sender? On the basis of the adults' visual performances (and widely shared correlons), the jogger concludes that they are the parents, and further infers that they most likely dressed the infant for the outing. Clearly, it is the receiver who has designated this couple, the inferred parents, as the probable senders – those who dressed (i.e., modified) the infant.

By changing a few details in this example, one can demonstrate how other senders might have been inferred. Suppose that the child were accompanied, not by two young adults, but by a solitary woman in her fifties who is wearing an outfit that performs visually like a domestic's uniform. The jogger infers, from the visual performances of the woman and her personal artifacts in this place, that she is probably a nanny taking her charge for a walk. Inferring the sender in this case is more difficult because there are several possibilities. Widely shared correlons permit the jogger to conclude that the nanny most likely dressed the child, and is therefore the sender. But what if she were simply conforming to the parents' usual practice of advertising their child's sex in public places? In the latter case, the jogger might infer that the parents played the sender role, through their interactions with the nanny. It is also possible that the parents actually object to identifying their child in this way, but were away on a trip. So the nanny, taking advantage of a seldom used gift, dressed the child as she preferred; in that event, the nanny decidedly would be the sender. Drawing on additional correlons, the jogger is apt to distinguish among these possibilities by inferring the most likely sender in this situation. Regardless of which sender the receiver identifies, his choice is arrived at through inference.

This example also makes clear that the process of inference does not ensure that the resultant information is correct or certain. Indeed, as archaeologists are the first to admit, the inferential process can produce erroneous or weak conclusions. Similarly, in everyday life we make do with probable inferences, hunches and guesses, and worse. Were it not so, lack of accurate inferences would cause paralysis, rendering us unable to respond to the cues of emitters in daily activities. Because interaction does usually proceed – i.e., to an investigator the activity appears to have a forward motion with respect to the focal interactor(s) – we can be sure that the accuracy of inferences rarely hinders human receivers.

A major cause of incorrect inferences and poor forecasts is faulty correlons. Indeed, people constantly acquire incomplete, imperfect, and erroneous relational knowledge through tuning. Ethnic, class, age, and gender stereotypes are examples of flawed correlons that, regrettably, generate responses just as effectively as ones that we, as social scientists, would regard as being correct. What is more, in groups where flawed correlons are held in common, responses based on them are treated by group members as skillful perform-ances. Even the hardwired correlons of artifacts can be less than perfect, as in a smoke alarm constantly cued by frying fish.

That correlons can be incorrect, as judged by modern science (cf. Stich 1996: 11–13), allows for the possibility that receivers sometimes infer senders and inscription events that lack materiality. For example, in many tribal societies, rainfall – a cloud's mechanical performance – is attributed by receivers to the action of a rain-making spirit. Similarly, a traditional healer might conclude that a sick person's symptoms (emissions) result from the malevolent use of a sorcerer's powers. The ancient Greeks situated the causes of some events in "malignant forces" related to "acts of gods" (Rosen 1995: 6). As the product of a receiver's inference, then, senders can even include spirits, ghosts, angels, gods, and other supernatural phenomena. Clearly, the require-ment that interactors have materiality (Chapter 2) can be relaxed for *inferred* interactors; the investigator may treat these purported agents as peculiar externs.

Artifacts that play supporting roles

Several additional concepts help the investigator to simplify – and thus study effectively – complex communication processes by calling attention to artifacts that play supporting roles. From the standpoint of the receiver, an artifact plays a supporting role when it alters another interactor's performance characteristics. For an example, let us return briefly to the Cypriot vessel discussed above. The archaeologist, it should be recalled, inferred that the potter had scraped the vessel's surface with a wooden tool. Thus, it was not contact between potter and pot that imparted the information, but the linked interactions among potter, wooden scraper, and pot. Artifacts like the wooden scraper, which facilitate inscription, are termed *sendtrons*.

Not surprisingly, an *emitron* is an artifact that enables or enhances an emitter's performances. The makeup used by mimes, for example, can be regarded as an emitron, permitting the mime's facial expressions – as visual performance – to stand out more clearly and be observed at a greater distance by the receiver than those of a bare face or a face painted less flamboyantly.

Finally, we arrive at *receptrons*, artifacts that facilitate reception. Many devices used in activities of observing, measuring, and counting – from multimillion-dollar telescopes and microscopes to a 39 cent plastic ruler – are receptrons, helping the receiver to register emissions. Although receptrons permeate scientific activities (see Hankins and Silverman 1995: ch. 1), some receptrons are personal artifacts, such as the bifocal glasses indispensable to so many academics. Seeing-eye and hearing-ear dogs can also be treated as receptrons.

The concepts of sendtron, emitron, and receptron permit the investigator precisely and flexibly to describe the participation of artifacts, as players of supporting roles, in complex communication processes. Thus, investigators can easily handle all sorts of "information" technology that seem to stymie conventional theories; in this way we obviate the need to devise special theories for dealing with "mediated" communication (e.g., Gumpert and Cathcart 1990; Lievrouw and Finn 1990).

Methodological implications

The theory presented above requires that a research question be formulated in relation to specific interactors in a particular activity and place. Once the context is defined, the investigator begins to delineate a communication process by indicating which interactor played the receiver role. In the next step, one specifies the interactors, including platial, situational, and activity artifacts, that performed emitter roles, and which was the salient emitter. Artifacts playing supporting roles can also be identified. Sender(s) and inscription events are inferred, as appropriate, depending on the correlons, inferences, and forecasts that the investigator imputes to the receiver. Finally, the investigator strives to explain the receiver's response as a consequence of the emissions that have been registered *and* the receiver's properties – i.e., tuning and personal artifacts (see Chapter 7).

The previous statements imply that the investigator must model the receiver's correlons in order to account for her inferences, forecasts, and responses. Indeed, the present theory entails a concern with the receiver's relational knowledge. Needless to say, modeling other people's correlons is highly problematic today because the social sciences have produced so few relevant principles.[4] Despite our fondest hopes, we cannot simply ask people what they know or administer verbal tests to elicit their relational knowledge – since much of it is entirely tacit (Hutchins 1995; Keller and Keller 1996; McDermott and Roth 1978; Reber 1993). As investigators undertake experiments and make ethnographic observations that attend to their subjects' tuning and personal artifacts and to the performances of platial and activity interactors – especially artifacts – principles useful for modeling correlons will eventually be developed.

Shared correlons and group responses

Given that relevant principles will be slow in coming, can the investigator interested in explaining responses somehow escape the need to model the correlons of an individual receiver? The answer is yes, so long as she is willing to adopt some simplifying assumptions: (1) the correlon(s) is deterministic, (2) a group of receivers has appropriate and identical tuning and personal artifacts, and (3) all other features of the communication process – i.e., interactors, activity, and place – are constant. Under these conditions, the investigator assumes that unspecified (deterministic) correlons establish a one-to-one mapping between emissions and response. Thus, identical responses among a group of receivers can be explained merely by invoking the emissions (Wheeless and Cook 1985: 260).

Though never met perfectly, these conditions might be best approximated in small, relatively homogeneous societies, where *major* differences in tuning vary mainly by age, sex, and gender (cf. Stephen and Harrison 1993). Thus, on the basis of the simplifying assumptions, an investigator could arrive at some first-approximation explanations of stereotypical responses.

In principle, this approach can be extended to more differentiated societies (*sensu* McGuire 1983) – those having more diverse activities, kinds of social roles, types of artifacts, and so on. In such societies, one can employ sociodemographic characteristics for forming smaller, more homogeneous groups whose members, because they presumably share deterministic correlons, should respond identically (cf. Schiffer 1995b). In making this move, the investigator is, in effect, treating sociodemographic characteristics as proxy measures of tuning. For example, she might assume that all well-educated, Anglo adult males, living in a nuclear-family household in a particular neighborhood and employed in similar jobs, should, by virtue of shared but unspecified correlons, respond alike in the same communication process. Alternatively, the investigator could assume that the people playing specific *social* roles in a given activity possess identical, deterministic correlons, which would generate the same response. Needless to say, using sociodemographic generalizations to predict/explain group responses is precisely the move that permits many sociologists and sociocultural anthropologists to ply their traditional trades.

Although avoiding the modeling of correlons, this strategy of explanation regrettably ignores the biological component of tuning, neglects individual variation in responses, treats people as if they responded automatically (not unlike smoke detectors), and reproduces an orthodox cultural or societal determinism. At best, this strategy is a stop-gap measure (see also Chapter 7). As behavioral archaeologists have argued (e.g., Rathje 1979), over the long term we must obtain the principles for modeling the relational knowledge possessed by individual receivers in order to explain responses (for other contributions to "cognitive" archaeology, see Byers 1994; Davidson and Noble 1989; Gibson and Ingold 1993; Keller and Keller 1996; Marshack 1989; Mellars and Gibson 1996; Mithen 1996; Rathje 1979; Renfrew 1982; Renfrew and Zubrow 1994; Schiffer 1992b: ch. 7; Schiffer and Miller 1999; Schiffer and Skibo 1987; Whitley 1992; Wynn 1989, 1991, 1993; Young and Bonnichsen 1984).

Modeling correlons and individual receiver responses

In another common strategy that eschews the modeling of correlons, the investigator imputes to a person an intent or goal, and this seemingly accounts for a given performance (cf. Dipert 1993). I contend that this mode of explanation is scientifically unsatisfactory (cf. Bostrom and Donohew 1992; Smith 1977: 265). Assigning causal efficacy to motives derives implicitly from the sender-focused perspective that permeates conversations in modern Western – and many other – societies. Indeed, intent and goal are concepts that we employ constantly in inferring reasons for other people's performances (Berger and Calabrese 1975; D'Andrade 1995: 158–163; Edwards 1994; Ehrenhaus 1988; Giddens 1993: 89–93; Goffman 1974: 22; Mills 1940; Sperber 1996: 147; Stich 1996: chs 2–4). The motives we identify are simply shorthands that, in lieu of a scientific causal analysis, help us to explain/predict the behavior of others. Though lacking a scientific foundation, in everyday life these kinds of inferences and forecasts do contribute to responses and thus facilitate the forward motion of activities.

I submit that accounting for someone's performance by invoking an intent or motive is misguided (cf. Gould 1990: 235–237). This is so not only because inferences about intent lack universality among human societies (DuBois 1993; Robbins 1997; Rosen 1995), but also because there are no scientific tools for identifying motives in specific cases (Schiffer and Miller 1999). In carrying out a scientific analysis, the investigator must reconceptualize an individual's given performance – e.g., putting on eye shadow, purchasing a watermelon, answering a question – by treating it *as a receiver's response in a communication process*. Thus, explaining a person's performance – any performance – is transformed from interminable discourse over intent into our familiar problem of explaining a receiver's response. And, in constructing such an explanation, the investigator cannot avoid the need to model the correlons of individual receivers.

When explaining responses of Western receivers, the investigator's models of correlons can incorporate Western indigenous concepts, including intent, goal, and motive. In a process akin to a double hermeneutic circle, the investigator may impute *to the receiver* a correlon or correlons incorporating these concepts; when keyed in by appropriate emissions, the correlon(s) generated the response. Let us take an example, which I keep simple by ignoring the context-defining correlons that would be required for a complete explanation.

Suppose that a woman and man are walking slowly along a downtown street, occasionally peering into store windows, when a masked man carrying a gun suddenly darts out the front door of a shop. The couple, as receivers, are cued by the masked man's visual performance and respond immediately by crouching down behind a nearby trash bin. In an effort to account for this response, the investigator may construct the couple's shared correlon as follows: "a gun-brandishing robber, trying to get away from the scene of the crime (imputed goal), might want to harm anyone who gets in the way (imputed intent)."

Although the theory permits the investigator to model a *receiver's* correlons (and thus inferences) using concepts like goal and intent, I suggest that this move often adds little to the response's explanation. With reference to the previous example, a much simpler correlon, focusing on a forecast, also suffices. To wit, "a gun-brandishing robber might shoot somebody nearby." This correlon is just as effective in explaining the couple's hiding response as one presuming that the receivers attribute goals or intent to the "robber." Is it possible to devise an even simpler correlon? Yes, indeed. The investigator need only assume that the people possess a generalized correlon to the effect that "encounters with gun-waving robbers should be avoided." Investigators who find this formulation a bit too stark are free to fashion correlons with greater embellishment. I merely emphasize that Western indigenous concepts can be used in modeling a Western receiver's correlons, but they are often superfluous. Thus, by Morgan's "canon of parsimony" (Wasserman 1993: 214), we should prefer the simplest correlon(s) that can explain the response. To underscore the value of modeling correlons with as little clutter as possible, I now turn to a more detailed and complex example.

On a recent trip to the Hopi Reservation, my wife Annette, son Jeremy, and I visited the homes and shops of a dozen or so potters on First Mesa, seeking an anniversary gift for old friends. Since my first journey in 1968 to Hopi − a series of quite isolated Indian villages in northern Arizona − dramatic changes had taken place. For example, many families now live in a low-density suburbia extending miles from Polacca, the village at the foot of First Mesa, and in their electrified homes are televisions, refrigerators, and countless other trappings of modernity. Despite the changes, potters are still at work, their wares more visible to tourists than during any of our previous visits.

Oddly enough, I was struck not by the large-scale changes at Hopi but by the conversations between potters and their visitors. Without prompting, potters divulged the meanings of their painted designs to utter strangers. In one home, for example, we were invited into a large room where pottery was made and also displayed to customers. On several large cafeteria-type tables lay potting materials and tools, a book on historic Hopi pottery (Wade and McChesney 1981), and a few finished vessels. Gently grasping a small jar still warm from firing, the artisan pointed proudly to the design she had painted repeatedly around the pot; it was, she said, a "water bird." This design was apparently laden with traditional meanings that we were privileged to share. Decades ago, when we had ventured to ask Hopi potters what their designs meant, the usual answer was "they are just designs." Why, I wondered, are these Hopi potters now so forthcoming with symbolic interpretations? Impressed by the potter as well as the pot, we bought the jar with the "water bird" design and, upon returning home, placed it temporarily on our mantel.

I now undertake a simplified analysis of the activity, "a Hopi artisan selling a pot to an Anglo tourist." Of special interest are the potter's acoustic performances and the customer's response: to purchase or not purchase the pot. This activity takes place in the Hopi potter's shop, and the conspicuous platial and activity interactors help to key in the context-defining correlons of both potter and tourist. From the standpoint of the customer–receiver, the potter is inferred to be the sender – the person who painted the design. As an emitter, the pot performs visually and tactilely; but the potter herself is also an emitter, furnishing information in diverse performances that help to cue the customer's response. In modern times, some Hopi potters are supplying interpretations of design symbolism through acoustic, visual, and tactile performances.

What caused the change over the past few decades in the performances of Hopi potters during selling activities? I hypothesize that the new-found eagerness of many potters to furnish meanings for their designs stems from larger changes in pottery marketing. Decades ago, most Hopi potters disposed of their wares wholesale to museum buyers or to traders; relatively few pots were sold at retail to the occasional tourist who turned up, uninvited, at the mesas. However, in recent years the Hopi mesas themselves have become a tourist destination. Thus, some Hopi potters, while still selling their wares wholesale, have opened retail shops in or adjacent to their homes, especially on First Mesa; these locales are identified prominently with signs advertising "pottery."

I hypothesize that Hopi potters, on the basis of persistent questioning from tourists, have learned (i.e., acquired a correlon) that the latter expect painted designs to have a deep symbolic significance. Further, I suggest that some potters have been retuned, acquiring a correlon that is used to forecast that a sale is more likely when the customer's expectations are met. Thus, in responding as a receiver to visitor queries in their shops, Hopi potters now add acoustic performances – discussions of symbolism – to accompany the visual and tactile performances of vessels offered for sale. From these diverse performances, the customer–receiver may infer that the potter is not only skilled in her craft but is also a knowledgeable, traditional Hopi. These emissions are more likely to cue a purchase if the receiver is a tourist tuned to the trappings of apparent Indian authenticity (cf. Eaton 1994). In light of increased interaction between potters and the end-purchasers of their products, it is not surprising that artisans are now tuned to be more customer friendly, employing verbal performances, in responses to customer queries, that increase the likelihood of a sale.

Discussion and conclusion

The archaeologically informed, receiver-oriented theory of communication presented here is distinguished from all others in the social sciences by the following *set* of postulates:

1 Interactors play three major roles – sender, emitter, and receiver – in all communication processes.
2 The major roles can be played by any person, artifact, or extern having the requisite performance characteristics.
3 As sendtrons, emitrons, and receptrons, artifacts may also play supporting roles in communication processes.
4 A communication process, which consists of four events – inscription, emission, reception, and response, is delineated by the investigator and studied with reference to a particular context (defined by an activity *and* a place).
5 Communication processes are permeated by the performances of personal, activity, situational, and platial artifacts.
6 The investigator is required to designate a receiver and, with respect to that receiver, identify the interactors playing emitter roles.
7 The receiver obtains information from emitters performing in many modes.
8 Receivers construct inferences about senders and inscription events using correlons that map to emissions and are keyed in hierarchically; the receiver can also employ correlons to formulate forecasts.
9 The receiver's response is cued by emitter performance(s), including that of the salient emitter, and is influenced by the receiver's tuning.
10 Ideally, explanation of a response in a specific communication process requires the investigator to model the receiver's relevant correlons, inferences, and forecasts.
11 Depending on how one delineates a communication process, any performance of any person can be treated as a receiver response.

The new theory necessarily includes the response of the receiver. That is because the receiver effects further interaction, causing what appears – to the investigator – as the activity's forward motion, usually with respect to a focal interactor. Needless to say, the forward motion of every activity involves, and depends upon, communication processes. What is more, because any person's performance can be regarded as a receiver's response, there is no need to distinguish theoretically between communication – defined in terms of communication processes – and human behavior, defined as performance.

Perhaps the new theory's greatest strength, beyond its obvious simplicity compared to competing theories (e.g., Patterson 1995), is that it finally frees students of communication from the two-body model based on language. The more general theory gives the investigator ample flexibility for analyzing all communication, especially that involving artifacts and externs; no communication phenomena are ruled out a priori because they fail to conform to the two-body model. In addition, the theory allows the same phenomenon to be handled in different ways, ensuring that a creative investigator always has the tools for studying any communication process, no matter how seemingly bizarre or complex. Finally, with its emphasis on the artifact emissions that help define contexts, contribute to inferences and forecasts, and cue responses, the theory supports the claim (Chapter 1) that artifacts participate in virtually all human communication.

Chapter 6

Basic communication processes

Introduction

The theory of communication set forth above is both abstract and, in important respects, counterintuitive. In this chapter, I make the theory more accessible to readers by showing how it can be used for describing communication processes in everyday activities. Through numerous examples, I also demonstrate the theory's versatility for handling communication processes of many sorts, including those ignored by students of communication in the other social sciences.

The examples are presented within a framework of *basic communication processes* (BCPs), which occur in every activity. BCPs are defined on the basis of all possible permutations of people, artifacts, and externs playing the three major communication roles. In any activity, no matter how complex, the investigator can discern instances of one or more BCPs (so long as there is at least one active interactor).[1]

Although examples are supplied for every BCP, they are somewhat simplified. Place and activity are seldom specified in detail; thus, it is assumed that receivers have keyed in appropriate context-defining correlons. In addition, the receiver's forecasts and responses are often omitted. Moreover, only BCPs having a person as the receiver are presented here, and it is also assumed that the emitter under discussion is the salient emitter. Finally, in choosing examples, I favored those in which the receiver constructs inferences explicitly. Despite these constraints, the examples should furnish the reader with a deeper appreciation for how the theory's concepts enable the analysis of real-world communication processes.

Processes with three interactors

In the first set of BCPs, the three major communication roles are always played by three *different* interactors. In the notation employed below, the interactor listed in the first position is the sender, the second is the emitter, and the receiver is third. BCPs have also been numbered consecutively throughout the chapter for ease of reference.

1 Person, person, person

On the basis of someone's performances (the emitter), a receiver makes inferences about another person (the sender). An example of BCP 1 was presented in the previous chapter, involving three women in a beauty shop. In countless comparable activities, receivers obtain information in identical BCPs from people whose visual performances have been modified by manicurists, barbers, hair stylists, and so on. These instances of BCP 1 commonly include sendtrons (e.g., manicurist's tools) and emitrons (e.g., shaped and painted fingernails).

In some cases of BCP 1, the modifications to a person's body are more than superficial. For example, male students in German universities often took part, until very recently, in ritual duels that usually left distinctive facial scars. Whenever I, as a receiver, encounter an elderly German man with a scarred face (emitter), I infer that someone (sender) had, with a sword (sendtron), bestowed this badge of honor upon him during his college days. Depending on the context, my response might consist merely of a change in facial expression. Similarly, receivers viewing the results of dentistry and surgery on another person (emitter) proffer innumerable inferences about the dentist, doctor, or inscription event.

BCP 1 also encompasses far subtler cases of communication. A friend of mine, also an archaeologist, was taught theory in graduate school by Robert C. Dunnell, one of the discipline's leading theorists. He knows Dunnell's ideas so well that sometimes, when the two of us discuss theory, I – as receiver – swear that Dunnell's words are coming out of his mouth. On the basis of this inference, I might respond, "I see your lips moving but I hear Dunnell." My response rests on the inference that Dunnell's pedagogical activities (inscription) had modified biochemical structures in my friend's nervous system, which as correlons were partly responsible for his acoustic emissions in theoretical debates. Having studied Dunnell's articles (e.g., 1978, 1980), I am appropriately tuned to make this inference, for my correlons allow recognition of his favorite phrases. Closely related to this example are cases in which receivers infer that a person's emissions were affected by teaching from a third person or group, as in the promotion of religious, corporate, and political ideologies through "brainwashing."

Intriguing examples of BCP 1 also come from witchcraft accusations and epidemiology. When illness strikes in some societies, the afflicted person seeks the help of a shaman or curer. Often the shaman (a receiver tuned by years of apprenticeship and practice) registers performances of the sick person (emitter), perhaps employing receptrons such as quartz crystals and fetishes. The shaman may infer that the illness stems from the malevolent actions of a sorcerer (the sender), who is sometimes named. Among the Gururumba, a group in highland New Guinea, a person's illness is at times attributed merely to the inadvertent yet harmful thoughts of another (Newman 1965: 87). Similarly, federal medical researchers at the Centers for Disease Control in Atlanta, Georgia, employing high-tech receptrons, offer inferences about person-to-person disease transmission.

2   Person, artifact, person

In this communication process, a person infers, from artifact emissions, something about a second person (the sender) or the inscription event. Not surprisingly, BCP 2 occurs in the inferential activities of the archaeologist (see Chapter 4), but also inheres in many, more mundane, activities.

Let us take, for example, a social worker visiting a single-parent family in a run-down neighborhood. While waiting for the parent to get dressed for the interview, the social worker looks around, registering in a reconnaissance activity the performances of platial and activity artifacts. To this appropriately tuned receiver, these artifacts emit volumes about the parent's child-rearing skills. In the living room/dining room area squats a large entertainment center, dominated by a 35-inch TV performing loudly. Nearby is a coffee table boasting an assortment of junk-food packages, liquor bottles and dirty glasses, and an ashtray overflowing with cigarette butts. Across the room is a soiled couch that exudes stuffing from large tears and reeks of urine. The ceiling light is broken, and the only illumination, beyond sunlight diffusing through closed curtains, comes from a decrepit pole lamp lurking in a corner. Nowhere in the public area of this apartment, however, does the social worker see a single newspaper, magazine, book, or even a writing instrument – with the exception of *TV Guide*. Together, the memorable emissions of these artifacts permit the social worker to infer an absence of good parenting skills, and he responds by making notations to that effect on a clipboard. In this case, the parent is inferred to be the sender, responsible for modifying the room by emplacing various artifacts there. Although the social worker will eventually conduct the interview, it is unlikely that the conclusion about poor parenting skills would be altered by the parent's acoustic emissions in subsequent communication processes.

Although complex, this example illustrates the many kinds of inferences that people routinely make on the basis of platial artifacts performing in and around someone else's dwelling. More familiar examples are conclusions about a neighbor's fastidiousness from a home's front yard and exterior, or a family's social position from their car, house, and living room furniture.

Also involving BCP 2 are activities relating to literary works, art objects, and musical instruments. From a novel, painting, or sculpture, for example, a critic might infer something about activities in the creator's life that shaped the work. Likewise, scholars offer judgments about each other's intelligence and research skills from books and articles. Similarly, a musical instrument's acoustic and visual emissions are the basis of a listener's inferences about sundry senders, such as musician, conductor, concert master, or composer.

The playing of chess, cards, Monopoly, and similar games furnishes additional activity contexts in which BCP 2 looms large. To wit, a receiver makes inferences and forecasts about other players from their facial expressions, postures, movement of game pieces, cards, and so on. When chess is played by grand masters, for example, a player–receiver employs the predictive capability of correlons to forecast his opponent's likely sequence of moves.

In a social scientist's laboratory, a student recruit (receiver) is handed a questionnaire (salient emitter). The student's responses (as pencil marks on the questionnaire) in this context, which is defined by platial interactors and experimental activities, rest often on forecasts about which answers the experimenter (sender) is likely to regard as "correct."

Instances of BCP 2 are not uncommon in the animal kingdom, as several examples demonstrate. In some spider species, the female (receiver) tactilely registers her web's vibrations (emissions). On the basis of their amplitude and frequency, she infers whether an intruder is potential mate or prey, and responds accordingly (Savory 1977: 304–311). Similarly, a female bower bird carefully regards a male's construction (the bower), judging his suitability as a mate (cf. Frings and Frings 1977: 112; Smith 1977: 251–252). And, from chemical emissions of glandular secretions deposited in the environment, beavers and many other mammals infer the territorial boundaries of conspecifics (e.g., Albone 1984: 87, 94; Peters 1980: 73–75).

3   Person, extern, person

In BCP 3, someone makes inferences about another person or inscription events on the basis of an extern's emissions. There is no shortage of intriguing examples of BCP 3, since we are constantly obtaining information from people-modified externs. For example, in a tuna-canning plant, the visual emissions of a tuna, partially dismembered by one worker (sender), cue the cutting activities of a second worker (receiver). In Sahuaro National Park, just west of Tucson, I have observed ironwood trees that bear old scars on their trunks. As a receiver, I infer from these scars (emitter) that, decades ago, someone (anonymous sender) tried to chop down the tree with an axe (a sendtron) but eventually abandoned the task, having discovered that ironwood is not misnamed.

The reader may respond with some puzzlement to the examples of BCP 3 just provided, pointing out that externs, once modified by people (cut-up tuna, chopping marks on a tree), have become artifacts. Thus, it might be argued that BCPs 2 and 3 are really the same. Indeed, the broad definition of artifact furnished in Chapter 2 does permit this conclusion. On the other hand, since the definition of extern is somewhat protean (Chapter 2), an investigator could treat slightly modified "natural" interactors as externs. In the final analysis, how one handles such judgments should depend on the research problem being addressed. In the present context, that of demonstrating the generality and versatility of the new communication theory, I find it useful to define extern expansively.

4   Artifact, person, person

In BCP 4, the receiver constructs an inference that an artifact has modified another person (emitter); the receiver treats the artifact as a causal agent. The most common examples are furnished by accidents involving artifacts. For example, a receiver encounters someone lying on the street (salient emitter), pinned down by a large wooden beam. The receiver infers that the person's condition has been caused by the collapse of an old, decaying billboard (sender). Many other cases of people modified by cars, weapons, tools, machinery, sports equipment, and so forth conform to BCP 4 so long as the artifact itself is the inferred sender.

5   Artifact, artifact, person

The receiver infers that one artifact (emitter) has been modified by another artifact (sender), treating the latter as if it were an independent agent (as in BCP 4). Such BCPs occur in forensics and archaeological analysis. For example, a ballistics expert concludes that a particular gun (sender) had fired the bullet (emitter) being studied. Likewise, a historical archaeologist examines an old beer can (emitter) and determines that it was manufactured entirely by a machine (sender).

Less esoteric examples of BCP 5 come from craft activities. Potters who fire their pots in bonfires need to know when to add more fuel. Employing the correlon that the fire's thermal performance alters the color of the pots being fired (emitters), the potter judges whether the fire (sender) is hot enough. Cooks make similar inferences about an oven's heat by registering the smell, appearance, touch, and taste of cooking food, adjusting the oven accordingly.

6   Extern, artifact, person

A person infers that the sender is an extern that has modified an artifact. It turns out that almost all artifacts have been modified by interactions with externs, such as the sun's ultraviolet light, insects, and floodwaters (Schiffer 1987: chs 7–9), and the emissions of altered artifacts furnish information to human receivers. Deterioration, weathering, and decay are of particular interest to materials scientists, engineers, architects, archaeologists, and museum conservators, but inferences about such processes also inhere in ordinary activities. Not uncommonly, someone cleaning out a refrigerator encounters UFOs – unidentified fermenting objects (Annette Schiffer, personal communication, 1996) – such as a misshapen, cantaloupe-like mass bristling with black and grey fuzzy spots. On the basis of the object's emissions, the person infers an attack of mold (sender) and responds in a manner not difficult to imagine. Likewise, in seeking the cause of a blighted or stunted crop (emitter), farmers sometimes infer (through correlons supplied by their religion) that an unhappy god has taken vengeance upon them.

7   Extern, person, person

The receiver acquires information from the performances of a second person who has been altered by an extern. Because modifications to people are attributed to a variety of natural and supernatural agents, including falling trees, viruses, extreme heat and cold, carnivores, spirits, demons, and mosquitoes, examples of BCP 7 abound in behavioral systems.

Imagine someone encountering a friend (emitter) at a dinner party whose normally pale skin is bright crimson. Without hesitation, the receiver infers that his friend has spent too much time at the beach, basking in the sun (sender). Doctors make comparable diagnoses, inferring that a patient's condition (emission) resulted from interactions with, for example, a microbial pathogen or noxious plant such as poison ivy. In still other diagnostic activities, a traditional healer might conclude that a person's aberrant emissions were caused by a malingering ancestor's spirit (e.g., Elkin 1977: 160). Among the Inkas of Peru, curers attributed broken bones or dislocated joints to the displeasure of the resident spirit where the injury took place (Mason 1968: 225). Receivers also attribute the power to heal or improve a patient's condition to externs, such as herbs that are eaten or applied to the body or the action of a guardian angel.

8   Artifact, extern, person

In BCP 8, someone infers an artifact sender from an extern's emissions; this BCP is commonly found in the activities of environmental sciences.

Several decades ago, scientists became alarmed that many trees in the forests high above the coastal plain of southern California were failing to thrive. Employing high-tech receptrons, the investigators determined that the trees (emitters) had been adversely affected by smog (sender) from the Los Angeles Basin. Today, scientists attribute changes in plants, animals, entire ecosystems, and even the earth's atmosphere to interactions with artifacts such as chemical pollutants.

Not surprisingly, my favorite example of BCP 8 comes from archaeology. Many an archaeologist has long wished that, like Superman, she had X-ray vision to reveal the whereabouts of the artifacts buried in sites. Happily, in recent years we have been able to employ instruments that register emissions passing through, or reflecting from, the ground under foot, and these receptrons can disclose the locations of buried artifacts (e.g., Weymouth 1986). With ground-penetrating radar (receptron), the archaeologist scans a site and obtains a map of subsurface "anomalies" – zones where the reflection of radar waves differs from the natural (i.e., unmodified) dirt. From this map (receptron), the appropriately tuned archaeologist identifies subsurface houses or trash areas (senders).

9   Extern, extern, person

Making inferences about interactions between externs is of consummate concern in sciences such as geology, paleontology, archaeology, and astronomy, as the following examples show. Through instruments (receptrons) in observatories and on spacecraft, planetary scientists have been registering the chemical, electromagnetic, and other performances of the planets in our solar system (e.g., McSween 1993). When Mercury's pock-marked face finally came into view, planetary scientists inferred that it had been repeatedly struck by meteors and asteroids (senders). Closer to home, geoscientists reconstruct the composition of the earth's ancient atmosphere (sender) from the chemical performance of fossils (emitters) obtained from cores drilled in deep-sea sediments. These inferences depend on a host of expensive instruments (receptrons) and on correlons about the chemical interactions between the ancient atmosphere and the microorganisms that thrived then.

Modern scientists are not the only people whose activities involve BCP 9. A traditional hunter, for example, observes footprints, damaged vegetation, the openings to burrows, scats, and other extern emissions, and infers (or forecasts) where prey animals have been (or are going). Likewise, an unusually large number of game animals showing up at the predicted time and place might be attributed to a benevolent spirit.

Processes with two interactors

The theory stipulates that an individual interactor can, in some communication processes, play more than one major role (Chapters 4 and 5). In this section I present BCPs in which interactors play dual roles; those played by the same interactor are not italicized.

10   Person, person, person

From the receiver's point of view, another person is both sender and emitter. Although this BCP is roughly equivalent to the two-body model, the difference is that the receiver treats the sender as having modified his own body with personal artifacts, thereby affecting his performances as an emitter.

On the basis of sundry emissions, including those from clothing, perfume and cologne, badges and insignia, jewelry, and so forth, the receiver constructs inferences about the sender (see Chapter 3 for innumerable examples).

11 *Person,* person, person

Can a person act as both emitter and receiver, inferring, from his own emissions, something about another person (a sender)? This does not sound like a very promising BCP, yet it accommodates cases of communication that might otherwise be overlooked. In the months after breaking my hip while roller skating, during bathing activities I (as receiver) scrutinized the scar on my thigh that remained from surgery to install a pin and plate. On the basis of the scar's visual and tactile emissions, I inferred that the surgeon (sender) had used scalpel, needle, and sutures (sendtrons) skillfully. Similar inferences may be built around the modifications imparted by hair stylists, tattoo artists, manicurists, makeup artists, dentists, orthodontists, liposuction-ists, and so on.

12 Person, *person,* person

In this communication process, someone modifies a second person and, on the basis of the latter's emissions, constructs inferences about, for example, the inscription event. BCP 12 pervades everyday activities.

When one person alters another, be it through surgery, application of makeup, filling a tooth, or styling hair, the craftsperson monitors the effects of his or her interactions (the inscription event) on the second person's emissions. In this way, the craftsperson plays both receiver and sender roles. The receiver's inferences demonstrably affect responses – that is, the craftsper-son's next interaction with the other person. Needless to say, this kind of communication process usually involves sendtrons (e.g., scalpels, drills, brushes, combs, and mousse).

13 Person, *artifact,* person

Someone secures information from an artifact (emitter), makes inferences about her own interactions (as sender) with that artifact, and then responds. Structurally parallel to BCP 12, BCP 13 is found in many activities, and is widespread among artifact-making and -using animals.

In playing both receiver and sender roles, craftspeople constantly monitor – through artifact emissions – the effects of their own performances as sender (see the duck-carving example in Chapter 7). The emissions clearly cue the craftsperson's response, which advances the artifact's life history. By craft activities, I ask the reader to conjure up more than images of a painter dabbing colors on a canvas or a child assembling a model airplane. For, as an archaeologist, I include among the crafts virtually any activity in which a person's sequential interactions modify an artifact or transform materials into products. Thus, baking bread, preparing herbal medicine, and framing a house all qualify as crafts. Craft activities usually involve sendtrons, such as pans and oven, mortar and pestle, and hammers and saws.

BCP 13 also inheres in artifact-maintenance activities, such as cleaning a carburettor, vacuuming the rug, washing dishes, and shining shoes. Needless to say, the investigator can consider maintenance artifacts to be sendtrons, such as screwdriver and solvent; vacuum cleaner; dishwashing detergent, water, sponge; and shoe polish, applicator, brush, and buffing cloth.

Although the information passed between a person and her work is one of the most common communication processes in behavioral systems, it goes largely unmentioned in the communication literature. This is not surprising given that craft and maintenance activities often take place in the absence of verbal performance.

It should also be noted that the most mundane person–artifact interactions can also be treated as instances of BCP 13, such as closing a door, grasping a grapefruit, or walking on the carpet. In these interactions, forecasts figure importantly in constructing a skillful response (Jeannerod 1997).

14 Person, extern, person

BCP 14 is structurally analogous to both BCPs 12 and 13, in that a person is acting as both sender and receiver, except that the performances of an extern rather than an artifact cue the receiver's response. This BCP is found widely in the activities of nonindustrial societies. Through tuning, people learn how to interact skillfully with the plants, animals, and minerals in their environments in ways that promote the forward motion of procurement and processing activities. In addition, any sequence of interactions between a person and an extern involves BCP 14, as in climbing a tree. Thus, among all BCPs, this one is doubtless the most primitive and widespread in the animal kingdom; and, like BCP 13, it is overlooked by social scientists.

15 Artifact, person, person

A person (receiver) makes inferences about artifact senders and responds on the basis of changes in his own emissions. This requires the receiver to infer that an artifact acted as an independent agent. Instances come from industrial activities, where machines sometimes interact mechanically with people in an abnormal manner. Someone whose hand is crushed by an automatic printing press, for example, speedily constructs an inference as to the sender and responds by screaming and – if possible – withdrawing the mauled member.

16   *Extern*, person, person

BCP 16 is structurally parallel to BCP 15; the difference is that someone who plays both emitter and receiver roles infers an extern (not artifact) as the sender. This BCP also resembles BCP 7 in terms of the kinds of senders likely to be inferred, such as disease-causing organisms, supernatural phenomena, and bad air. For example, a person with an overall reddening of exposed skin or an itchy rash on a leg might make inferences about the likely sender, such as the sun, poison ivy, or an angry god. Clearly, most self-diagnoses, and remedies administered, by an afflicted person are examples of inferences and responses conforming to BCP 16.

17   Artifact, artifact, *person*

In BCP 17, someone infers from an artifact's emissions that the artifact itself was the sender. A great many compound artifacts, from computers to aircraft, consist of parts that sometimes fail to interact properly, as indicated by the artifact's emissions. A specialist is then enlisted to infer which part or parts caused the faulty performance, and a response takes place, such as replacing the allegedly defective part. Decades ago, when my 1956 Plymouth developed a clanking sound, but still had no other untoward emissions, I took it to a nearby dealer for a diagnosis. Even before the hood went up, the mechanic (receiver) had concluded that the water pump (sender) was responsible for the odd noise. Diagnosis of malperforming automobiles and other compound artifacts today usually requires not only specialists but also expensive receptrons.

Examples of BCP 17 are common among the analytical activities of archaeologists. For example, in examining a stone spearpoint under the microscope, the archaeologist sometimes finds "polished" zones near the base. This visual performance is taken as evidence for the inference that the spear point had indeed been attached to a wooden shaft. Friction between the two components caused a change in light reflectance that, according to the archaeologist's correlates (e.g., Keeley 1980; Vaughan 1985), is characteristic of wood–stone contact.

18   Extern, extern, *person*

Structurally parallel to BCP 17, BCP 18 requires that a person infer, from an extern's emissions, something about the latter's own performance in an inscription event. Surprisingly, people do treat some externs as being capable of modifying themselves. An example comes from harvesting wild fruit, such as blackberries. In this activity, the picker infers from a berry's visual and perhaps tactile emissions that it is ripe – having modified itself over time – an inference that cues the picker to pluck it from the bush. From the receiver's point of view, then, sender and emitter are the same extern.

Processes with one interactor

There remains but one additional BCP that meets the constraints set forth in this chapter's introduction, that of one person playing all three roles.

19 Person, person, person

A person infers, from her own performances as an emitter, that she is the sender. Monitoring oneself, as an indication of the efficacy of one's previous performances, is a constant feature of modern life in Western and westernized societies, and doubtless in others as well. Thus, it is not difficult to find examples of BCP 19, given some latitude in delineating inscription events and a liberal interpretation of sendtron.

Many people incessantly monitor their weight, using receptrons such as scales or mirrors. In observing oneself, an individual constructs inferences from these emissions about how well a diet is doing. In this case, one can even consider food and drugs to be slow-acting sendtrons, which gradually modify someone's visual performance. (Faulty correlons, which lead to incorrect inferences, cause diseases such as anorexia and bulimia.)

People also monitor their own performances in activities such as combing hair, lathering on sunscreen, and trimming nails. Obviously, these communication processes can be regarded as instances of BCP 13, in which the emitter role is played by an artifact. But it is also possible to handle these kinds of communication by allowing the person to play all three major roles. In so doing, the investigator treats artifacts such as combs and nail-trimmers as sendtrons used in the inscription event; a trimmed nail becomes an emitron, as does combed hair. The person constructs inferences about his or her own performances as the sender.

BCP 19 also describes other communication phenomena that social scientists usually ignore. For example, a receiver can register the performances of his or her own organs and tissues, such as abdominal pain (see LeDoux 1996: 258–259 on "bodily sensations"). The person can then infer the physiological state responsible for his own body's performances (e.g., hunger). (In principle, investigators wielding scientific instruments as receptrons can independently confirm these internal emissions.) Responses such as obtaining food demonstrate that this communication process involves a consequential engagement with the material medium (see Chapter 7).

Final remarks

The preceding list of BCPs along with corresponding examples has shown the fruitfulness of the general theory in allowing investigators to recognize how deeply processes of inference are embedded in all human activities. Virtually no realm of human endeavor is free from communication processes in which a receiver constructs inferences about senders or inscription events and responds on the basis of those inferences. It is also apparent that communication processes are interwoven with all behavior in that they facilitate engagement with the material medium, and thus enable the forward motion of activities. Moreover, the preceding examples demonstrate, perhaps more convincingly than the theory itself, how thoroughly communication processes are pervaded by artifacts. Finally, this chapter supports the new theory's claim to great generality by showing how it deftly handles many communication phenomena that, in light of other theories, are opaque or invisible.

Having worked through diverse examples, which show the theory's utility for describing concrete communication processes, we are now ready to return to the book's major project. In the following chapter, then, I develop in detail a precise relationship between behavior and communication. This furnishes a foundation for presenting a model of receiver response that applies as well to any human behavior.

Chapter 7

Explaining performance

A general model of receiver response

Introduction

The goal of explaining variability in human behavior is widely espoused across the social sciences, but the most general explanatory question has been framed in many ways. The formulations presented in Chapter 5 make it possible to pose the question in a way that establishes a profound identity between human behavior and communication. Before reiterating this identity, however, I must tie together some loose ends.

The new theory specifies that, in any communication process, interactors play three major roles: sender, emitter, and receiver. These roles have been delineated in some detail (Chapter 5) and extensive examples supplied (Chapter 6). So far, differences in the roles have been emphasized, but now is the time to call attention to their commonalities. As it turns out, each role entails a performance: during inscription, the sender performs relative to the emitter (and vice versa); emitter and receiver both perform in interactions during emission and reception events; and, in responding, the receiver performs in relation to other interactors.

As already noted in Chapter 5, the key premise for unifying the roles is that any performance of an active interactor, such as a person, can be considered a receiver's response. This premise follows directly from the theory's receiver orientation in that the investigator always designates the receiver in a specific communication process. Thus, when one person speaks to another, this acoustic performance can be regarded as a response, the final event of a communication process in which the speaker has just been the receiver. Having designated the receiver, the investigator can then delineate the appropriate communication process. Similarly, when a makeup artist applies paint to another's face, her performance can be treated as the response of a receiver, and the communication process specified accordingly. The unification of roles allows us to appreciate that both behavior (as a given performance) and communication (as a receiver's response) are one. Although some artifacts and externs are active interactors, this chapter focuses exclusively on human receivers.

The explanatory question

That all human performances are receiver responses leads me to formulate the general question about behavior as follows: what explains a receiver's response? This question calls upon us to construct a general model of the factors creating variability in the responses of human receivers. Integrating and elaborating ideas presented in Chapter 5, I present a cognitive model that does exactly that (for other models, see Barker *et al.* 1988; Patterson 1995). Although cognitive models should be compatible with the general findings of neuroscience (e.g., Deacon 1997; Jeannerod 1997), such models cannot, without undue reductionism, be usefully expressed in terms of brain anatomy and patterns of neuron activation.

The general determinants of a receiver's response lie in (1) emitter performances and (2) receiver-specific factors — i.e., tuning (as correlons), and properties and performance characteristics (which are strongly affected by personal artifacts and receptrons). As promised in Chapter 4, the present model greatly expands the functions of correlons, emphasizing the correlon-laden cognitive processes that intervene between reception and response.

Many investigators might balk at my formulation of the explanatory question, preferring to ask: what caused the individual to act in this way? The latter question has more intuitive appeal than one focused on receiver responses, but it also brings along lots of unneeded baggage. For example, "act" in the conventional question is liable to be interpreted narrowly as an individual's muscular movements (Chapter 2). This contradicts the major thrust of the present work, which is to view human behavior as performance in relation to other interactors in the material medium (Hutchins 1995; Walker, Skibo, and Nielsen 1995), for only some muscular movements are performances, consequentially taking part in interactions. In addition, the conventional question also immediately suggests that a person's actions or comportment reflects deep-seated individual traits such as "values," "attitudes," and "personality," which Western indigenous theories — and some social scientists — suggest have overriding effects across diverse contexts. Such a view unacceptably deemphasizes the contextual factors of activity and place, especially artifact performances, that demonstrably influence responses.

Finally, in adopting the conventional question, one is also likely to accept, tacitly to be sure, premises of Western indigenous theories about human agency. In particular, by treating individuals always as conscious, goal-oriented agents, these theories lead us to expect that people can supply "reasons for" performances — their own and those of others (Skinner 1974; Stich 1996: ch. 3). Thus, it is believed that an investigator can obtain explanatorily relevant information simply by asking someone: why did you do this? or why did she do that? Let us term the answers to such questions *commentary*, recognizing that it is an individual's account of her own or another's performances. (I shall expand the concept of commentary, as we go along, to include any utterance elicited by an investigator in interview activities.)

Regrettably, the commentaries that suffice in natural conversations, which as acoustic performances cue responses and thus contribute to an activity's forward motion, cannot supply *scientific* answers to explanatory questions, even when the questions are asked by social scientists (cf. T. Jones 1995: 26). To argue otherwise is to give consciousness an omniscience that it clearly cannot have. For, in accepting commentary at face value, one must assume that people are completely aware of their own cognitive processes; this is a transparent absurdity, since at the very least one could never bring into consciousness the cognitive process that is itself creating consciousness (LeDoux 1996: 29, 32). A more defensible assumption, mirroring a move made by Freudians, structuralists, and others, is that the operation of many, perhaps most, cognitive processes is utterly inaccessible to an individual's conscious probing (cf. LeDoux 1996: 21; Mithen 1996: 148–149, 190–191). Moreover, as Stich (1996: 14) puts it, "there is good reason to think that much of the information (or misinformation) that we use in predicting and explaining people's behavior is stored in a way that makes it inaccessible to conscious access." Indeed, because many correlons cannot easily be expressed verbally (Chapter 4), commentary must exclude much relational knowledge relevant to explaining performance (LeDoux 1996: 31–32; cf. Karmiloff-Smith 1992: 21–23).

Unfortunately, most terms used by social scientists when discussing behavior and communication, such as intent, goal, purpose, meaning, and symbol, originate in the indigenous theories of Western societies; constituted as correlons, these indigenous theories generate commentary. I submit that it is advantageous to eschew these ethnocentric and temporocentric terms when building scientific theories and models. But how should investigators treat the ubiquitous commentaries that people provide as "explanations of" or "reasons for" their own or another's performances? The answer is surprisingly simple: any instance of commentary, which is mainly an acoustic performance, can be handled as a receiver's response – no different from any other human performance. In short, commentary is not acceptable as explanation but must itself be explained.[1]

The model

Employing an electrical metaphor enjoying some currency in discussions of cognitive processes, I suggest that emissions activate a response circuit. Thus, received emissions are conducted through a set of cognitive operations in a person's nervous system, the last one of which generates the response. My model of the response circuit consists of the following cognitive operations:

registration, weighting, inference, mapping, selection, and execution. Some operations encompass several suboperations, and these are identified and discussed below.

The cognitive processes are labeled *operations* in preference to "stages" because the details of information flow, especially in the brain, are known at present only sketchily. More than likely, flows of information, as electrochemical interactions among neurons, exhibit a massive parallelism (cf. Loftus and Schooler 1985; Quinlan 1991), for the cognitive operations can occur simultaneously, doubtless in different areas of the nervous system, and draw upon sundry kinds of stored knowledge – including correlons – that are also widely distributed (Deacon 1997; Jeannerod 1997; LeDoux 1996). Moreover, the operations are apt to take place sometimes in one sequence, sometimes in another, depending on tuning and contextual factors. In view of this expectable complexity, it would be unwise to model information processing as an invariant series of stages. Nonetheless, for purposes of model building at the scale needed to furnish a general account of receiver responses, I present the cognitive operations in a "logical" order with registration at the beginning and execution at the end. Of overriding importance is that these operations be present and, in some manner, working in a coordinated fashion to effect a response.

Registration

Registration (cf. Ackerman 1990: 305; Fabrega 1977: 435; Halloran 1985: 32; LeDoux 1996: 53) is the reception or monitoring of emissions by a receiver's sensory apparatus; registration may be conscious or nonconscious, explicit or implicit, and voluntary or involuntary. During wakefulness, people monitor their sensory fields, continuously registering emissions in all modes from many interactors performing simultaneously, including emissions from their own bodies. Registration is affected by many factors, including the receiver's tuning, performance characteristics, personal artifacts, and receptrons.

Individual differences in mode-specific performance characteristics contribute to variability in responses. Although most people's sensory performance characteristics fall into a "normal" range (e.g., almost everyone can recognize faces in daylight at a distance of three feet without glasses), some people have acute vision and others are blind. These differences are grounded in a person's biological properties, the result of genetic, developmental, aging, and experiential factors (e.g., Corso 1981).

Matching is the ability of someone's senses to register emissions in a particular performance mode. For example, a person born blind or who has lost his sight through injury is unable to match any visual performance. Likewise, no human being can register the ultrasound emissions of small rodents or the radio-frequency broadcasts of cellular phones. Most people,

however, are able to match the smell of garlic and the mechanical performance of a biting dog.

Even when emitters and receivers are matched in a given sensory mode,
there can be differences in the efficiency or quality of reception, which are
also expressed as performance characteristics. Compared to an individual of
normal hearing, for example, a hearing-impaired person is unable to register
as faithfully acoustic emissions in ordinary conversations. It should be noted
that some registration impairments are short term, such as those caused by
drugs or head colds that temporarily reduce the sensitivity of taste, smell, and
hearing. Needless to say, people enjoying extraordinary performance in a
particular sensory mode are eagerly sought for certain occupations; wine
tasters and scent designers, for example, seem to have unusually acute chemical
senses (Ackerman 1990).

Variation in matching directly affects responses. When there is a mismatch,
for example, the response circuit is truncated because emissions in that mode
cannot cue a response. In the case of a match, the response circuit continues to
process the information and a response ensues; alternatively, registration may
affect only a person's tuning (i.e., creating new correlons and modifying old
ones). Whereas all registration can affect tuning, only registration that leads
directly to a response is of concern here.

Receptrons can substantially enhance a person's sensory performance
characteristics. Examples of personal artifacts in common use as receptrons are
glasses and hearing aids. Similarly, some people can improve their night vision
by eating more foods, like carrots, containing beta carotene. In scientific,
engineering, military, and medical activities of industrial societies, countless
costly receptrons extend human senses, enabling receivers to "see" on
computer screens the birth of stars, the movement of submarines deeply
submerged on the other side of the world, and brain metabolism, and to
"hear" the pulses of pulsars and the discourse of dolphins. These stunning feats
are accomplished by receptrons that convert emissions unmatchable by
humans – e.g., far infrared and radio-frequency radiation, magnetic and
electrical fields – into forms, such as visible light or audible sound, that can be
registered; in effect, these receptrons are transducers.

As already noted (Chapter 6, BCP 19), humans, along with many higher
animals and some machines, register internal emissions from their own organs,
tissues, and limbs, and these can cue responses, such as messaging a sore arm
muscle, urinating, eating, and scratching one's leg. I emphasize that these
responses need not be automatic, like reflexes. Indeed, throughout hominid
evolution, humans have acquired greater cortical control over many sensori-
motor systems that in other animals operate entirely as reflexes (Deacon 1997;
Jeannerod 1997; LeDoux 1996). For example, an ambitious junior executive,
meeting with his company's president, could register a desperate urge to pee,
but might simply hold it.[2]

Platial and activity emitters, many of which are artifacts, usually have strong and direct effects on registration. For example, at low light levels and in deep water, color vision is profoundly impaired even in someone who can register all colors (Coren *et al.* 1994: 170); similarly, conversation may be difficult between two people with excellent hearing on a very windy day; and a gentle touch may not be felt through a heavy coat. Thus, reception can be influenced by any contextual factor that affects distances between emitters and receivers, furnishes distractions or interferences, or attenuates the emission relative to the receiver. On the other hand, emitrons improve registration by increasing an emission's apparent or actual amplitude. For example, a megaphone used at a swimming competition enables swimmer–receivers more easily to hear the starter's commands. Similarly, a receiver can discern the sex of a person wearing sex-specific headgear, clothing, and shoes at a greater distance than someone sporting a unisex outfit.

Weighting

In all animals, the output of registration consists of electrochemical signals from sensory organs (Coren *et al.* 1994). These signals serve as input to other cognitive operations occurring in the spinal cord and brain, including weighting. A largely implicit operation, weighting determines which emissions from which emitters matter; that is, which ones actually contribute to cuing a response. Weighting chooses among the sensory signals furnished by registration, allowing only those that are privileged or weighted to be passed through, in series and/or in parallel, to other operations (compare to "filtering," Coren *et al.* 1994: 521–524; Pashler 1998: 14).

Because correlons are ordinarily keyed in hierarchically (Chapter 5), the emissions of context-defining platial and activity interactors are always weighted (except, perhaps, by infants, young children, and dysfunctional adults); thus, multiple emissions can be weighted more or less simultaneously. Also weighted are the performances of additional activity interactors, especially the salient emitter. Weighting can be illustrated by a common craft activity: a man carving a wooden duck on the front porch. The carver in this activity plays both sender and receiver (see Chapter 6, BCP 13); the duck is the salient emitter, the carving knife a sendtron.

As carving begins, emissions of platial and activity interactors, such as the porch, sunlight, and chair, are weighted and key in context-defining correlons. Subsequently, the tactile and visual performances of the bird, after each stroke of the knife, are weighted, and thus influence the carver's response – usually, but not always, another knife stroke. At the same time, however, someone may enter the activity area, performing visually and acoustically; these latter emissions can be immediately weighted and yield a response, perhaps a glare or greeting. In addition, the carver can be simultaneously registering – that is, mostly listening to – a football game on a nearby TV. The TV's visual performance is weighted when the carver stops carving to look at an instant replay. Externs can be weighted again: as the sun begins to set, for example, the carver finds it increasingly difficult to see his work; thus, he may glance at the sky which, along with the attenuated visual performance of the duck, cues the carver to turn on the porch light or conclude carving for the day.

In a conventional account of this activity, the investigator might employ the term "attention" to describe shifts in registering various emissions (e.g., Coren *et al.* 1994: ch. 15; Hanneman 1975: 38–39; Kelly 1981: 124; Kinchla 1992; Kubey and Csikszentmihalyi 1990; Pashler 1998; Wheeless and Cook 1985). Thus, attention would mainly denote a shift in attending to (i.e., registering) an emitter's performance, as in the turn from viewing the duck to the TV. However, a given performance can be the focus of attention – i.e., registered faithfully, even consciously – yet not be weighted (cf. Deacon 1997: 258–259). In any activity, then, a person's attention can be moving constantly among emitters without cuing a response (apart from the largely reflex responses that facilitate registration itself, such as the movement of head and eyes in visual interactions [cf. Coren *et al.* 1994; Jeannerod 1997: 11–12]). In the present model, only registered performances that contribute to cuing a (nonregistration) response are said to be weighted, whether or not they attract attention.

A number of performances quite predictably attract attention (Kelly 1981: 124), though having no necessary effect on responses, and can mislead investigators. Hawkins *et al.* (1992: 224–228) have summarized the main properties of emitters that contribute to attention-getting performances in a variety of modes (see also Ackerman 1990; Hayden 1998; Wheeless and Cook 1985: 264). Among the properties that enhance the "noticeability" of emissions are large size, loud sounds, bright colors, movement, repetition, contrast with background, and isolation or separation from background. Obviously, these regularities are zealously exploited by people in the marketing professions to call attention to their products through displays and advertisements (Hawkins *et al.* 1992). That a TV performing visually and acoustically has many of these properties perhaps explains why TVs are "a magnet for attention" (Kubey and Csikszentmihalyi 1990: 37; see also Armstrong *et al.* 1991).

Noticeability is a performance characteristic doubtless grounded in hardwired correlons (Hayden 1998), some of which people share with other mammals, perhaps even reptiles, fish, and insects. That animals infer the presence of predators, food, or potential mates from attention-grabbing performances suggests why hardwired correlons might have arisen through natural selection. Yet it would be a mistake to treat human responses to such performances simply as reflexes, for, as a trip to the supermarket would demonstrate, people learn not to weight many highly noticeable emissions.

A return to the duck-carving example illustrates that weighting is strongly affected by learned correlons. On the basis of correlons acquired during previous carving episodes (and perhaps from reading books on carving wooden animals or watching other carvers at work), specific visual and tactile performances of the duck are weighted, and these ordinarily cue the next knife strokes. Similarly, the carver's correlons allow the voice of the TV's play-by-play announcer or crowd noise to be weighted, almost automatically, so that he can look up in time for a replay. Tuning also determines when the declining level of light is weighted, thus cuing an appropriate response.

Inference

Weighted sensory inputs are passed through to correlons in the inference operation, which produces information about places, activities, interactors (senders and/or emitters), and interactions (cf. Kelly 1981: 76–82; Tversksy and Hemenway 1983). This operation yields low-level inferences (through an *identification* suboperation) and high-level inferences (through an *assignment* suboperation); needless to say, both kinds of inference affect responses.

Identification

Operating on weighted emissions, the identification suboperation places interactors and interactions into simple categories, such as tree, old man, my aunt Brenda, dangerous animal, carpet, hairy woodpecker, hot weather, red light, grimace, jazz band, "flipping the bird," shiny coin, a waving hand. Additional correlons combine simple categories into complex ones that identify activities and places, such as reading a book in the bedroom, playing shuffleboard in the park, and carving a duck on the front porch. In short, correlons link specific performances to simple categories, as well as simple categories to complex ones. It should be evident that individual variation in the correlons employed in identification contributes to dissimilar inferences and responses.

Many investigators assume that categories (simple and complex) are easily accessible to an investigator who merely monitors a subject's acoustic and gestural performances. Indeed, by applying "eliciting frames" (e.g., McDermott and Roth 1978: 333), cognitive anthropologists and others have sought to reveal indigenous categories for many domains of phenomena, ranging from firewood to diseases. The investigator organizes the informants' responses, a set of related categories, into overarching classificatory systems such as taxonomies and paradigms (e.g., Atran 1990; Berlin 1992; D'Andrade 1995).

When studying indigenous classifications, the investigator should never forget that the elicited categories consist entirely of commentary; the implicit cognitive categories that actually underlie responses may not be directly accessible to the informant or the investigator (cf. Burling 1964). From the standpoint of the present project, then, the investigator's task is to posit categories that, by helping the receiver to key in correlons, contribute to responses – whether or not such categories arise in commentary.

The human ability to classify, to create cognitive categories, is nothing special (Byrne 1995; Deacon 1997: 90; Delius 1992; Hauser 1996: ch. 7), for in animals "Categorization is essential to all cognitive processes" (Roitblat and von Fersen 1992: 691). Pigeons and chimpanzees, for example, can generalize from specific cases, such as the picture of one tree, to a general category "tree" having an infinite number of particular instances (e.g., Vauclair 1996: 14–16; Wasserman 1993: 217–218). Doubtless, the cognitive mechanisms enabling the acquisition of correlons, through direct experience, for constructing and applying categories are evolutionarily ancient, at least in mammals. Alone among animals, however, humans are able to talk about their purported categories (i.e., supply commentary to an investigator).

Assignment

Operating upon identifications of places, activities, interactors, and interactions, the assignment suboperation generates, also by means of correlons, higher-level inferences. The latter often make reference to a particular interactor, such as the sender; and, as noted in Chapters 3–6, inferences about senders come in countless varieties (see also Stamp et al. 1994: 184–187). Some inferences posit a person's dispositions (e.g., eager to please, lazy, skillful) or psychological states, such as being angry or jealous. Inferences can also describe an interactor's condition (e.g., a sender/emitter is ready to become a receiver) or the character of particular interactions (e.g., a baseball strikes someone in the face); still others implicate a person's ethnicity, religion, wealth, social role, prestige, expert knowledge, etc. In general, high-level inferences may describe any property or quality of an interaction, interactor, activity, or place. Learned correlons largely determine which high-level inferences a receiver constructs, consciously and nonconsciously, on the basis of particular emissions in a given communication process.

The inference operation, especially the assignment suboperation, works mostly in a nonconscious manner in everyday activities despite the ease with which an investigator can access abundant and seemingly relevant commentary. A contrived example makes this clear. Suppose that an omnipresent investigator is privy to a host of interactions taking place between employees in an insurance company's head office. This company has achieved considerable diversity in its white-collar workforce and has, through sensitivity training, attempted to tune its white employees to treat alike both black and white colleagues. When the investigator asks white employees, in a formal interview in their offices, about their "attitudes" toward blacks, they are apt to respond that blacks as a group are as intelligent, friendly, and hardworking as whites. Moreover, they might also claim to interact with each person as an individual, regardless of ethnicity. Put into the terms of the present model, then, they claim that their responses are unaffected by ethnicity inferences. Unwilling to accept this commentary at face value, our investigator records and analyzes a large sample of actual person–person interactions in the workplace – e.g., "social" office visits, water-cooler conversations, *ad hoc* groups that go out together for lunch, and "spontaneous" birthday parties – and finds that, in fact, the interaction patterns are intelligible only if one posits ethnicity as an inference that influences responses. If the investigator were to follow the same people throughout all of their daily activities over several months, she might discover that ethnicity inferences have even more pronounced effects on responses in other contexts. Clearly, despite commentary claiming that these enlightened people are ethnicity blind, their real-world responses betray the involvement of ethnicity-based correlons. Apparently, we cannot assume that commentary about inferences furnishes the correlons that actually come into play when someone is responding (cf. T. Jones 1995).

Mapping

In mapping, previously created inferences are operated upon by additional correlons and thereby yield a *response repertoire* (Dawkins and Dawkins 1973; Hanneman 1975: 36; King 1994: 8). Thus, responses are mapped "on" to the inferences, and are also mapped "out" or delineated. Needless to say, responses are place-, activity-, interactor-, and interaction-specific. Although sometimes capable of providing rich commentary about possible responses, people usually delineate alternatives nonconsciously. Mapping has two suboperations, *novelty* and *forecasting*.

An important feature of the present model is the insistence that responses, with the likely exception of reflexes, are selected from a set of alternatives (cf. Smith 1977: 87). That specific alternatives are always possible, if not always highly probable, permits us to explain why identical factors of place, activity, interactors, and interactions can cue, at different times, different responses by the same person.

Discussions in Chapter 5 imply that the response repertoire is strongly affected by a person's properties and thus performance characteristics. For example, in food-preparation activities, an individual with tiny hands could be incapable of opening, unaided, jars with large lids, and so has a different response repertoire than someone with massive hands. Similarly, a tourist who cannot read French is apt to have a range of responses to street signs in Paris that differs from a native Parisian's. Even transient properties, such as those induced by drugs, food, and fatigue, can affect response repertoires, as can personal artifacts insofar as they alter someone's properties and performance characteristics. To take an obvious example of the latter, imagine a football player on the sidelines but dressed in street clothes; he would be unable to enter the game in response to the coach's call.

In the activities of everyday life, receivers register the same emissions from the same emitters, again and again, leading to recurrent inferences. Under these conditions, the mapping operation uses correlons, more or less automatically, to generate a set of responses, each of which has − for that given set of factors − a specific probability (cf. Smith 1977: 128). Thus, one can represent the response repertoire, for common communication processes, as a set of specific responses along with their corresponding probabilities: $p(R1)$, $p(R2)$,...$p(Rn)$. Response probabilities can assume many statistical distributions, ranging from one response with a probability of 1.0, to ten responses each having a probability of 0.10; most everyday cases, I expect, lie between these extremes. This formulation enables the investigator to model virtually any response repertoire for high-frequency communication processes. Even when dealing with a communication process of low frequency, the investigator is at least forced to consider the set of alternatives that the receiver's mapping operation might have yielded. An example can flesh out the mapping operation and illustrate the importance of tuning in delineating the response repertoire.

Imagine a college classroom with a male student, the receiver, seated at a desk, registering the instructor's lecture performance (in visual and acoustic modes) and taking notes. At some point the student concludes that the instructor has been repeating herself. On the basis of this inference, the instructor and her performances have been placed into the category of "terminally boring lecture," and a corresponding response repertoire is mapped out. Among the student's possible responses are (1) putting his head down on the desk and snoozing, (2) reading the campus newspaper, (3) leaving class, (4) remaining seated but ceasing to take notes, and (5) continuing to monitor the lecturer while taking notes and exhibiting a new facial expression that tuned receivers infer as "boredom." This set consists of the responses that the student has produced previously in identical contexts, and were readily generated by his correlons. Each response, therefore, has an a priori probability. Let us assume that the student's correlons yield a highly skewed distribution of response probabilities, in that he almost always nods off.

Mapping need not end with the delineation of previously executed responses. Sometimes, especially if the receiver has never met the same set of factors in a communication process, a *novelty* suboperation is activated for generating new responses. The novelty suboperation, which may involve consciousness, can use existing correlons generatively or fashion new ones. In particular, indigenous theories (Chapter 4), which are abstract correlons having generative capabilities, can contribute to the creation of novel responses. For example, Americans, who participate in the world's most intense consumer society (Schiffer and Majewski n.d.), seem to possess an arsenal of indigenous theories that account − in general terms − for the comings and goings of consumer products, such as the vested interest, technological constraint, and consumerist theories (Schiffer n.d.). When someone encounters a new case to explain, whose details are utterly unknown, these theories help generate appropriate responses. In short, indigenous theories empower people by giving them the flexibility to fashion novel yet skilled performances when confronted with unfamiliar phenomena (see also Greene and Geddes 1993). The novelty suboperation can also activate diverse cognitive processes, such as problem-solving, that create new correlons (see also Boden 1990), thereby contributing to new responses.

Forecasting, a second suboperation, often comes into play in mapping. As noted in Chapter 4, correlons, being relational knowledge, can be used predictively. Thus, forecasts of future interactions of senders and/or emitters can be bundled with each response in the repertoire, thereby affecting its probability. For example, the bored student in the previous example may forecast, on the basis of correlons about the instructor's previous responses to snoozing students, how she will respond to him when he puts his head down on the desk.

Many investigators recognize a role for "anticipation" or "expectations" in interpersonal communication (e.g., Burgoon *et al.* 1996), but they have not generalized such notions beyond the two-body model. Forecasting is in fact rather common in everyday activities, including those having artifacts as major role players. Whenever a tennis player responds to a ball arriving on her side of the net, she must forecast not only where her own swing (as a response) will place the ball, but also the other player's position on the court when it arrives. Virtually all sports and games entail these kinds of correlon-based forecasts; the more skillful players, of course, have an arsenal of finely honed correlons. Likewise, when skillfully driving automobiles, riding bicycles and motorcycles, even steering grocery carts, we forecast the effects of our own potential responses on other interactors. The result is an adjustment of probabilities for responses in the repertoire.

Forecasting at times becomes conscious and explicit, especially in activities of "group decision-making" undertaken by various social units, from play groups, to engineering teams, to corporate boards (Hiltz *et al.* 1986). These deliberative processes have been studied at length as special phenomena simply – I maintain – because they are explicit. In fact, they merely represent an especially conspicuous form of forecasting.

Selection

In the selection operation, a response is chosen. I submit that whenever the response repertoire contains more than one response, selection must involve a stochastic element. For example, let us assume that when a person enters his kitchen for the first time in the morning, emissions of platial artifacts, tuning, and so forth contribute to mapping out a repertoire of two responses, each of which has a probability of 0.5: (1) open the refrigerator and take out the orange juice bottle or (2) open the cupboard door and remove a can of coffee. Which response is generated on a given morning is entirely the result of chance, utterly indeterminant (*contra* Watson 1930: 183). In most cases, however, different responses have different probabilities; and, in a surprisingly large number of cases, one response might be highly probable. In high school classes, for example, the bell ringing at the hour's end cues a nearly uniform response among students, as each one noisily stuffs papers, pen, and books into a backpack (if they have not done so already) and stands up.

Like mapping, selection is carried out consciously or nonconsciously. Precisely the necessity of choosing among alternatives might have contributed to the evolution of consciousness in animals (Crisp 1996: 313; Griffin 1991; but see Mithen 1996: 147). That selection is sometimes conscious and explicit is perhaps responsible for the availability of copious commentary that apparently accounts for choices. Although commentary provides a person's post hoc "reasons" (or rationalization) for choosing a response, the reasons might not implicate the actual causal factors. This problem is exacerbated because people, in offering indigenous explanations, seldom recognize that selection can be partly stochastic. How often, for example, does someone's explanation for a performance acknowledge that "this is what I do about 30 percent of the time" when cued by the salient emitter in that context?

Execution

Not surprisingly, the response circuit's last operation is execution. In executing a response, the receiver carries out a performance that usually consists of several discrete interactions in multiple modes. Even in a conversation between two people, a response often involves an utterance, a change in facial expression, and a postural adjustment along with performances of the original receiver's personal artifacts. Similarly, in carving a duck, the artisan may respond to the duck's emissions by making postural adjustments, changing his facial expression, groaning or humming, repositioning the duck with one hand, and applying the knife with the other. (Because he is alone, his sounds and facial expressions do not consequentially engage the material medium; thus, they do not take part in interactions.)

Tuning looms large in execution. For the tuned receiver, execution of routine performances ordinarily depends on performance-specific "programs," sometimes called "motor schemas" (Jeannerod 1997: 51–52, 160). Varying in complexity and duration of execution, programs include stifling a sneeze, lighting a match, reciting a poem, and planting a narcissus bulb. Programs are stored in the nervous system as complex correlons, which activate particular muscles and muscle groups of the organs and tissues that create speech (e.g., tongue, lips, larynx, diaphragm), facial expressions (e.g., eyes, eyelashes, eyebrows, lips, nose, cheeks, jaw), gestures and other movements (e.g., arms, wrists, fingers), and postures and gaits (arms, legs, torso, head). Once the response has been selected and execution begun, programs function more-or-less automatically (Barker *et al.* 1988: 206; Deacon 1997: 237; Karmiloff-Smith 1992: 16; but see Pashler 1998, Chapter 8), often with no awareness on the part of the person. (Surprisingly, awareness of cues from a salient emitter sometimes *follows* the receiver's response [Jeannerod 1997: 84–86].)

When a response is novel, and thus the receiver lacks stored programs, much of the execution operation can come into consciousness, as a person painstakingly activates appropriate muscles and muscle groups (Deacon 1997: 237). This is a difficult process (Barker *et al.* 1988: 207; Pashler 1998), often requiring simultaneous activation of multiple motor systems and thus conscious, parallel processing in the brain. Recall, for example, how hard it was learning to ride a bicycle and to pronounce words in a second language. However, once these responses are learned – i.e., performance-specific programs are in place – their execution is unproblematic and becomes mostly nonconscious. The necessity of "manually" activating many motor systems in novel contexts is yet another factor that could have contributed to the emergence of consciousness early in the evolution of animals (cf. Griffin 1991).

Discussion

By framing the general question of what causes human behavior in terms of receiver response, I have established an unexpected and far-reaching unity between behavior and communication. I now consider some general issues in the social sciences that might be illuminated by the new formulations.

Criteria of explanation

The first issue concerns the criteria of explanation. Let me begin by asking: In terms of the model, what constitutes an adequate explanation of a specific response? I remind the reader that commentary supplied by someone about his own or another's performance is not an acceptable explanation. In fashioning a scientific explanation of a response, the investigator must go well beyond commentary to identify the causal factors in a communication process.

The receiver-response model suggests that two sets of factors are causally relevant: (1) weighted performances of platial and activity emitters, and (2) the person's tuning, performance characteristics, and personal artifacts. Another way to put this is that an explanation must pinpoint the emitter performances that, in the presence of particular correlons and other receiver-specific factors, cued the response. What is more, the investigator has to approximate the set of correlons keyed in during that response circuit; i.e., model the correlons that established linkages among cognitive operations, from registration to response.

In no case will meeting these requirements be easy, but the scientific explanation of receiver responses — and thus behavior — is in principle possible.

Many explanations will be probabilistic in that, although the investigator has specified all relevant emissions and receiver-specific factors, the response was simply one of several that could have been executed under those conditions. Most social scientists, who routinely interpret statistical associations in causal terms, are comfortable with stochastic processes, believing that with better models, better data, and better statistics the correlations will rise, leaving little variance unexplained. In contrast, the receiver-response model leads to the expectation that cognitive processes have an irreducible stochastic component that should be especially noticeable in the explanation of low-probability responses.

How is it possible, in general, to explain events having low probabilities? Fortunately, the Statistical Relevance model (e.g., W. Salmon 1971; M. Salmon 1982) clarifies the explanation of low-probability events. According to this model, the investigator assembles, as causal factors, any conditions or variables that stand in a statistically relevant relationship to the event being explained. Thus, all factors that affect the probability of a particular event's occurrence are identified and accorded explanatory relevance, even if the event's probability in light of these factors remains low. Happily, the receiver-response model is compatible with the Statistical Relevance model: weighted emissions, correlons, and performance characteristics (including the effects of personal artifacts) comprise the statistically relevant sets of factors making up a causal explanation, regardless of the response's specific probability. Albert Einstein's misgivings notwithstanding, in science there is no shame in admitting that many processes are stochastic and that some events are not strictly determined.

Explanation of group responses

Sociologists and anthropologists are seldom disturbed by randomness in individual responses because they usually deal with people responding in the aggregate, groups whose behaviors exhibit statistical patterns. Investigators strive to identify the combination of social and demographic variables that yields the highest correlation with the aggregate behavior of interest. Thus, we learn that individuals are more likely to engage in criminal activities if they come from low-income families, broken homes, and high-crime neighborhoods (e.g., Gottfredson and Hirschi 1990), or that patrilocal marital residence is more often practiced by people who are residentially mobile, live in small groups, and obtain food by hunting and gathering (Steward 1955).

In my view, these kinds of explanations, whose causal factors are variables such as household type, income, ethnicity, religion, and type of settlement pattern, fail to pinpoint actual causality (see also Sperber 1996: 2, 99). To put these kinds of explanatory factors into the most favorable light possible, it can be said they are merely proxy measures of potentially shared life-history activities (and thus tuning). Individuals participating in those activities are apt to have acquired similar correlons that can, in the presence of appropriate emissions, give rise to similar responses (Chapter 5). Regrettably, these explanations are transparently inadequate, since income, ethnicity, neighborhood, and so forth cannot be efficient or proximate causes of any specific performance. Thus, social and demographic factors have no causal efficacy beyond indicating a potential for shared life-history experiences, and thus shared correlons. It is the latter that, as tuning, actually contribute to similarities (and differences) in individual responses.

An example of the problem is provided by the responses of urban teenagers when interacting with "literacy artifacts" (Gerardo Bernache, personal communication, 1990), such as books, magazines, and newspapers. As is well known, many people from low-income households read poorly and reluctantly when required to perform in high-school classroom activities. Yet, in these same contexts, some people coming from low-income households read quite well. Likewise, although many people from middle- and upper-income households are proficient readers, some are not.

In seeking an explanation for these patterns of behavioral variability, the investigator should first assess the role played by impaired vision and learning disabilities that can affect reading-related performances. Because these biological factors will account for only a small percentage of the variability in reading performances, the remaining variability must be attributed to reading-related correlons acquired experientially.

It goes almost without saying that sociodemographic categories do not capture the relevant differences and similarities in life-history experiences that contribute to variability in reading-related correlons (cf. Teachman 1987). Even in seemingly homogeneous, low-income households, people grow up participating in varied sets of activities, and so have obtained different correlons; in some instances, they may have acquired correlons more typical of people raised in middle- and upper-income households. For example, let us hypothesize that children are more likely to read avidly and well if their homes contain many books, magazines, and newspapers; if their hours of TV viewing are limited; if they see their parents and siblings reading; and if they are read to as infants and small children. While it can be anticipated that most low-income, urban households lack literacy artifacts, in some such households they might abound. After all, parents can buy used books and magazines very cheaply at yard sales, rummage sales, and thrift shops. What is causally relevant to explaining an individual's responses in reading activities, then, is not household income, family composition, parents' educational level and occupations, or neighborhood. What matters, rather, is whether that person has participated, usually at home, in literacy activities from a young age, thereby acquiring correlons appropriate for skillful performance.

Evidently, social scientists interested in explaining behavioral variability will have to finger the life-history activities that demonstrably affect the acquisition of specific correlons. Thus, the search for explanation cannot stop after the identification of statistically significant associations – empirical generalizations – between aggregate responses and sociodemographic variables; instead, these patterns should be the starting point for isolating the life-history experiences – particularly those involving interactions with relevant artifacts – that created individual differences in tuning. From the standpoint of the present work, then, explanations applying at the group level alone are patently inadequate in a true causal sense.

Goals and purposes

An investigator who registers one person's performances over a period of hours and days would notice that she shifts – sometimes sporadically, sometimes periodically – from activity to activity. Engagements in a given activity vary from lengthy (e.g., watching a movie from start to finish) to fleeting (e.g., turning on a light switch when entering a room), and sometimes alternate regularly, with one seemingly embedded in another, as in eating snacks during a movie.

In Western societies, we make sense of activity changes, and of persistent participation in one activity, by postulating that a person is attempting to reach a given goal or achieve a certain purpose, such as having a clean room or a nicely carved duck (Jeannerod 1997: ch. 5; Noble and Davidson 1996: 216–217; Wilson 1995). Although invoking goals and purposes to account for someone's sequence of activities gives us a level of understanding adequate for conversation in everyday life and cues our responses, such accounts (as commentary) are not scientific explanations, even when proffered by scientists. Fortunately, the present work has already supplied the conceptual tools needed for handling varied sequences of activity engagement.

Our task is that of rephrasing the question in behavioral terms: how can an investigator explain an individual's sequence of performances? When put this way, the question implies its own answer. To wit, every performance of every individual – in sequences long and short, in activities old and new – is a receiver's response in a communication process. Thus, explaining a change in a person's activity engagement simply requires the investigator to isolate the communication process whose response results in an activity change. Because such responses are no more difficult to explain than any others, the causes will always lie in emissions and receiver-specific factors. In this framework, then, invoking a receiver's goals and purposes is unnecessary, for the latter are little more than the teleology that permeates commentary in Western and westernized societies.

Conclusion

This chapter has presented a model of the cognitive operations intervening between emitter performances and a receiver's response. The operations of this generalized response circuit are registration, weighting, inference, mapping, selection, and execution. The last operation, execution, is the response, a performance usually carried out in many modes. Because any performance of any person is a receiver's response, the model is capable of explaining, generally, any and all human behavior. More precisely, the model can direct the investigator's attention to the specific factors – e.g., emitter performances, correlons, and the receiver's performance characteristics (based in part on personal artifacts) – that effect a given response.

The model of receiver response, along with formulations in earlier chapters, gives substance to the claim that both behavior and communication intimately involve artifacts. Not only do emitters, whose performances key in correlons and cue responses, consist largely of artifacts, but responses almost always include performances of personal artifacts and interactions with other activity artifacts. Moreover, the most common basic communication processes in everyday life involve people–artifact interactions (Chapter 6). In short, neither human behavior nor communication can be abstracted from the material medium and studied apart from artifacts if these phenomena are to be explained scientifically.

Regrettably, conventional ontology and theory have prevented social scientists from appreciating that diverse and sustained people–artifact interactions are the most distinctive and important feature of human life. Rather than recognizing behavior and communication as artifact-laden phenomena, investigators have subordinated the understanding of all human performances to theories and models built originally to make sense of language. As a result, people are treated as actors playing the game of life according to shared, language-like social and cultural rules. The skewed vision of human life – i.e., behavior, communication, and their causes – that has emerged from the social sciences is no longer adequate for investigators applying their intellectual products to real-world problems.

I hope that the ideas presented in this book will provoke other social scientists to rethink their ontology and theory, laying a foundation for designing empirical research projects that can illuminate the causes of "natural" – i.e., ethnographically observed – human behavior. The eminently testable formulations furnished above are merely a starting point for building a new science of behavior, without regard to disciplinary boundaries, that incorporates into every model and theory the ubiquitous people–artifact interactions of the material medium.

Glossary

Active emitter   By virtue of having a sensory apparatus, an active emitter is also capable of playing a receiver role in a communication process. See also *passive emitter*.

Activity   A set of sequentially related interactions, occurring in a particular location, among a set of interactors which includes at least one person or artifact. Activity is an important analytic unit for studies of behavior and communication. See also *reference activity*.

Activity artifacts   The artifacts taking part in a given activity, which are drawn from personal, situational, and platial artifacts.

Appropriately tuned receiver   Someone who possesses the relational knowledge (correlons) needed for constructing inferences/forecasts from, and responding skillfully to, emissions in a specific communication process. See also *tuning*.

Artifact   Any material phenomenon that exhibits one or more properties produced by a given species. Artifacts of interest in the present work are those phenomena produced, replicated, or otherwise brought wholly or partly to their present form through the actions of people. These artifacts include portable objects, structures, domesticated plants and animals, and modifications to the human body such as tattoos and styled hair. See also *activity*, *personal*, *platial*, and *situational artifacts*.

Assignment   A suboperation of inference in the response circuit, assignment generates high-level inferences about the properties or qualities of an interaction, interactor, activity, or place.

Basic communication process   Every activity contains one or more of nineteen basic communication processes, which are defined on the basis of all possible permutations of people, artifacts, and externs playing the three major communication roles.

Behavior   Relational phenomena, definable at several scales, involving people. In the present work, definitions of behavior are provided at two scales: (1) any performance of a person that engages one or more other interactors consequentially, and (2) all interactions in a behavioral system.

Behavioral system   A large-scale analytic unit comprising the entire set of interactions taking place with reference to a specific group of people (e.g., a household, community, or society), during an interval of time.

Chemical interaction   A chemical transfer or change taking place between interactors.

Cognitive operations   The six processes that make up the response circuit: registration, weighting, inference, mapping, selection, and execution.

Commentary   An utterance elicited by an investigator in interview activities, especially explanations of an individual's own or another's performances.

Communication   An interactor acquires information, through inference, from the performances of other interactors (emitters).

Communication process   The passage of consequential information from interactor to interactor, culminating in a receiver's response. A communication process is situated in the reference activity and consists of four sequential events: inscription, emission, reception, and response.

Complex interaction   Interactions involving compound interactors, more than two interactors, multiple interaction modes, or several interaction zones on one or more interactors.

Compound interactor   Any combination of interactors that interacts as a single entity, such as artifacts consisting of many parts. Because people are combined with personal artifacts, such as clothing and jewelry, they tend to be compound interactors. See also *macroartifact*.

Context   The context of a communication process is a specific activity transpiring in a given place. See also *reference activity*.

Correlate   A relational statement of archaeological knowledge which the investigator employs to link an interactor's present-day performances to its past interactions. Correlates are a subset of correlons.

Correlons   The relational knowledge that makes possible the inferences obtained, and forecasts constructed, by a receiver in a communication process. More generally, correlons infuse the cognitive operations of the response circuit. The correlons of a human receiver, which arise through diverse mixes of learning and hardwiring, cannot be directly observed but must be modeled by the investigator.

Cuing   Specific emissions that lead immediately to (or "cue") the receiver's response.

Electrical interaction   The flow of electrons or ions between parts of an interactor or between interactors.

Electromagnetic interaction   An interaction that takes place on the basis of electromagnetic radiation, such as light or radio waves.

Emissions   The performances, in one or more interaction modes, by the emitter(s) in a communication process.

Emitron   An artifact playing a supporting role in a communication process by facilitating the emitter's performances. See also *sendtron* and *receptron*.

Emitter   One of the three major interactor roles in a communication process. From emitter performances, in one or more interaction modes, the receiver obtains information through inference. See also *salient*, *active*, and *passive emitter*.

Execution   An operation of the response circuit that effects the response.

Extern   A type of interactor which arises independently of people, such as sunlight and clouds, wild plants and animals, rocks and minerals, and landforms.

Focal interactor   The interactor that appears to be choreographing the performances of other interactors in an activity, thus giving impetus to the activity's forward motion and advancing its own life history.

Forecasting   A suboperation of mapping in the response circuit, forecasting furnishes expectations of future interactions of other interactors. Forecasts can be bundled with responses in the response repertoire, thereby affecting their probabilities.

Formal trace   Chemical, physical, or biological properties of an interactor – i.e., those pertaining to its form – that have been affected by previous interactions and can serve as evidence for inference. See also *locational*, *relational*, and *quantitative trace*.

Hierarchical organization of correlons   The postulate that the correlons of a human receiver are organized hierarchically by place, activity, interactor, and interaction. See also *keying in of correlons*.

Human behavior   See *behavior*.

Identification   A suboperation of inference in the response circuit, identification places interactors and interactions into simple categories (a type of interactor or interaction) and combines simple categories into complex ones (such as activity and place). See also *assignment*.

Indigenous theories   Abstract correlons, having generative capabilities, that contribute to the creation of novel responses in the response circuit. See also *novelty*.

Inference   A conclusion about something arrived at through reasoning from evidence. More specifically, for the present project, an inference is any information about a past interactor or interaction that is supported by evidence (performances of interactors) and relational knowledge (correlons). Finally, in the response circuit, inference is the cognitive operation that produces information about places, activities, interactors (senders and/or emitters), and interactions. Inference, as a cognitive operation, contains two suboperations: identification and assignment.

Inscription   In a communication process, the sender imparts information by modifying the emitters' properties (formal, locational, relational, quantitative).

Interaction   Any matter–energy transaction taking place between two or more interactors. The discrete interaction is the minimal observational unit in the material medium. See also *interaction modes*.

Interaction modes   Interactions may occur in one or more of five major modes: mechanical, chemical, thermal, electrical, and electromagnetic.

Interaction zone   The actual place on an interactor that takes part in a specific interaction.

Interactor   Any form of matter or energy capable of participating in interactions. The three major types of interactor are people, artifacts, and externs. See also *compound, focal, primary, secondary,* and *tertiary interactor.*

Interactor roles   In a communication process, interactors play three major roles: sender, emitter, and receiver.

Keying in of correlons   Because correlons are organized hierarchically, they are keyed in sequentially by the performances of different emitters (pertaining to place, activity, interactor, and interaction). See also *hierarchical organization of correlons.*

Life history   The specific sequence of interactions that occurs during a given interactor's existence. Discrete interactions in a life history are often aggregated into activities or processes or stages.

Locational trace   An interactor's location of occurrence, which has been affected by previous interactions and can serve as evidence for inference. See also *formal, relational,* and *quantitative trace.*

Macroartifact   Particularly obtrusive compound artifacts, such as horse and rider, car and driver, a cultivated field, and the air over industrial cities.

Mapping   An operation of the response circuit, mapping leads to the enumeration of a response repertoire. Mapping contains two suboperations: novelty and forecasting.

Matching   The ability of someone's senses to register emissions in a particular performance mode. Matching is a suboperation of registration in the response circuit.

Material medium   The material world which humans help shape and to which they respond. It is constituted by interactors, which can be any form of matter or energy, including people, artifacts, and externs.

Mechanical interaction   Physical contact occurring between interactors.

Mediation   The special case of communication in which an artifact plays the emitter role when the sender is a person.

Novelty   A suboperation of mapping in the response circuit, novelty generates new responses.

Operations   See *cognitive operations.*

Passive emitter   These interactors lack a sensory apparatus and so cannot play a receiver role. See also *active emitter.*

Performance   One interactor's minimal engagement with another in a discrete interaction. A performance can occur in any interaction mode.

Performance characteristic   A capability, competence, or skill that could be exercised by an interactor – i.e., "come into play" – in a specific performance. See also *sensory performance characteristic.*

Personal artifact   Any artifact compounded with a person, such as tattoos, makeup, earrings, clothing, shoes. Personal artifacts dramatically affect an individual's properties and thus performance characteristics.

Platial artifact   Any artifact that resides in a "place" – a specific location or set of locations, indoors or outdoors, including portable artifacts stored there, semi-portable objects (e.g., furniture), and more or less permanent architectural features.

Primary interactor   In an activity, the interactors whose performances are essential for advancing the focal interactor's life history. See also *secondary* and *tertiary interactor*.

Property   Any quality or quantity – chemical, physical, biological – that is intrinsic to an interactor and can be measured in relation to a standardized scale in a laboratory. An interactor's properties, such as shape, size, color, hardness, and weight, influence but do not determine performance characteristics.

Quantitative trace   Frequencies and relative frequencies of interactors which have been affected by previous interactions and can serve as evidence for inference. See also *formal*, *locational*, and *relational trace*.

Receiver   One of the three major roles that interactors play in a communication process. The receiver registers the performances of emitters in the reference activity and, on the basis of this evidence, constructs inferences (and forecasts) and responds. In order to play a receiver role, an interactor must have a sensory apparatus and be capable of responding.

Receiver response circuit   See *response circuit*.

Reception   The receiver in a communication process registers the emissions of activity and platial interactions. On the basis of these registered performances, the receiver employs correlons for constructing inferences and forecasts. See also *registration*.

Receptron   An artifact playing a supporting role in a communication process by facilitating reception by the receiver. See also *emitron* and *sendtron*.

Reference activity   The activity, designated by the investigator, which serves to anchor the study of a specific communication process. The reference activity is always the one in which the receiver takes part.

Registration   In the response circuit, registration is the operation that receives or monitors emissions by employing the sensory apparatus. See also *matching*.

Relational trace   An interactor's location in relation to another interactor. Interactors that co-occur are said to be associated; associations have been affected by previous interactions and can serve as evidence for inference. See also *formal*, *locational*, and *quantitative trace*.

Response   The last event of a communication process, in which the receiver, acting upon information yielded through inference, performs in one or more modes.

Response circuit   The correlate-laden cognitive operations that produce a human receiver's response. The response circuit consists of six cognitive operations: registration, weighting, inference, mapping, selection, and execution.

Response repertoire   An enumeration of responses produced by the mapping operation of the response circuit. A response repertoire can be represented, for common communication processes, as a set of specific responses along with their corresponding probabilities; the latter are based on the interactor's history of responses in the same communication process.

Retuning   The acquisition, often experientially, of new correlons or the remodeling of old ones. See also *tuning*.

Salient emitter   The emitter whose performances lead the receiver to formulate specific inferences/forecasts and cue the response.

Secondary interactor   In any activity, the interactors that play indirect, yet necessary roles, in advancing the focal interactor's life history. See also *primary* and *tertiary interactor*.

Selection   An operation of the response circuit, selection chooses the response.

Sender   One of the three major roles that interactors play in a communication process. A sender imparts information to a second interactor (the emitter) by modifying one or more of its properties (formal, locational, relational, quantitative). The latter affect the emitter's performances in the reference activity and serve as evidence for the receiver's inference. As a product of the receiver's inference, senders may be natural or supernatural.

Sendtron   An artifact playing a supporting role in a communication process by facilitating the sender's performances during inscription. See also *emitron* and *receptron*.

Sensory performance characteristic   A performance characteristic involving any of the senses: sight, touch (and pain), hearing, smell, and taste. Thus, one can speak of visual, acoustic, olfactory, and tactile performance characteristics.

Situational artifacts   These arrive with people or turn up at a place for the conduct of an activity.

Tertiary interactor   In an activity, those interactors whose performances are not entirely necessary for advancing the focal interactor's life history. See also *primary* and *secondary interactor*.

Thermal interaction   When one interactor warms or cools another.

Trace   Properties of an interactor that have been affected by past interactions in its life history. Traces affect an interactor's present-day performances and can thus serve as the evidential basis of inference. See also *formal*, *locational*, *relational*, and *quantitative trace*.

Tuning   The genetic and experiential processes through which a receiver obtains correlons. See also *appropriately tuned receiver* and *retuning*.

Weighting   In the response circuit, the weighting operation determines which emissions from which emitters matter; that is, which ones will be passed through to other cognitive operations.

Notes

1 Introduction

1 By "human" is meant entirely modern *Homo sapiens*, which evolved about 100,000 to 300,000 years ago with a brain and cognitive organization identical to our own. Nonetheless, some formulations in this book may apply as well to earlier hominids and to other, contemporary animal species.

2 I do not confine the meaning of "rules" to scientific laws. Rather, rule is a flexible concept that accommodates generalizations of any scale or scope (Schiffer 1996b), from universal laws to an individual-specific regularity (see Chapter 4).

2 What is human behavior?

1 Obviously, one could divide up the universe of interactors in countless ways. I have employed this tripartite division because it accords with an evolutionary hypothesis (inspired by Mithen 1996; see also Bard 1991; Cosmides and Tooby 1987; Karmiloff-Smith 1992; Sperber 1996: ch. 6; Tooby and Cosmides 1992; Wynn 1989). To wit, I suggest that cognitive processes evolved in our distant ancestors to facilitate interactions with externs, conspecifics (people, eventually), and diverse artifacts – in that order. First, as animals our primitive mammalian forebears evolved the ability to interact with externs during locomotion as well as in foraging and predator-avoidance activities. Second, in the more social Great Apes, cognitive processes evolved for dealing with conspecifics such as the abilities to keep track of kin, forge alliances and work groups, and manipulate the behavior of others. Third, in the most recent stage of hominid evolution, *Homo sapiens* evolved cognitive processes that enable interaction with myriad artifact types in countless activities. I further hypothesize that cognitive neuroscientists will find, in *natural* contexts (see Chapter 4 for the definition of context), significant differences in the way humans process information pertaining to the three kinds of interactors (for hypotheses on the evolutionary relationships between tools and cognition, see the papers in Gibson and Ingold 1993, Mellars and Gibson 1996, Noble and Davidson 1996, and Wynn 1989). Regrettably, use of the term "object" by psychologists and cognitive scientists, which indiscriminately designates both externs and artifacts (e.g., D'Andrade 1995: 150; Karmiloff-Smith 1992), has obscured possible differences in cognitive processes.

2 Although Hutchins (1995) does not define performance, his usage is similar to mine, for he focuses on the linked interactions among people and artifacts in activities – navigation systems in particular.

3   In employing the term "behavioral system," I emphatically deny any implication that these units are naturally bounded, well integrated, unchanging, or homeostatically regulated (for critiques of such systems-theory assumptions, see Athens 1977; Brumfiel 1992; Salmon 1978). Rather, "system" refers to an assemblage of interacting parts that forms a complex whole.

4   The choreography metaphor eventually needs to be unpacked and demystified; even so, it is a useful device that enables us sometimes to distinguish between activity interactors and uninvolved platial interactors.

5   As strictly defined above, a performance relates to only one interaction; however, in view of the many complex interactions that take place, it is usually necessary to expand the definition to include a person's simultaneous participation in many interactions. This broadened definition of performance is employed especially in Chapter 7.

3 Artifacts and "interpersonal" communication

1   The timing of performances also has communicative effects and cross-cuts all communication modes.

5 A general theory of communication

1   To the extent that behavior-modification therapies ignore context, and most do, their chances of success are diminished.

2   It goes almost without saying that the findings of many social-science experiments conducted in laboratories cannot be generalized beyond these highly contrived contexts.

3   The theory also predicts other incompatibilities. In particular, an individual's "attitudes" and "values," which are usually treated by social scientists as context-invariant personal traits, should differ according to the activity/place in which they are elicited or inferred (see Schiffer 1992b: ch. 7). This suggests the futility of trying to predict a person's responses in one context on the basis of her "values" and "attitudes" elicited from questionnaires filled out in a different – often laboratory – context.

4   It is important to acknowledge that, when modeling correlons in the course of fashioning a scientific explanation of a receiver's response, the investigator engages in a process that many sociocultural anthropologists would call "interpretation" (Sperber 1996: ch. 2). Understood as the modeling of correlons, "interpretation" need not be a shadowy, intuitive exercise, for the new communication theory gives guidance on how to model correlons in an explicit and replicable manner.

6 Basic communication processes

1   The framework of BCPs presented here should enable investigators to develop new classifications of activities on the basis of the BCPs they contain. Communication-based activity classifications would be indispensable for evaluating, with archaeological evidence, hypotheses about cognitive evolution (e.g., Chapter 2, note 1). One hypothesis is that the selective pressures favoring modern human cognition arose when, repeatedly, person–receivers took part in activities having diverse BCPs with artifact senders and emitters.

7 Explaining performance

1   In complex organisms such as humans, a concordance between the causal factors identified in both commentary and in a scientific explanation could sometimes arise, for evolution has produced behavioral flexibility by allowing aspects of some decision-making processes to become conscious and explicit (Deacon 1997). For example, if a briskly walking woman comes to a sudden stop at a street corner, both she and the investigator are apt to implicate heavy traffic and a red light as causally relevant factors. In principle, it should be possible to pinpoint, in future research, the kinds of contexts in which the factors identified in commentary and in a scientific explanation might coincide.

2   That people monitor their own physiological states, implicitly and explicitly, gives the investigator another way, beyond emotion-flavored correlons (Chapter 4), to include "affect" in the receiver-response model (see also Byrne 1992). Indeed, both simple and complex emotions can be treated as physiological states (cf. Barker *et al.* 1988: 203; Ekman 1993; Lewis 1995), measurable in principle by an investigator employing appropriate receptrons (e.g., LeDoux 1996: 292; Stein and Oatley 1992). I submit that the monitoring of one's own physiological states can be handled like any other kind of registration. As such, the effects of emotions, which can cue responses, are readily accommodated by the receiver-response model (cf. Easterbrook 1959). Needless to say, the incorporation of affect into cognitive models is long overdue (Hutchins 1995: ch. 9; LeDoux 1996: ch. 2).

References

Ackerman, D. 1990 *A Natural History of the Senses*. Random House, New York.

Aghazadeh, Fereydoun (ed.) 1994 *Advances in Industrial Ergonomics and Safety VI*. Taylor & Francis, London.

Albone, Eric S. 1984 *Mammalian Semiochemistry: The Investigation of Chemical Signals Between Mammals*. John Wiley & Sons, Chichester.

Appadurai, A. (ed.) 1986 *The Social Life of Things*. Cambridge University Press, Cambridge.

Arensberg, Conrad M. 1972 "Culture as Behavior: Structure and Emergence." *Annual Review of Anthropology* 1: 1–26.

Armstrong, G. Blake, Greg A. Boiarsky, and Marie-Louise Mares 1991 "Background Television and Reading Performance." *Communication Monographs* 58: 235–253.

Athens, J. Stephen 1977 "Theory Building and the Study of Evolutionary Process in Complex Societies." In Lewis R. Binford (ed.) *For Theory Building in Archaeology: Essays on Faunal Remains, Aquatic Resources, Spatial Analysis, and Systemic Modeling*, pp. 353–384. Academic Press, New York.

Atran, S. 1990 *Cognitive Foundations of Natural History: Towards an Anthropology of Science*. Cambridge University Press, Cambridge.

Babad, Yael E., Irving E. Alexander, and Elisha Y. Babad 1983 "Returning the Smile of the Stranger: Developmental Patterns and Socialization Factors." *Monographs of the Society for Research in Child Development*, 48 (5).

Bard, Kim A. 1991 "'Social Tool Use' by Free-Ranging Orangutans: A Piagetian and Developmental Perspective on the Manipulation of an Animate Object." In Sue Taylor Parker and Kathleen Rita Gibson (eds) *"Language" and Intelligence in Monkeys and Apes: Comparative Developmental Perspectives*, pp. 356–378. Cambridge University Press, Cambridge.

Barker, Deborah R., Larry L. Barker, and Margaret F. Hauser 1988 "Origins, Evolution, and Development of a Systems-Based Model of Intrapersonal Processes: A Holistic View of Man as Information Processor." In Brent D. Ruben (ed.) *Information and Behavior*, vol. 2, pp. 197–215. Transaction Books, New Brunswick, NJ.

Barnes, Ruth and Joanne B. Eicher (eds) 1992 *Dress and Gender: Making and Meaning in Cultural Contexts*. Berg, New York.

Barrett, Karen 1993 "The Development of Nonverbal Communication of Emotion: A Functionalist Perspective." *Journal of Nonverbal Behavior* 17: 145–169.

Basso, Keith 1996 *Wisdom Sits in Places*. University of New Mexico Press, Albuquerque.

Baudrillard, J. 1983 "The Precession of Simulacra." *Art and Text* 11: 3–46.

Beck, Benjamin B. 1980 *Animal Tool Behavior: The Use and Manufacture of Tools by Animals*. Garland STPM Press, New York.

—— 1986 "Tools and Intelligence." In R.J. Hoage and Larry Goldman (eds) *Animal Intelligence: Insights into the Animal Mind*, pp. 135–147. Smithsonian Institution Press, Washington, DC.

Beranek, Leo 1962 *Music, Acoustics and Architecture*. Wiley, New York.

Bergeman, C.S. 1997 *Aging Differently: Genetic and Environmental Influences on Development in Later Life*. Sage, Thousand Oaks, CA.

Berger, Charles R. 1991 "Communication Theories and Other Curios." *Communication Monographs* 58: 101–113.

—— and Richard J. Calabrese 1975 "Some Explorations in Initial Interaction and Beyond: Toward a Developmental Theory of Interpersonal Communication." *Human Communication Research* 1: 99–112.

—— and S.H. Chaffee (eds) 1987 *Handbook of Communication Science*. Sage, Newbury Park, CA.

Berlin, Brent 1992 *Ethnobiological Classification: Principles of Categorization of Plants and Animals in Traditional Societies*. Princeton University Press, Princeton, NJ.

Betzig, L. (ed.) 1996 *Human Nature: A Critical Reader*. Oxford University Press, New York.

Bickman, Leonard 1974 "The Social Power of a Uniform." *Journal of Applied Social Psychology* 4: 47–61.

Binford, Lewis R. 1962 "Archaeology as Anthropology." *American Antiquity* 28: 217–225.

—— 1982 "The Archaeology of Place." *Journal of Anthropological Archaeology* 1: 5–31.

Birdwhistell, Ray L. 1970 *Kinesics and Context: Essays on Body Motion Communication*. University of Pennsylvania Press, Philadelphia.

Bloch, Maurice 1990 "Language, Anthropology and Cognitive Science." *Man* 6: 183–198.

Blom, Jan-Petter and John J. Gumperz 1972 "Social Meaning in Linguistic Structure: Code-Switching in Norway." In John J. Gumperz and Dell Hymes (eds) *Directions in Sociolinguistics: The Ethnography of Communication*, pp. 407–434. Holt, Rinehart & Winston, New York.

Boden, M. 1990 *The Creative Mind: Myths and Mechanisms*. Weidenfeld & Nicolson, London.

Boesch, Christophe, Paul Marchesi, Nathalie Marchesi, Barbara Fruth, and Frédéric Joulian 1994 "Is Nut Cracking in Wild Chimpanzees a Cultural Behaviour?" *Journal of Human Evolution* 26: 325–338.

Bohannon, Paul 1988 "Beauty and Scarification Amongst the Tiv." In Arnold Rubin (ed.) *Marks of Civilization: Artistic Transformations of the Human Body*, pp. 77–82. Museum of Cultural History, University of California, Los Angeles.

Bohner, Gerd, Kimberly Crow, Hans-Peter Erb, and Norbert Schwarz 1992 "Affect and Persuasion: Mood Effects on the Processing of Message Content and Context Cues and on Subsequent Behaviour." *European Journal of Social Psychology* 22: 511–530.

Bonner, John T. 1980 *The Evolution of Culture in Animals*. Princeton University Press, Princeton, NJ.

Bostrom, Robert and Lewis Donohew 1992 "The Case for Empiricism: Clarifying Fundamental Issues in Communication Theory." *Communication Monographs* 59: 109–129.

Bourdieu, P. 1977 *Outline of a Theory of Practice*. Cambridge University Press, Cambridge.

Boyatzis, Chris J. and Malcolm W. Watson 1993 "Preschool Children's Symbolic Representation of Objects Through Gestures." *Child Development* 64: 729–735.

Boyd, Donna 1996 "Skeletal Correlates of Human Behavior in the Americas." *Journal of Archaeological Method and Theory* 3: 189–251.

Brain, Robert 1979 *The Decorated Body*. Hutchinson, London.

Brantingham, P. Jeffrey 1998 "Mobility, Competition, and Plio-Pleistocene Hominid Foraging Groups." *Journal of Archaeological Method and Theory* 5: 57–98.

Braun, David P. 1983 "Pots as Tools." In Arthur Keene and James Moore (eds) *Archaeological Hammers and Theories*, pp. 107–134. Academic Press, New York.

Bronner, Simon J. 1986 *Grasping Things: Folk Material Culture and Mass Society in America*. University of Kentucky Press, Lexington.

—— 1989 *Consuming Visions: Accumulation and Display of Goods in America, 1880–1920*. Norton, New York.

—— 1992 (ed.) *American Material Culture and Folklife: A Prologue and Dialogue*. Utah State University Press, Logan.

Brumfiel, Elizabeth M. 1992 "Distinguished Lecture in Archaeology: Breaking and Entering the Ecosystem – Gender, Class, and Faction Steal the Show." *American Anthropologist* 94: 551–567.

—— and Timothy Earle (eds) 1987 *Specialization, Exchange, and Complex Societies*. Cambridge University Press, Cambridge.

Bruton, Michael N. (ed.) 1989 *Alternative Life-History Styles of Animals*. Kluwer, Norwell, MA.

Buck, Peter H. 1959 *Vikings of the Sunrise*. University of Chicago Press, Chicago, IL.

Burgoon, Judee K. 1978 "Nonverbal Communication." In Michael Burgoon and Michael Ruffner (eds) *Human Communication*, pp. 129–170. Holt, Rinehart & Winston, New York.

——, David B. Buller, and W. Gill Woodall 1996 *Nonverbal Communication: The Unspoken Dialogue*. 2nd edn. McGraw-Hill, New York.

—— and Joseph B. Walther 1990 "Nonverbal Expectancies and the Evaluative Consequences of Violations." *Human Communication Research* 17: 232–265.

Burgoon, Michael and Michael Ruffner 1978 *Human Communication*. Holt, Rinehart & Winston, New York.

Burling, Robbins 1964 "Cognition and Componential Analysis: God's Truth or Hocus-Pocus?" *American Anthropologist* 66: 20–28.

—— 1993 "Primate Calls, Human Language, and Nonverbal Communication." *Current Anthropology* 34: 25–54.

Busemeyer, Jerome R. and In Jae Myung 1992 "An Adaptive Approach to Human Decision Making: Learning Theory, Decision Theory, and Human Performance." *Journal of Experimental Psychology: General* 121: 177–194.

Byers, A. Martin 1994 "Symboling and the Middle–Upper Palaeolithic Transition: A Theoretical and Methodological Critique." *Current Anthropology* 35: 369–399.

Byrne, Donn 1992 "The Transition from Controlled Laboratory Experimentation to Less Controlled Settings: Surprise! Additional Variables are Operative." *Communication Monographs* 59: 190–198.

Byrne, Richard 1995 *The Thinking Ape: Evolutionary Origins of Intelligence*. Oxford University Press, Oxford.

Cahill, Spencer E. 1989 "Fashioning Males and Females: Appearance Management and the Social Reproduction of Gender." *Symbolic Interaction* 12: 281–298.

Cameron, Catherine M. and Steve A. Tomka (eds) 1993 *Abandonment of Settlements and Regions: Ethnoarchaeological and Archaeological Approaches*. Cambridge University Press, Cambridge.

Carr, Christopher 1995 "Building a Unified Middle-Range Theory of Artifact Design: Historical Perspectives and Tactics." In Christopher Carr and Jill E. Neitzel (eds) *Style, Society, and Person*, pp. 151–258. Plenum, New York.

—— and Jill E. Neitzel (eds) 1995 *Style, Society, and Person*. Plenum, New York.

Cartmill, Matt 1990 "Human Uniqueness and Theoretical Context in Paleoanthropology." *International Journal of Primatology* 11: 173–192.

Cash, Thomas F., Kathryn Dawson, Pamela Davis, Maria Bowen, and Chris Galumbeck 1989 "Effects of Cosmetics Use on the Physical Attractiveness and Body Image of American College Women." *The Journal of Social Psychology* 129: 349–355.

Casmir, Fred L. (ed.) 1994 *Building Communication Theories: A Socio/Cultural Approach*. Erlbaum, Hillsdale, NJ.

Chambers, Bernice G. 1951 *Color and Design: Fashion in Men's and Women's Clothing and Home Furnishings*. Prentice Hall, New York.

Charness, Neil 1985 *Aging and Human Performance*. Wiley, New York.

Cherry, Colin 1966 *On Human Communication: A Review, a Survey, and a Criticism*. 2nd edn. MIT Press, Cambridge, MA.

Chung, Po-Pui and Kwok Leung 1988 "Effects of Performance Information and Physical Attractiveness on Managerial Decisions about Promotion." *The Journal of Social Psychology* 128: 791–801.

Clifford, M.M. and E. Walster 1973 "The Effect of Physical Attractiveness on Teacher Expectations. *Sociology of Education* 46: 248–258.

Cohen, I. Bernard 1990 *Benjamin Franklin's Science*. Harvard University Press, Cambridge, MA.

Conkey, Margaret W. and Christine Hastorf (eds) 1990 *The Uses of Style in Archaeology*. Cambridge University Press, Cambridge.

Cordwell, J.M. and R.A. Schwarz 1979 *The Fabrics of Culture: The Anthropology of Clothing and Adornment*. Mouton, The Hague.

Coren, Stanley, Lawrence M. Ward, and James T. Enns 1994 *Sensation and Perception*. Harcourt Brace, Fort Worth, TX.

Corso, John F. 1981 *Aging Sensory Systems and Perception*. Praeger, New York.

Cosmides, L. and J. Tooby 1987 "From Evolution to Behaviour: Evolutionary Psychology as the Missing Link." In J. Dupré (ed.) *The Latest and the Best: Essays on Evolution and Optimality*, pp. 277–306. Cambridge University Press, Cambridge.

Cott, Hugh B. 1940 *Adaptive Coloration in Animals*. Methuen, London.

Craik, Jennifer 1994 *The Face of Fashion: Cultural Studies in Fashion*. Routledge, London.

Crick, Malcolm R. 1982 "Anthropology of Knowledge." *Annual Review of Anthropology* 11: 287–313.

Crisp, Roger 1996 "Evolution and Psychological Unity." In Marc Bekoff and Dale Jamieson (eds) *Readings in Animal Cognition*, pp. 309–321. MIT Press, Cambridge.

Croney, John 1980 *Anthropometry for Designers*. Batsford, London.

Crowley, David J. (ed.) 1994 *Communication Theory Today*. Stanford University Press, Stanford, CA.

Crystal, David 1975 "Paralinguistics." In J. Benthall and Ted Polhemus (eds) *The Body as a Medium of Expression*, pp. 162–174. E.P. Dutton, New York.

Csikszentmihalyi, Mihaly and Eugene Rochberg-Halton 1981 *The Meaning of Things: Domestic Symbols and the Self*. Cambridge University Press, Cambridge.

Dance, Frank E.X. (ed.) 1967 *Human Communication Theory: Original Essays*. Holt, Rinehart & Winston, New York.

D'Andrade, Roy 1995 *The Development of Cognitive Anthropology*. Cambridge University Press, Cambridge.

Daniel, Glyn and Colin Renfrew 1988 *The Idea of Prehistory*. Edinburgh University Press, Edinburgh.

David, Fred 1992 *Fashion, Culture, and Identity*. University of Chicago Press, Chicago, IL.

Davidson, Iain and William Noble 1989 "The Archaeology of Perception: Traces of Depiction and Language." *Current Anthropology* 30: 125–155.

Dawkins, R. 1982 *The Extended Phenotype*. W.H. Freeman, San Francisco, CA.

—— and M. Dawkins 1973 "Decisions and the Uncertainty of Behavior." *Behaviour* 45: 83–103.

Deacon, Terrence W. 1997 *The Symbolic Species: The Co-Evolution of Language and the Brain*. Norton, New York.

de Certeau, Michael 1984 *The Practice of Everyday Life*. University of California Press, Berkeley.

Deetz, James F. 1977 "Material Culture and Archaeology: What's the Difference?" In Leland Ferguson (ed.) *Historical Archaeology and the Importance of Material Things*, pp. 9–12. The Society for Historical Archaeology, Special Publication Series, No. 2.

Delia, J.G. 1987 "Communication Research: A History." In C.R. Berger and S.H. Chaffee (eds), *Handbook of Communication Science*, pp. 20–98. Sage, Beverly Hills, CA.

Delius, Juan D. 1992 "Categorical Discrimination of Objects and Pictures by Pigeons." *Animal Learning & Behavior* 20: 301–311.

Dembo, Adolfo and J. Imbelloni 1978 "Body Alteration and Adornment: A Pictorial Essay." In Ted Polhemus (ed.) *The Body Reader: Social Aspects of the Human Body*, pp. 154–173. Pantheon Books, New York.

Dipert, Randall R. 1993 *Artifacts, Art Works, and Agency*. Temple University Press, Philadelphia.

Dittmar, H. 1992 *The Social Psychology of Material Possessions: To Have is to Be*. St. Martin's Press, New York.

Domjan, Michael 1993 *The Principles of Learning and Behavior*. Brooks/Cole, Pacific Grove, CA.

Doty, R.L. 1985 "The Primates: III. Humans." In R.E. Brown and D.W. MacDonald (eds) *Social Odours in Mammals*, Vol. 2, pp. 804–832. Clarendon Press, Oxford.

———, P.A. Green, C. Ram, and S.L. Yankell 1982 "Communication of Gender from Human Breath Odors: Relationship to Perceived Intensity and Pleasantness." *Hormones and Behavior* 16: 13–22.

Douglas, Mary and B. Isherwood 1979 *The World of Goods*. Allen Lane, London.

DuBois, John W. 1993 "Meaning Without Intention: Lessons from Divination." In J.H. Hill and J.T. Irvine (eds) *Responsibility and Evidence in Oral Discourse*, pp. 48–71. Cambridge University Press, Cambridge.

Duncan, Starkey, Jr. 1969 "Nonverbal Communication." *Psychological Bulletin* 72(2): 118–137.

Dunnell, Robert C. 1978 "Style and Function: A Fundamental Dichotomy." *American Antiquity* 43: 192–202.

——— 1980 "Evolutionary Theory and Archaeology." *Advances in Archaeological Method and Theory* 3: 35–99.

Earle, Timothy and J. Ericson (eds) 1977 *Exchange Systems in Prehistory*. Academic Press, New York.

Easterbrook, J.A. 1959 "The Effect of Emotion on Cue Utilization and the Organization of Behavior." *Psychological Review* 66: 183–201.

Eaton, Linda B. 1994 "The Hopi Craftsman Exhibition: The Creation of Authenticity." *Expedition* 36(1): 24–32.

Edwards, Derek 1994 "Imitation and Artifice in Apes, Humans, and Machines." *American Behavioral Scientist* 37: 754–771.

Ehrenhaus, Peter 1988 "Attributing Intention to Communication: Information as the Interpretation of Interaction." In Brent D. Ruben (ed.) *Information and Behavior*, Vol. 2, pp. 248–270. Transaction Books, New Brunswick, NJ.

Eisenberg, Abne M. and Ralph R. Smith, Jr. 1971 *Nonverbal Communication*. Bobbs-Merrill, Indianapolis, IN.

Ekman, Paul 1985 *Telling Lies*. Norton, New York.

——— 1993 "Facial Expressions and Emotion." *American Psychologist* 48: 384–392.

——— and Wallace V. Friesen 1967 "Head and Body Cues in the Judgment of Emotion: A Reformulation." *Perceptual and Motor Skills* 24: 711–724.

——— and ——— 1969 "The Repertoire of Nonverbal Behavior: Categories, Origins, Usage, and Coding." *Semiotica* 1: 49–98.

———, E. Richard Sorenson, and Wallace V. Friesen 1969 "Pan-Cultural Elements in Facial Displays of Emotion." *Science* 164: 86–88.

Elkin, A.P. 1977 *Aboriginal Men of High Degree*. 2nd edn. St. Martin's Press, New York.

Eyman, Scott 1997 *The Speed of Sound: Hollywood and the Talkie Revolution, 1926–1930*. Simon & Schuster, New York.

Fabrega, Horacio, Jr. 1977 "Culture, Behavior, and the Nervous System." *Annual Review of Anthropology* 6: 419–455.

Fahie, J.J. 1884 *A History of Electric Telegraphy to the Year 1837*. E. & F.N. Spon, London.

Fast, Julius 1971 *Body Language*. Pocket Books, New York.

Fellman, Sandi 1986 *The Japanese Tattoo*. Abbeville Press, New York.

Fix, Michael and Raymond J. Struyk (eds) 1993 *Clear and Convincing Evidence: Measurement of Discrimination in America*. Urban Institute Press, Lanham, MD.

Fleagle, John G. 1998 *Primate Adaptation and Evolution*. 2nd edn. Academic Press, New York.

Fletcher, Roland 1996 "Organized Dissonance: Multiple Code Structures in the Replication of Human Culture." In H.D.G. Maschner (ed.) *Darwinian Archaeologies*, pp. 61–86. Plenum, New York.

Fortner, Robert S. 1994 "Mediated Communication Theory." In Fred L. Casmir (ed.) *Building Communication Theories: A Socio/Cultural Approach*, pp. 209–240. Erlbaum, Hillsdale, NJ.

Foucault, Michel 1972 *The Archaeology of Knowledge*. Harper Torchbooks, New York.

Fox, Robin 1979 "The Evolution of Mind: An Anthropological Approach." *Journal of Anthropological Research* 35: 138–156.

Fridlund, Alan J. 1994 *Human Facial Expression: An Evolutionary View*. Academic Press, San Diego, CA.

Friedel, Robert, Paul Israel, and Bernard S. Finn 1987 *Edison's Electric Light: Biography of an Invention*. Rutgers University Press, New Brunswick, NJ.

Frings, Hubert, and Mable Frings 1977 *Animal Communication*. 2nd edn. University of Oklahoma Press, Norman.

Fritz, John M. 1972 "Archaeological Systems for Indirect Observation of the Past." In M.P. Leone (ed.) *Contemporary Archaeology*, pp. 135–157. Southern Illinois University Press, Carbondale.

Fry, Robert (ed.) 1980 "Models and Methods in Regional Exchange." *Society for American Archaeology, Papers* 1.

Galef, Bennet G., Jr. 1990 "Tradition in Animals: Field Observations and Laboratory Analyses." In Marc Bekoff and Dale Jamieson (eds) *Interpretation and Explanation in the Study of Animal Behavior. Volume 1: Interpretation, Intentionality, and Communication*, pp. 74–95. Westview Press, Boulder, CO.

Gallagher, Winifred 1993 *The Power of Place: How Our Surroundings Shape Our Thoughts, Emotions, and Actions*. HarperCollins, New York.

Gallistel, C.R. 1990 *The Organization of Learning*. MIT Press, Cambridge.

Gibson, Kathleen R. and Timothy Ingold (eds) 1993 *Tools, Language and Cognition in Human Evolution*. Cambridge University Press, Cambridge.

Giddens, Anthony 1993 *New Rules of Sociological Method*. 2nd edn. Stanford University Press, Stanford, CA.

Gillin, John 1948 *The Ways of Men: An Introduction to Anthropology*. Appleton-Century, New York.

Glassie, Henry 1975 *Folk Housing in Middle Virginia: A Structural Analysis of Historical Artifacts*. University of Tennessee Press, Knoxville.

Goffman, Erving 1959 *The Presentation of Self in Everyday Life*. Doubleday, Garden City, NJ.

—— 1974 *Frame Analysis: An Essay on the Organization of Experience*. Harper & Row, New York.

Gordon, Deborah M. 1995 "The Development of Organization in an Ant Colony." *American Scientist* 83(1): 50–57.

Gottfredson, Michael R. and Travis Hirschi 1990 *A General Theory of Crime*. Stanford University Press, Stanford, CA.

Gould, Richard A. 1990 *Recovering the Past*. University of New Mexico Press, Albuquerque.

Gouran, Dennis S., Randy Y. Hirokawa, Michael C. McGee, and Laurie L. Miller 1994 "Communication in Groups: Research Trends and Theoretical Perspectives." In

Fred L. Casmir (ed.) *Building Communication Theories: A Socio/Cultural Approach*, pp. 241–268. Erlbaum, Hillsdale, NJ.

Greene, John O. and Deanna Geddes 1993 "An Action Assembly Perspective on Social Skill." *Communication Theory* 3: 26–49.

Greenfield, Patricia M. 1991 "Language, Tools and Brain: The Ontogeny and Phylogeny of Hierarchically Organized Sequential Behavior." *Behavioral and Brain Sciences* 14: 531–595.

Griffin, Donald R. 1991 "Progress Toward a Cognitive Ethology." In C.A. Ristau (ed.) *Cognitive Ethology: The Minds of Other Animals*, pp. 3–17. Erlbaum, Hillsdale, NJ.

—— 1992 *Animal Minds*. University of Chicago Press, Chicago, IL.

Gross, A.L. and B. Ballif 1991 "Children's Understanding of Emotion from Facial Expressions and Situations: A Review." *Developmental Psychology* 23: 388–399.

Gross, Samuel R. and Robert Mauro 1989 *Death and Discrimination: Racial Disparities in Capital Sentencing*. Northeastern University Press, Boston, MA.

Gumerman, George J. IV 1997 "Food and Complex Societies." *Journal of Archaeological Method and Theory* 4: 105–139.

Gumpert, Gary and Robert Cathcart 1990 "A Theory of Mediation." In Brent D. Ruben and Leah A. Lievrouw (eds) *Mediation, Information, and Communication. Information and Behavior, Vol. 3*, pp. 21–36. Transaction Books, New Brunswick, NJ.

Haberlandt, Karl 1994 *Cognitive Psychology*. Allyn & Bacon, Boston.

Hakken, D. 1993 "Computing and Social Change: New Technology and the Workplace Transformation." *Annual Review of Anthropology* 22: 107–132.

Hall, Bradford 1992 "Theories of Culture and Communication." *Communication Theory* 2: 50–70.

Hall, D. Geoffrey 1991 "Acquiring Proper Nouns for Familiar and Unfamiliar Animate Objects: Two-Year-Olds' Word-Learning Biases." *Child Development* 62: 1142–1154.

Hall, Edward T. 1966 *The Hidden Dimension*. Doubleday, New York.

Hall, K.R.L. 1963 "Tool-Using Performances as Indicators of Behavioral Adaptability." *Current Anthropology* 4: 479–494.

Halloran, James D. 1985 "Information and Communication: Information is the Answer, but What is the Question?" In Brent D. Ruben (ed.) *Information and Behavior*, Vol. 1, pp. 27–39. Transaction Books, New Brunswick, NJ.

Handy, W.C. 1923 "Tattooing in the Marquesas." *Bernice P. Bishop Museum Bulletin* 1.

Hankins, Thomas L. and Robert J. Silverman 1995 *Instruments and the Imagination*. Princeton University Press, Princeton, NJ.

Hanneman, Gerhard J. 1975 "The Study of Human Communication." In Gerhard J. Hanneman and William McEwen (eds) *Communication and Behavior*, pp. 21–49. Addison-Wesley, Reading, MA.

Hard, Robert J., Raymond P. Mauldin, and Gerry R. Raymond 1996 "Mano Size, Stable Carbon Isotope Ratios, and Macrobotanical Remains as Multiple Lines of Evidence of Maize Dependence in the American Southwest." *Journal of Archaeological Method and Theory* 3: 253–318.

Hardcastle, Valerie Gray 1996 *How to Build a Theory in Cognitive Science*. State University of New York Press, Albany.

Harper, Nancy 1979 *Human Communication Theory: The History of a Paradigm*. Hayden Book Co., Rochelle Park, NJ.

Harris, Marvin 1964 *The Nature of Cultural Things*. Random House, New York.

Harrison, Randall P. 1989 "Nonverbal Communication." In Sarah S. King (ed.) *Human Communication as a Field of Study*, pp. 113–125. State University of New York Press, Albany.

—— and Wayne W. Crouch 1975 "Nonverbal Communication: Theory and Research." In Gerhard J. Hanneman and William McEwen (eds) *Communication and Behavior*, pp. 76–97. Addison-Wesley, Reading, MA.

Haslett, Beth 1987 *Communication: Strategic Action in Context*. Erlbaum, Hillsdale, NJ.

Hauser, Marc D. 1996 *The Evolution of Communication*. MIT Press, Cambridge, MA.

Hawkins, D.I., R.J. Best, and K.A. Coney 1992 *Consumer Behavior: Implications for Marketing Strategy*. 5th edn. Irwin, Homewood, IL.

Hayden, Brian 1998 "Practical and Prestige Technologies: The Evolution of Material Systems." *Journal of Archaeological Method and Theory* 5: 1–55.

Heath, Robert L. and Jennings Bryant 1992 *Human Communication Theory and Research: Concepts, Contexts, and Challenges*. Erlbaum, Hillsdale, NJ.

Heilbron, J.L. 1982 *Elements of Early Modern Physics*. University of California Press, Berkeley.

Herman, Louis M. and Palmer Morrel-Samuels 1996 "Knowledge Acquisition and Asymmetry Between Language Comprehension and Production: Dolphins and Apes as General Models for Animals." In Marc Bekoff and Dale Jamieson (eds) *Readings in Animal Cognition*, pp. 289–306. MIT Press, Cambridge, MA.

Heron, Carl and Richard P. Evershed 1993 "The Analysis of Organic Residues and the Study of Pottery Use." *Archaeological Method and Theory* 5: 247–284.

Heslin, R. and T. Alper 1983 "Touch: A Bonding Gesture." In J.M. Wiemann and R.P. Harrison (eds) *Nonverbal Interaction*, pp. 47–75. Sage, Beverly Hills, CA.

Hewes, G.W. 1957 "The Anthropology of Posture." *Scientific American* 196: 123–132.

Hill, Elizabeth M., Elaine S. Nocks, and Lucinda Gardner 1987 "Physical Attractiveness: Manipulation by Physique and Status Displays." *Ethology and Sociobiology* 8: 143–154.

Hiltz, S.R., K. Johnson, and M. Turoff 1986 "Experiments in Group Decision Making: Communication Process and Outcome in Face-to-Face Versus Computerized Conferences." *Human Communication Research* 13: 225–252.

Hodder, Ian 1982 *Symbols in Action*. Cambridge University Press, Cambridge.

—— (ed.) 1987 *The Archaeology of Contextual Meanings*. Cambridge University Press, Cambridge.

—— (ed.) 1989 *The Meaning of Things: Material Culture and Symbolic Expression*. Unwin Hyman, London.

Hull, David L. 1988 *Science as a Process: An Evolutionary Account of the Social and Conceptual Development of Science*. University of Chicago Press, Chicago, IL.

Hulse, Stewart H., Harry Fowler, and Werner K. Honig 1978 *Cognitive Processes in Animal Behavior*. Erlbaum, Hillsdale, NJ.

Hunsberger, Bruce, and Brenda Cavanagh 1988 "Physical Attractiveness and Children's Expectations of Potential Teachers." *Psychology in the Schools* 25: 70–74.

Hutchins, Edwin 1995 *Cognition in the Wild*. MIT Press, Cambridge, MA.

Hymes, Dell 1967 "The Anthropology of Communication." In Frank E. Dance (ed.) *Human Communication Theory: Original Essays*, pp. 1–39. Holt, Rinehart & Winston, New York.

Ingersoll, Daniel W., Jr. and Gordon Bronitsky (eds) 1987 *Mirror and Metaphor: Material and Social Constructions of Reality*. University Press of America, Lanham, MD.

Jakobs, Esther, Antony S.R. Manstead, and Agneta H. Fischer 1996 "Social Context and the Experience of Emotion." *Journal of Nonverbal Behavior* 20: 123–146.

Jeannerod, Marc 1997 *The Cognitive Neuroscience of Action*. Blackwell, Oxford.

Jerrard, Jane 1992 *Goldilocks & the Three Bears*. New Seasons Publishing.

Jones, Doug 1995 "Sexual Selection, Physical Attractiveness, and Facial Neotony: Cross-Cultural Evidence and Implications." *Current Anthropology* 36: 723–748.

Jones, S.E. and A.E. Yarbrough 1985 "A Naturalistic Study of the Meanings of Touch." *Communication Monographs* 51: 37–55.

Jones, Timothy W. 1995 *Archaeology as Archaeology*. Ph.D. dissertation, University of Arizona. University Microfilms, Ann Arbor, MI.

Joseph, Nathan 1986 *Uniforms and Nonuniforms: Communicating Through Clothing*. Greenwood Press, New York.

Kaiser, Susan B. 1985 *The Social Psychology of Clothing and Personal Adornment*. Macmillan, New York.

——, Margaret Rudy, and Pamela Byfield 1985 "The Role of Clothing in Sex-Role Socialization: Person Perceptions Versus Overt Behavior." *Child Study Journal* 15: 83–97.

Kalick, S. Michael 1988 "Physical Attractiveness as a Status Cue." *Journal of Experimental Social Psychology* 24: 469–489.

Karmiloff-Smith, Annette 1992 *Beyond Modularity: A Developmental Perspective on Cognitive Science*. MIT Press, Cambridge, MA.

Karraker, Katherine H. 1990 "Infant Physical Attractiveness and Facial Expression: Effects on Adult Perceptions." *Basic and Applied Social Psychology* 11: 371–385.

Katovich, Michael A. and William A. Reese, II 1993 "Postmodern Thought in Symbolic Interaction: Reconstructing Social Inquiry in Light of Late-Modern Concerns." *The Sociological Quarterly* 34: 391–411.

Keeley, Lawrence 1980 *Experimental Determination of Stone Tool Uses: A Microwear Analysis*. University of Chicago Press, Chicago, IL.

Keller, Charles M. and Janet Dixon Keller 1996 *Cognition and Tool Use: The Blacksmith at Work*. Cambridge University Press, New York.

Kellerman, Kathy, Scott Broetzmann, Tae-Seop Lim, and Kenji Kitao 1989 "The Conversation Mop: Scenes in the Stream of Discourse." *Discourse Processes* 12: 27–61.

Kelly, John C. 1981 *A Philosophy of Communication: Explorations for a Systematic Model*. Centre for the Study of Communications and Culture, London.

Kendon, Adam 1985 "Behavioural Foundations for the Process of Frame Attunement in Face-to-face Interaction." In G.P. Ginsburg, M. Brenner, and M. von Cranach (eds) *Discovery Strategies in the Psychology of Action*, pp. 229–253. Academic Press, London.

—— 1993 "Human Gesture." In Kathleen R. Gibson and Tim Ingold (eds) *Tools, Language and Cognition in Human Evolution*, pp. 43–62. Cambridge University Press, Cambridge.

—— 1997 "Gesture." *Annual Review of Anthropology* 26: 109–128.

Kinchla, R.A. 1992 "Attention." *Annual Review of Psychology* 43: 711–742.

King, Barbara 1994 *The Information Continuum*. SAR Press, Santa Fe, New Mexico.

Kirk-Smith, M.D. and D.A. Booth 1980 "Effects of Androstenone on Choice of Location in Other's Presence." In H. van der Starre (ed.) *Olfaction and Taste VII*, pp. 397–400. IRL Press, London.

Knapp, A. Bernard 1996 "Archaeology Without Gravity: Postmodernism and the Past." *Journal of Archaeological Method and Theory* 3: 127–158.

Knapp, Mark L. and Judith A. Hall 1992 *Nonverbal Communication in Human Interaction.* Harcourt Brace Jovanovich, Fort Worth, TX.

Krippendorff, Klaus 1975 "Information Theory." In Gerhard J. Hanneman and William McEwen (eds) *Communication and Behavior,* pp. 351–389. Addison-Wesley, Reading, MA.

Krueger, Dorothy L. and Nancy L. Harper 1988 "Information, Behavior, and Meaning." In Brent D. Ruben (ed.) *Information and Behavior,* Vol. 2, pp. 54–73. Transaction Books, New Brunswick, NJ.

Kubey, Robert and Mihaly Csikszentmihalyi 1990 *Television and the Quality of Life: How Viewing Shapes Everyday Experience.* Erlbaum, Hillsdale, NJ.

Kuhn, Thomas 1970 *The Structure of Scientific Revolutions.* 2nd edn. University of Chicago Press, Chicago, IL.

Labows, John N. and George Preti 1992 "Human Seriochemicals." In Steve Van Toller and G.H. Dodd (eds) *Fragrance: The Psychology and Biology of Perfume,* pp. 69–90. Elsevier, London.

Lal, Barbara B. 1995 "Symbolic Interaction Theories." *American Behavioral Scientist* 38: 421–441.

LaMotta, Vincent M. and Michael B. Schiffer n.d. "Formation Processes of House Floor Assemblages." In Penelope Allison (ed.) *The Archaeology of Household Activities.* Routledge, London.

Larsen, Clark S. 1987 "Bioarchaeological Interpretations of Subsistence Economy from Human Skeletal Remains." *Advances in Archaeological Method and Theory* 10: 339–445.

Latour, Bruno 1993 *We Have Never Been Modern.* Harvard University Press, Cambridge, MA.

Lautman, Victoria 1994 *The New Tattoo.* Abbeville Press, New York.

Lave, Jean and Etienne Wenger 1991 *Situated Learning: Legitimate Peripheral Participation.* Cambridge University Press, Cambridge.

Lawrence, Denise L. and Setha M. Low 1990 "The Built Environment and Spatial Form." *Annual Review of Anthropology* 19: 453–505.

LeDoux, Joseph 1996 *The Emotional Brain: The Mysterious Underpinnings of Emotional Life.* Simon & Schuster, New York.

Lemonnier, Pierre 1992 "Elements for an Anthropology of Technology." *University of Michigan, Museum of Anthropology, Anthropological Papers,* no. 88.

Leone, Mark P. 1977 "The New Mormon Temple in Washington, D.C." In Leland Ferguson (ed.) *Historical Archaeology and the Importance of Material Things,* pp. 43–61. The Society for Historical Archaeology, Special Publication Series, No. 2.

—— and Parker B. Potter, Jr. (eds) 1989 *The Recovery of Meaning: Historical Archaeology in the Eastern United States.* Smithsonian Institution Press, Washington D.C.

Leroi-Gourhan, André 1993 *Gesture and Speech.* MIT Press, Cambridge, MA.

Lévi-Strauss, Claude 1963 *Structural Anthropology.* Basic Books, New York.

Lewin, Roger 1992 *Complexity: Life at the Edge of Chaos.* Macmillan, New York.

Lewis, Michael 1995 "Self-Conscious Emotions." *American Scientist* 83: 68–78.

Lieberman, Philip 1991 *Uniquely Human: The Evolution of Speech, Thought, and Selfless Behavior.* Harvard University Press, Cambridge, MA.

Lievrouw, Leah A. and T. Andrew Finn 1990 "Identifying the Common Dimensions of Communication: The Communication Systems Model." In Brent D. Ruben and Leah A. Lievrouw (eds) *Mediation, Information, and Communication. Information and Behavior* series, Vol. 3, pp. 37–65. Transaction Books, New Brunswick, NJ.

Littlejohn, Stephen W. 1991 *Theories of Human Communication.* Wadsworth, Belmont, CA.

Loftus, Elizabeth and Jonathan W. Schooler 1985 "Information-Processing Conceptualizations of Human Cognition: Past, Present, and Future." In Brent D. Ruben (ed.) *Information and Behavior,* Vol. 1, pp. 225–250. Transaction Books, New Brunswick, NJ.

Longacre, William A. and James M. Skibo 1994 *Kalinga Ethnoarchaeology: Expanding Archaeological Method and Theory.* Smithsonian Institution Press, Washington D.C.

MacDonald, David W. 1980 "Patterns of Scent Marking with Urine and Faeces Amongst Carnivore Communities." *Symposia of the Zoological Society of London* 45: 107–139.

Marshack, Alexander 1989 "Evolution of Human Capacity: The Symbolic Evidence." *Yearbook of Physical Anthropology* 32: 1–34.

Mascia-Lees, Frances E. and Patricia Sharpe (eds) 1992 *Tattoo, Torture, Mutilation, and Adornment: The Denaturalization of the Body in Culture and Text.* State University of New York Press, Albany.

Mason, J. Alden 1968 *The Ancient Civilizations of Peru.* Penguin Books, Harmondsworth.

Matsumoto, D. 1991 "Cultural Influences on Facial Expressions of Emotion." *Southern Communication Journal* 56: 128–137.

McBurney, D.H., J.M. Levine, and P.H. Cavanaugh 1977 "Psychophysical and Social Ratings of Human Body Odor." *Personality and Social Psychology Bulletin* 3: 135–138.

McCracken, Grant 1988 *Culture and Consumption.* Indiana University Press, Bloomington.

McDermott, R.P. and David R. Roth 1978 "The Social Organization of Behavior: Interactional Approaches." *Annual Review of Anthropology* 7: 321–345.

McGrew, W.C. 1992 *Chimpanzee Material Culture: Implications for Human Evolution.* Cambridge University Press, Cambridge.

—— 1993 "The Intelligent Use of Tools: Twenty Propositions." In Kathleen R. Gibson and Tim Ingold (eds) *Tools, Language and Cognition in Human Evolution,* pp. 151–170. Cambridge University Press, Cambridge.

McGuire, Randall H. 1983 "Breaking Down Cultural Complexity: Inequality and Heterogeneity." *Advances in Archaeological Method and Theory* 6: 91–142.

—— 1995 "Behavioral Archaeology: Reflections of a Prodigal Son." In James M. Skibo, William H. Walker, and Axel E. Nielsen (eds) *Expanding Archaeology,* pp. 162–177. University of Utah Press, Salt Lake City.

McNeill, D. 1992 *Hand and Mind: What Gestures Reveal About Thought.* University of Chicago Press, Chicago, IL.

McPhee, Robert D. and Steven R. Corman 1995 "An Activity-Based Theory of Communication Networks in Organizations, Applied to the Case of a Local Church." *Communication Monographs* 62: 132–151.

McSween, Harry Y. 1993 *Stardust to Planets: A Geological Tour of the Solar System.* St. Martin's Press, New York.

Mehrabian, A. and S.R. Ferris 1967 "Inference of Attitudes from Nonverbal Communication in Two Channels." *Journal of Consulting Psychology* 31: 248–252.

Mellars, Paul and Kathleen R. Gibson (eds) 1996 *Modelling the Early Human Mind*. McDonald Institute, Cambridge University, Cambridge.

Mendoza-Denton, Norma 1996 "'Muy Macha': Gender and Ideology in Gang-Girls' Discourse About Makeup." *Ethnos* 61: 47–63.

Meyrowitz, Joshua 1990 "Using Contextual Analysis to Bridge the Study of Mediated and Unmediated Behavior." In Brent D. Ruben and Leah A. Lievrouw (eds) *Mediation, Information, and Communication. Information and Behavior*, Vol. 3, pp. 67–94. Transaction Books, New Brunswick, NJ.

Mickleburg, Rod 1996 "'Ugly' Student Rejected by Universities in China." *Arizona Daily Star*, 15 October, p. A-2. Tucson, AZ.

Milberg, Sandra and Margaret S. Clark 1988 "Moods and Compliance." *British Journal of Social Psychology* 27: 79–90.

Miller, Daniel 1985 *Artefacts as Categories: A Study of Ceramic Variability in Central India*. Cambridge University Press, Cambridge.

—— 1987 *Material Culture and Mass Consumption*. Basil Blackwell, London.

—— 1994 *Modernity, An Ethnographic Approach: Dualism and Mass Consumption in Trinidad*. Berg, Providence, Rhode Island.

—— 1995 "Consumption and Commodities." *Annual Review of Anthropology* 19: 453–505.

Mills, C.W. 1940 "Situated Actions and Vocabularies of Motives." *American Sociological Review* 5: 904–913.

Mithen, Steven 1996 *The Prehistory of the Mind*. Thames & Hudson, London.

Montagu, Ashley 1978 *Touching: The Human Significance of the Skin*. 2nd edn. Harper & Row, New York.

Montepare, Joann M. and Leslie A. Zebrowitz 1993 "A Cross-Cultural Comparison of Impressions Created by Age-Related Variations in Gait." *Journal of Nonverbal Behavior* 17: 55–68.

Moriarty, Sandra E. 1996 "Abduction: A Theory of Visual Interpretation." *Communication Theory* 6: 167–187.

Moynihan, Martin 1985 *Communication and Noncommunication by Cephalopods*. Indiana University Press, Bloomington.

Musello, Christopher 1992 "Objects in Process: Material Culture and Communication." *Southern Folklore* 49: 37–59.

Nagel, Ernest 1961 *The Structure of Science*. Harcourt, Brace & World, New York.

Nelson, Charles A. (ed.) 1994 *Threats to Optimal Development: Integrating Biological, Psychological, and Social Risk Factors*. The Minnesota Symposia on Child Psychology, Vol. 27. Erlbaum, Hillsdale, NJ.

Neupert, Mark A. and William A. Longacre 1994 "Informant Accuracy in Pottery Use-Life Studies: A Kalinga Example." In W.A. Longacre and J.M. Skibo (eds) *Kalinga Ethnoarchaeology: Expanding Archaeological Method and Theory*, pp. 71–82. Smithsonian Institution Press, Washington D.C.

Newell, Allen 1990 *Unified Theories of Cognition: The William James Lectures, 1987*. Harvard University Press, Cambridge, MA.

Newman, Philip L. 1965 *Knowing the Gururumba*. Holt, Rinehart & Winston, New York.

Nielsen, Axel E. 1995 "Architectural Performance and the Reproduction of Social Power." In James M. Skibo, William H. Walker, and Axel E. Nielsen (eds) *Expanding Archaeology*, pp. 47–66. University of Utah Press, Salt Lake City.

Noble, William and Iain Davidson 1996 *Human Evolution, Language and Mind: A Psychological and Archaeological Inquiry*. Cambridge University Press, Cambridge.

Nolan, Michael J. 1975 "The Relationship Between Verbal and Nonverbal Communication." In G.J. Hanneman and W. McEwen (eds) *Communication and Behavior*, pp. 98–119. Addison-Wesley, Reading, MA.

O'Brien, Michael J. and T.D. Holland 1995 "Behavioral Archaeology and the Extended Phenotype." In J.M. Skibo, W. Walker, and A. Nielsen (eds) *Expanding Archaeology*, pp. 143–161. University of Utah Press, Salt Lake City.

——, ——, R.J. Hoard, and G.L. Fox 1994 "Evolutionary Implications of Design and Performance Characteristics of Prehistoric Pottery." *Journal of Archaeological Method and Theory* 1: 259–304.

Olson, Scott R. 1994 "Renewed Alchemy: Science and Humanism in Communication Epistemology." In Fred L. Casmir (ed.) *Building Communication Theories: A Socio/Cultural Approach*, pp. 49–85. Erlbaum, Hillsdale, NJ.

Oudshoorn, Nelly 1994 *Beyond the Natural Body: An Archeology of Sex Hormones*. Routledge, London.

Parker, S.T., R.W. Mitchell, and M.L. Boccia (eds) 1994 *Self-Awareness in Animals and Humans: Developmental Perspectives*. Cambridge University Press, New York.

Pashler, Harold E. 1998 *The Psychology of Attention*. MIT Press, Cambridge, MA.

Patrik, Linda E. 1985 "Is There an Archaeological Record?" *Advances in Archaeological Method and Theory* 8: 27–62.

Patterson, Miles L. 1995 "A Parallel Process Model of Nonverbal Communication." *Journal of Nonverbal Behavior* 19: 3–29.

Peacock, Brian and Waldemar Karwowski (eds) 1993 *Automotive Ergonomics*. Taylor & Francis, London.

Peacock, James L. and Dorothy C. Holland 1993 "The Narrated Self: Life Stories in Process." *Ethos* 21: 367–383.

Pearce, John M. 1987 *Introduction to Animal Cognition*. Erlbaum, Hillsdale, NJ.

Perriault, Jacques 1981 *Mémoires de l'Ombre et du Son: une Archéologie de l'Audio-Visuel*. Flammarion, Paris.

Peters, Roger 1980 *Mammalian Communication: A Behavioral Analysis of Meaning*. Brooks/Cole Publishing, Monterey, CA.

Petroski, Henry 1985 *To Engineer is Human: The Role of Failure in Successful Design*. St. Martin's Press, New York.

—— 1995 *Engineers of Dreams: Great Bridge Builders and the Spanning of America*. Alfred A. Knopf, New York.

Pfaffenberger, Bryan 1992 "The Social Anthropology of Technology." *Annual Review of Anthropology* 21: 491–516.

Pheasant, Stephen 1986 *Bodyspace: Anthropometry, Ergonomics and Design*. Taylor & Francis, London.

Philips, Susan U. 1980 "Sex Differences and Language." *Annual Review of Anthropology* 9: 523–544.

Piaget, J. 1952 *The Origins of Intelligence in Children*. Norton, New York.

Plomin, R., J.C. DeFries, G.E. McClearn, and M. Rutter 1997 *Behavioral Genetics*. 3rd edn. Freeman, San Francisco, CA.

Polhemus, Ted 1978a *Fashion and Anti-Fashion: Anthropology of Clothing and Adornment*. Thames & Hudson, London.

—— 1978b (ed.) *The Body Reader: Social Aspects of the Human Body*. Pantheon Books, New York.

Pospisil, Leopold 1963 *The Kapauku Papuans of West New Guinea*. Holt, Rinehart & Winston, New York.

Provine, Robert R. 1996 "Laughter." *American Scientist* 84(1): 38–45.

Prown, Jules D. 1980 "Mind in Matter: An Introduction to Material Culture Theory and Method." In Robert B. St. George (ed.) *Material Life in America, 1600–1860*, pp. 17–37.

—— 1993 "The Truth of Material Culture: History or Fiction?" In Steven Lubar and W. David Kingery (eds) *History from Things: Essays on Material Culture*, pp. 1–19. Smithsonian Institution Press, Washington, D.C.

Quimby, Ian M.G. (ed.) 1978 *Material Culture and the Study of American Life*. W.W. Norton, New York.

Quinlan, Philip T. 1991 *Connectionism and Psychology*. University of Chicago Press, Chicago, IL.

Radcliffe-Brown, A.R. 1933 *The Andaman Islanders*. 2nd edn. Cambridge University Press, Cambridge.

Radner, D. and M. Radner 1989 *Animal Consciousness*. Prometheus Books, Buffalo, New York.

Radzikhovskii, L.A. 1987 "Activity, Structure, Genesis, and Unit of Analysis." *Soviet Psychology* 25: 82–98.

Ramenofsky, Ann F. and Anastasia Steffen (eds) 1998 *Unit Issues in Archaeology*. University of Utah Press, Salt Lake City.

Rapoport, Amos 1990 *The Meaning of the Built Environment: A Nonverbal Communication Approach*. University of Arizona Press, Tucson.

Rathje, William L. 1979 "Modern Material Culture Studies." *Advances in Archaeological Method and Theory* 2: 1–37.

—— and Cullen Murphy 1992 *Rubbish! The Archaeology of Garbage*. HarperCollins, New York.

—— and Michael B. Schiffer 1982 *Archaeology*. Harcourt Brace Jovanovich, New York.

Reber, Arthur S. 1993 *Implicit Learning and Tacit Knowledge: An Essay on the Cognitive Unconscious*. Oxford University Press, Oxford.

Reid, J. Jefferson, Michael B. Schiffer, and William L. Rathje 1975 "Behavioral Archaeology: Four Strategies." *American Anthropologist* 77: 836–848.

Renfrew, Colin 1982 *Towards an Archaeology of Mind*. Cambridge University Press, Cambridge.

—— and Ezra B.W. Zubrow (eds) 1994 *The Ancient Mind: Elements of a Cognitive Archaeology*. Cambridge University Press, Cambridge.

Ristau, C. and P. Marler (eds) 1990 *Animal Cognition*. Erlbaum, Hillsdale, NJ.

Robbins, Joel 1997 "666, or Why is the Millennium on the Skin? Morality, the State and the Epistemology of Apocalypticism Among the Urapmin of Papua New Guinea." In P.J. Stewart and A. Strathern (eds) *Millennial Markers*, pp. 35–58. Centre for Pacific Studies, James Cook University of North Queensland, Townsville.

Rogel, M.J. 1978 "A Critical Evaluation of the Possibility of Higher Primate Reproductive and Sexual Pheromones." *Psychological Bulletin* 85: 810–830.

Roitblat, Herbert L. and Lorenzo von Fersen 1992 "Comparative Cognition: Representations and Processes in Learning and Memory." *Annual Review of Psychology* 43: 671–710.

Romero, Javier 1970 "Dental Mutilation, Trephination, and Cranial Deformation." In Robert Wauchope (ed.) *Handbook of Middle American Indians*, Vol. 9, pp. 50–67. University of Texas Press, Austin.

Romney, A.K., W.H. Batchelder, and S.C. Weller 1987 "Recent Applications of Cultural Consensus Theory." *American Behavioral Scientist* 31: 163–177.

——, S.C. Weller, and W.H. Batchelder 1986 "Culture and Concensus: A Theory of Culture and Informant Accuracy." *American Anthropologist* 88: 313–338.

Rosen, Lawrence 1995 "Introduction: The Cultural Analysis of Others' Inner States." In Lawrence Rosen (ed.) *Other Intentions: Cultural Contexts and the Attribution of Inner States*, pp. 3–11. School of American Research Press, Santa Fe, New Mexico.

Rosenthal, Robert and Bella M. DePaulo 1980 "Encoders vs Decoders as Units of Analysis in Research in Nonverbal Communications." *Journal of Nonverbal Behavior* 5: 92–103.

Roszell, Patricia, David Kennedy, and Edward Grabb 1989 "Physical Attractiveness and Income Attainment Among Canadians." *The Journal of Psychology* 123: 547–559.

Roux, V., B. Bril, and G. Dietrich 1995 "Skills and Learning Difficulties Involved in Stone Knapping: The Case of Stone-Bead Knapping in Khambhat, India." *World Archaeology* 27: 63–87.

Ruben, Brent D. and Leah A. Lievrouw (eds) 1990 *Mediation, Information, and Communication. Information and Behavior* series, Vol. 3. Transaction Books, New Brunswick, NJ.

Rubin, Arnold (ed.) 1988 *Marks of Civilization: Artistic Transformations of the Human Body*. Museum of Cultural History, University of California, LA.

Rye, Owen S. 1981 *Pottery Technology: Principles and Reconstruction*. Taraxacum, Washington, D.C.

Saarnio, David A. and David F. Bjorklund 1984 "Children's Memory for Objects in Self-Generated Scenes." *Merrill-Palmer Quarterly* 30: 287–301.

Salmon, Merrilee 1978 "What Can Systems Theory Do for Archaeology?" *American Antiquity* 43: 174–183.

—— 1982 *Philosophy and Archaeology*. Academic Press, New York.

Salmon, Wesley 1971 *Statistical Explanation and Statistical Relevance*. University of Pittsburgh Press, Pittsburgh, PA.

Savage-Rumbaugh and Karen E. Brakke 1996 "Animal Language: Methodological and Intepretive Issues." In Marc Bekoff and Dale Jamieson (eds) *Readings in Animal Cognition*, pp. 269–288. MIT Press, Cambridge, MA.

Savory, Theodore 1977 *Arachnida*. 2nd edn. Academic Press, London.

Scherer, Klaus R. 1972 "Judging Personality from Voice: A Cross-Cultural Approach to an Old Issue in Interpersonal Perception." *Journal of Personality* 40: 191–210.

Schiffer, Michael B. 1972 "Archaeological Context and Systemic Context." *American Antiquity* 37: 156–165.

—— 1975 "Behavioral Chain Analysis: Activities, Organization, and the Use of Space." In *Chapters in the Prehistory of Eastern Arizona, IV. Fieldiana: Anthropology* 65: 103–119.

—— 1976 *Behavioral Archeology*. Academic Press, New York.

—— 1978 "Methodological Issues in Ethnoarchaeology." In R.A. Gould (ed.) *Explorations in Ethnoarchaeology*, pp. 229–247. University of New Mexico Press, Albuquerque.

—— 1979 "A Preliminary Consideration of Behavioral Change." In Colin Renfrew and Kenneth Cooke (eds) *Transformations: Mathematical Approaches to Culture Change*, pp. 353–368. Academic Press, New York.

—— 1987 *Formation Processes of the Archaeological Record*. University of New Mexico Press, Albuquerque.

—— 1991 *The Portable Radio in American Life*. University of Arizona Press, Tucson.

—— 1992a "Archaeology and Behavioral Science: Manifesto for an Imperial Archaeology." In LuAnn Wandsnider (ed.) *Quandaries and Quests: Visions of Archaeology's Future*, pp. 225–238. Southern Illinois University, Carbondale, Center for Archaeological Investigations, Occasional Paper No. 20.

—— 1992b *Technological Perspectives on Behavioral Change*. University of Arizona Press, Tucson.

—— 1995a *Behavioral Archaeology: First Principles*. University of Utah Press, Salt Lake City.

—— 1995b "Social Theory and History in Behavioral Archaeology." In James M. Skibo, William H. Walker, and Axel E. Nielsen (eds) *Expanding Archaeology*, pp. 22–35. University of Utah Press, Salt Lake City.

—— 1996a "Some Relationships Between Behavioral and Evolutionary Archaeologies." *American Antiquity* 61: 643–662.

—— 1996b "Formation Processes of the Historical and Archaeological Records." In W. David Kingery (ed.) *Learning From Things: Method and Theory in Material Culture Studies*, pp. 73–80. Smithsonian Institution Press, Washington, D.C.

—— n.d. "Indigenous Theories, Scientific Theories, and Product Histories." In Paul Graves-Brown (ed.) forthcoming.

——, Tamara Butts, and Kimberly Grimm 1994 *Taking Charge: The Electric Automobile in America*. Smithsonian Institution Press, Washington, D.C.

—— and Teresita Majewski n.d. "Modern Material Culture Studies: Toward an Archaeology of Consumerism." In Teresita Majewski and Charles E. Orser, Jr. (eds) *International Handbook of Historical Archaeology*. Plenum, New York.

—— and Andrea R. Miller 1999 "A Behavioral Theory of Meaning." In James M. Skibo and Gary Feinman (eds) *Pottery and People: A Dynamic Interaction*. University of Utah Press, Salt Lake City.

—— and James M. Skibo 1987 "Theory and Experiment in the Study of Technological Change." *Current Anthropology* 28: 595–622.

—— and —— 1989 "A Provisional Theory of Ceramic Abrasion." *American Anthropologist* 91: 102–116.

—— and —— 1997 "The Explanation of Artifact Variability." *American Antiquity* 62: 27–50.

——, ——, Tamara C. Boelke, Mark A. Neupert, and Meredith Aronson 1994 "New Perspectives on Experimental Archaeology: Surface Treatments and Thermal Response of the Clay Cooking Pot." *American Antiquity* 59: 197–217.

Schleidt, Margret and Carola Genzel 1990 "The Significance of Mother's Perfume for Infants in the First Weeks of Their Life." *Ethology and Sociobiology* 11: 145–154.

Schlereth, Thomas J. and Kenneth L. Ames (eds) 1985 *Material Culture: A Research Guide*. University of Kansas Press, Lawrence.

Schneider, Jane 1987 "The Anthropology of Cloth." *Annual Review of Anthropology* 16: 409–448.

Sebeok, Thomas A. 1968 *Animal Communication: Techniques of Study and Results of Research*. Indiana University Press, Bloomington.

—— 1977 (ed.) *How Animals Communicate*. Indiana University Press, Bloomington.

Sept, Jeanne 1992 "Archaeological Evidence and Ecological Perspectives for Reconstructing Early Hominid Subsistence Behavior." *Archaeological Method and Theory* 4: 1–56.

Shafer, Harry J. 1985 "A Mimbres Potter's Grave: An Example of Mimbres Craft-Specialization?" *Bulletin of the Texas Archaeological Society* 56: 185–200.

Shanks, Michael 1992 *Experiencing the Past*. Routledge, London.

Shipman, Pat 1981 *Life History of a Fossil: An Introduction to Taphonomy and Paleoecology*. Harvard University Press, Cambridge, MA.

Sillitoe, Paul 1998 "The Development of Indigenous Knowledge: A New Applied Anthropology." *Current Anthropology* 39: 223–252.

Singh, Devendra 1993 "Adaptive Significance of Female Physical Attractiveness: Role of Waist-to-Hip Ratio." *Journal of Personality and Social Psychology* 65: 293–307.

Skibo, James M. 1992 *Pottery Function: A Use-Alteration Perspective*. Plenum, New York.

——, Axel E. Nielsen, and William H. Walker (eds) 1995 *Expanding Archaeology*. University of Utah Press, Salt Lake City.

—— and Michael B. Schiffer 1995 "The Clay Cooking Pot: An Exploration of Women's Technology." In James M. Skibo, Axel E. Nielsen, and William E. Walker (eds) *Expanding Archaeology*, pp. 80–91. University of Utah Press, Salt Lake City.

Skinner, B.F. 1953 *Science and Human Behavior*. Macmillan, New York.

—— 1974 *About Behaviorism*. Alfred A. Knopf, New York.

Smith, W. John 1977 *The Behavior of Communicating: An Ethological Approach*. Harvard University Press, Cambridge, MA.

Snowdon, Charles T. 1990 "Language Capacities of Nonhuman Animals." *Yearbook of Physical Anthropology* 33: 215–243.

Sober, Elliot 1984 *The Nature of Selection: Evolutionary Theory in Philosophical Focus*. MIT Press, Cambridge, MA.

Soppe, Herman J.G. 1988 "Age Differences in the Decoding of Affect Authenticity and Intensity." *Journal of Nonverbal Behavior* 12: 107–119.

Sovern, Michael I. 1973 *Cases and Materials on Racial Discrimination in Employment*. 2nd edn. West Publishing, St. Paul, MN.

Sperber, Dan 1975 *Rethinking Symbolism*. Cambridge University Press, Cambridge.

—— 1996 *Explaining Culture: A Naturalistic Approach*. Blackwell, Oxford.

—— and D. Wilson 1995 *Relevance: Communication and Cognition*. 2nd edn. Blackwell, Oxford.

Spielman, A.I., X.-N. Zeng, J.J. Leyden, and G. Preti 1995 "Proteinaceous Precursors of Human Axillary Odor: Isolation of Two Novel Odor-Binding Proteins." *Experientia* 51: 40–47.

Stamp, Glen H., Anita L. Vangelisti, and Mark L. Knapp 1994 "Criteria for Developing and Assessing Theories of Interpersonal Communication." In Fred L. Casmir (ed.) *Building Communication Theories: A Socio/Cultural Approach*, pp. 167–208. Erlbaum, Hillsdale, NJ.

Starrett, Gregory 1995 "The Political Economy of Religious Commodities in Cairo." *American Anthropologist* 97: 51–68.

Stein, N.L. and K. Oatley 1992 "Basic Emotions: Theory and Measurement." *Cognition and Emotion* 6: 161–168.

Stephen, Timothy and Teresa M. Harrison 1993 "Interpersonal Communication, Theory, and History." *Communication Theory* 3: 163–172.

Stevens, S.S. 1950 "Introduction: A Definition of Communication." *The Journal of the Acoustical Society of America* 22: 689–697.

Steward, Julian H. 1955 *Theory of Culture Change.* University of Illinois Press, Urbana.

Steward, Samuel M. 1990 *Bad Boys and Tough Tattoos: A Social History of the Tattoo with Gangs, Sailors, and Street-Corner Punks, 1950–1965.* Haworth Press, New York.

Stich, Stephen P. 1996 *Deconstructing the Mind.* Oxford University Press, New York.

Stoddart, D. Michael 1990 *The Scented Ape: The Biology and Culture of Human Odour.* Cambridge University Press, Cambridge.

Strathern, Andrew J. and Marilyn Strathern 1971 *Self-Decoration in Mt. Hagen.* Duckworth, London.

Streri, Arlette and Elizabeth S. Spelke 1988 "Haptic Perception of Objects in Infancy." *Cognitive Psychology* 20: 1–23.

Strzalko, J. and D.A. Kaszycka 1992 "Physical Attractiveness: Interpersonal and Intrapersonal Variability of Assessments." *Social Biology* 39: 170–176.

Sullivan, Alan P. 1978 "Inference and Evidence in Archaeology: A Discussion of the Conceptual Problems." *Advances in Archaeological Method and Theory* 1: 183–222.

Summerhayes, D.L. and R.W. Suchner 1978 "Power Implications of Touch in Male–Female Relationships." *Sex Roles* 4: 103–110.

Teachman, Jay D. 1987 "Family Background, Educational Resources, and Educational Attainment." *American Sociological Review* 52: 548–557.

Thayer, Stephen 1986 "History and Strategies of Research on Social Touch." *Journal of Nonverbal Behavior* 10: 12–28.

Theraulaz, Guy and Eric Bonabeau 1995 "Coordination in Distributed Building." *Science* 269: 686–688.

Thomas, Julian 1996 *Time, Culture and Identity.* Routledge, London.

Thompson, R.H. 1956 "The Subjective Element in Archaeological Inference." *Southwestern Journal of Anthropology* 12: 327–332.

—— 1958 "Modern Yucatecan Maya Pottery Making." *Society for American Archaeology, Memoirs* No. 15.

Tomasello, Michael, Sue Savage-Rumbaugh, and Ann Cale Kruger 1993 "Imitative Learning of Actions on Objects by Children, Chimpanzees, and Enculturated Chimpanzees." *Child Development* 64: 1688–1705.

Tooby, J. and L. Cosmides 1989 "Evolutionary Psychology and the Generation of Culture, Part I: Theoretical Considerations." *Ethnology and Sociobiology* 10: 29–49.

—— and —— 1992 "The Psychological Foundations of Culture." In J.H. Barkow, L. Cosmides, and J. Tooby (eds) *The Adapted Mind: Evolutionary Psychology and the Generation of Culture*, pp. 19–136. Oxford University Press, New York.

Trager, George L. 1958 "Paralanguage: A First Approximation." *Studies in Linguistics* 13(1–2): 1–12.

Tringham, Ruth, Glenn Cooper, George Odell, Barbara Voytek, and Anne Whitman 1974 "Experimentation in the Formation of Edge Damage: A New Approach to Lithic Analysis." *Journal of Field Archaeology* 1: 171–196.

Trudgill, Peter 1983 *Sociolinguistics: An Introduction to Language and Society.* Penguin, Harmondsworth.

Tucker, Joan S. and Ronald E. Riggio 1988 "The Role of Social Skills in Encoding Posed and Spontaneous Facial Expressions." *Journal of Nonverbal Behavior* 12: 87–97.

Tversky, Barbara and Kathleen Hemenway 1983 "Categories of Environmental Scenes." *Cognitive Psychology* 15: 21–149.

Ubelaker, Douglas H. 1978 *Human Skeletal Remains: Excavation, Analysis, Interpretation.* Taraxacum, Washington, D.C.

van Hooff, J.A. 1962 "Facial Expressions in Higher Primates." *Symposia of the Zoological Society of London* 8: 997–125.

Van Toller, Steve and G.H. Dodd (eds) 1992 *Fragrance: The Psychology and Biology of Perfume.* Elsevier, London.

Vauclair, Jacques 1996 *Animal Cognition: An Introduction to Modern Comparative Psychology.* Harvard University Press, Cambridge, MA.

Vaughan, Patrick 1985 *Use-Wear Analysis of Flaked Stone Tools.* University of Arizona Press, Tucson.

Veblen, Thorstein 1994 *The Theory of the Leisure Class.* Penguin Books, New York. Originally published 1899. Von Furstenberg, George, Bennett Harrison, and Ann R. Horowitz 1974 *Patterns of Racial Discrimination.* Lexington Books, Lexington, MA.

Wade, Edwin L. and Lea S. McChesney 1981 *Historic Hopi Ceramics: The Thomas V. Keam Collection of the Peabody Museum of Archaeology and Ethnology.* Peabody Museum Press, Harvard University, Cambridge, MA.

Wagley, Charles 1983 *Welcome of Tears: The Tapirapé Indians of Central Brazil.* Waveland Press, Prospect Heights, IL.

Walker, William H. 1995 "Ceremonial Trash?" In James M. Skibo, William H. Walker, and Axel E. Nielsen (eds) *Expanding Archaeology*, pp. 1–12. University of Utah Press, Salt Lake City.

—— 1998 "Where are the Witches of Prehistory?" *Journal of Archaeological Method and Theory* 5: 245–308.

——, Vincent M. LaMotta, and E. Charles Adams n.d. "Katsinas and Kiva Abandonment at Homol'ovi: A Deposit-Oriented Perspective on Religion in Southwest Prehistory." In Michelle Hegmon (ed.) *Regional Systems in the Southwest.* University of Colorado Press, Boulder.

——, James M. Skibo, and Axel E. Nielsen 1995 "Introduction: Expanding Archaeology." In James M. Skibo, William H. Walker, and Axel E. Nielsen (eds) *Expanding Archaeology*, pp. 1–12. University of Utah Press, Salt Lake City.

Walsh, P.B. 1983 *Growing Through Time: An Introduction to Adult Development.* Books/Cole, Monterey, CA.

Wasserman, E.A. 1993 "Comparative Cognition: Beginning the Second Century of the Study of Animal Intelligence." *Psychological Bulletin* 113: 211–228.

Watkins, M.J., E. Ho, and E. Tulving 1976 "Context Effects in Recognition Memory for Faces." *Journal of Verbal Learning and Verbal Behavior* 15: 505–517.

Watson, Bruce 1994 "In the Heyday of Men's Hats, Fashion Began at the Top." *Smithsonian*, March.

Watson, John B. 1930 *Behaviorism.* W.W. Norton, New York.

Weiner, Annette 1988 *The Trobrianders of Papua New Guinea.* Holt, Rinehart & Winston, New York.

—— and Jane Schneider (eds) 1989 *Cloth and Human Experience.* Smithsonian Institution Press, Washington D.C.

Weymouth, John W. 1986 "Geophysical Methods of Archaeological Site Surveying." *Advances in Archaeological Method and Theory* 9: 311–395.

Wheeless, Lawrence R. and John A. Cook 1985 "Information Exposure, Attention, and Reception." In Brent D. Ruben (ed.) *Information and Behavior*, Vol. 1, pp. 251–285. Transaction Books, New Brunswick, NJ.

White, Leslie 1959 *The Evolution of Culture*. McGraw-Hill, New York.

White, Randall 1989 "Production Complexity and Standardization in Early Aurignacian Bead and Pendant Manufacture: Evolutionary Implications." In P. Mellars and C. Stringer (eds) *The Human Revolution: Behavioural and Biological Perspectives on the Origins of Modern Humans*, pp. 366–390. Edinburgh University Press, Edinburgh.

Whitley, David S. 1992 "Prehistory and Post-Positivist Science: A Prolegomenon to Cognitive Archaeology." *Archaeological Method and Theory* 4: 57–100.

Whittaker, John C., Douglas Caulkins, and Kathryn A. Kamp 1998 "Evaluating Consistency in Typology and Classification." *Journal of Archaeological Method and Theory* 5: 129–164.

Wiessner, Polly 1984 "Reconsidering the Behavioral Basis for Style: A Case Study Among the Kalahari San." *Journal of Anthropological Archaeology* 3: 190–234.

Williams, Connie K. and Constance Kamii 1986 "How do Children Learn by Handling Objects?" *Young Children* 42(1): 23–26.

Williams, Frederick 1975 "Language and Communication." In G.J. Hanneman and William McEwen (eds) *Communication and Behavior*, pp. 59–75. Addison-Wesley, Reading, MA.

Wilson, Edward O. 1978 *On Human Nature*. Harvard University Press, Cambridge, MA.

Wilson, Steven R. 1995 "Elaborating the Cognitive Rules Model of Interaction Goals: The Problem of Accounting for Individual Differences in Goal Formation." *Communication Yearbook* 18: 3–25.

Wobst, H. Martin 1977 "Stylistic Behavior and Information Exchange." In C.E. Cleland (ed.) *Papers for the Director: Research Essays in Honor of James B. Griffin*, pp. 317–334. University of Michigan, Museum of Anthropology, Anthropological Papers, No. 61.

Worchel, Stephen 1986 "The Influence of Contextual Variables on Interpersonal Spacing." *Journal of Nonverbal Behavior* 10: 230–254.

Wyer, Robert S. and Donald E. Carlston 1979 *Social Cognition, Inference, and Attribution*. Erlbaum, New York.

Wylie, Alison 1985 "The Reaction Against Analogy." *Advances in Archaeological Method and Theory* 8: 63–111.

—— 1992 "The Interplay of Evidential Constraints and Political Interests: Recent Archaeological Research on Gender." *American Antiquity* 57: 15–35.

Wynn, Thomas 1989 *The Evolution of Spatial Competence*. University of Illinois Press, Urbana.

—— 1991 "Tools, Grammar, and the Archaeology of Cognition." *Cambridge Archaeological Journal* 1: 191–206.

—— 1993 "Two Developments in the Mind of Early *Homo*". *Journal of Anthropological Archaeology* 12: 299–322.

Young, David E. and Robson Bonnichsen 1984 *Understanding Stone Tools: A Cognitive Approach*. Center for the Study of Early Man, University of Maine at Orono.

Zahr, Lina 1985 "Physical Attractiveness and Lebanese Children's School Performance." *Psychological Reports* 56: 191–192.

Zedeño, M. Nieves 1997 "Landscapes, Land Use, and the History of Territory
Formation: An Example from the Puebloan Southwest." *Journal of Archaeological
Method and Theory* 4: 67–103.

Zipf, George K. 1949 *Human Behavior and the Principle of Least Effort*. Addison-Wesley,
Cambridge, MA.

Zuckerman, Miron, Kunitate Miyake, and Holley S. Hodgins 1991 "Cross-Channel
Effects of Vocal and Physical Attractiveness and Their Implications for Interpersonal Perception." *Journal of Personality and Social Psychology* 60: 545–554.

Index